*A Southern
Weave of Women*

A Southern Weave of Women

FICTION OF THE CONTEMPORARY SOUTH

LINDA TATE

THE UNIVERSITY OF GEORGIA PRESS

Athens and London

© 1994 by the University of Georgia Press
Athens, Georgia 30602
All rights reserved
Designed by Betty Palmer McDaniel
Set in 10.5 on 14 Berkeley Medium
by Tseng Information Systems, Inc.
Printed and bound by Thomson-Shore, Inc.
The paper in this book meets the guidelines for
permanence and durability of the Committee on
Production Guidelines for Book Longevity of the
Council on Library Resources.

Printed in the United States of America
98 97 96 95 94   C   5 4 3 2 1

Library of Congress Cataloging in Publication Data
Tate, Linda.
    A southern weave of women : fiction of the
contemporary South / Linda Tate.
        p. cm.
    Includes bibliographical references and index.
    ISBN 0-8203-1614-8 (alk. paper)
        1. American fiction—Southern States—History and
criticism. 2. Women and literature—Southern States—
History—20th century. 3. American fiction—Women
authors—History and criticism. 4. American fiction—20th
century—History and criticism. 5. Southern States—In
literature. 6. Family in literature. 7. Women in literature.
I. Title.
PS261.T3 1994
813'.54099287'0975—dc20   93-33744

British Library Cataloging in Publication Data available

To my own southern mothers:
Bonnie Landsbury Burrows
Marie Manley Landsbury
Fanny Preston Tate

They were women then
My mama's generation

. . .

How they battered down
Doors

. . .

To discover books
Desks
A place for us
How they knew what we
Must know
Without knowing a page
Of it
Themselves.

ALICE WALKER, "The Women"

[T]heir voices, their lives and words and stories are so clear, so familiar as if there have been no changes at all.

JILL MCCORKLE, *Tending to Virginia*

CONTENTS

Contents

*A Southern
Weave of Women*

INTRODUCTION

> I believe that the truth about any subject only comes when all the sides
> of the story are put together, and all their different meanings make one
> new one. Each writer writes the missing parts to the other writer's story.
> And the whole story is what I'm after.
>
> ALICE WALKER, "Beyond the Peacock: The Reconstruction of Flannery O'Connor"

*M*y grandmothers have always been, for me, models of strong
womanhood. And it is no coincidence that they are southern women.
Although both emigrated to the lower Midwest as young women, they
nevertheless retained their southernisms. Grandma Tate, who died when
I was six years old, made such a lasting impression on me that I have
felt her presence and her power envelop, protect, and nurture me more
than once in the many years since her death. As I grew older and asked
questions about her—always with a thirst to know and understand the
woman whose spirit my own echoed so deeply—I learned the family
apocrypha that made her loom even larger in my mind. Raised in western Kentucky, she married in her early teens, bore three daughters, and
left her husband and children in her late teens. She roamed the border
South and the lower Midwest for more than a decade afterward, working as a motorcycle rider in a circus and as a crew cook on Mississippi
riverboats. After she met my grandfather, a riverboat pilot and a Tennessee native, they married, had three sons, and lived on the river until
the eldest, my father, was ready to start school. As they settled down
into the more stable and typical life of landlubbers, my grandparents—
both half-Cherokee and half-white, probably Scotch-Irish—continued
to live the culture of the poor southern whites. Though they enjoyed a
higher standard of living than did their relatives who still lived in Kentucky and Tennessee, they nevertheless valued family and were active
in their fundamentalist church while paradoxically continuing to enjoy

music and dancing, my grandmother clogging in her kitchen to hillbilly music. Perhaps I loved my grandmother so much not simply because she was a strong and happy woman in her own right but also because she recognized a kindred spirit in me. I have always cherished above all the family legend that holds that, after seeing me dance day upon day, my Grandma Tate exclaimed, "You're never going to keep that girl from dancing!"

Although my Grandma Tate fueled my imagination, my Grandma Landsbury filled my life. I have had the special privilege of knowing and loving this strong southern woman all of my life. Grandma Landsbury's adventures, too, have taken on the stature of family legend, and I have learned them as she has told the stories to me again and again. Raised on a farm in northeastern Arkansas with five sisters and two brothers by a loving mother and an intelligent if tyrannical father, my grandmother grew up with a passion for knowledge. Always someone who enjoyed reading, writing, and spelling, she became a schoolteacher for two years in rural Arkansas, a somewhat typical course of events for a young un-married woman in the early 1920s. But country schoolteaching was not enough for my grandmother, so she left for the big city with her sister in 1928. Having bobbed her hair and now living in a boardinghouse and working at a St. Louis factory, my grandmother boldly left behind her restrictive southern upbringing. Eventually three of her siblings moved to St. Louis, very effectively re-creating a tightly knit sense of extended southern family. She married my grandfather, a native St. Louisan, at the late age of twenty-four and delayed having her two children until she was well into her thirties. She continued to work in the factory and later worked in a cafeteria. After the birth of her first child, my mother, she attended a revival and returned to the fundamentalist religion of her upbringing. Like my Grandma Tate, Grandma Landsbury has always been a fun-loving and young-minded grandmother (even though she is now in her late eighties), and more important to me, she has always been outspoken and upfront about what she thinks and feels. Though I love spending sunny afternoons sitting in her kitchen as she prepares supper, and though I adore her lavish flower gardens, it is her feistiness that has always drawn me to her. I have often liked to think that if she were a young woman today she might be taking a path in life similar to my own.

Though both of my grandmothers provided me strong and bold models of southern womanhood, they also presented the consequences of restrictive southern culture. I saw that her southern upbringing had forced my Grandma Tate into an early marriage and bleak poverty in her early teens. Likewise, I saw that a restrictive southern society could not provide the educational and career opportunities that might have made my Grandma Landsbury happy to stay there. Moreover, I saw that both—not unlike other southern women—found their greatest sources of happiness in their families and in their evangelical faiths. My own interest in southern women's studies grew out of a need to understand my grandmothers and their lives, their place within their culture and its effect upon my own life. But though my studies—particularly when they involved male treatments of southern male literature (and this was most of the time)—helped me to identify the negative and oppressive forces that shaped my grandmothers' lives, they did not go a long way toward helping me appreciate the positive qualities they displayed as southern women.

Partially this is because my grandmothers—and countless others like them, both past and present—do not fall within traditional conceptions of southern womanhood. First, though they suffered their own forms of patriarchal and cultural oppression, they were also feisty, gutsy, and adventurous women, hardly the sheltered women of popular myth. Second, as poor white women, they can hardly be understood within the framework of the upper-middle-class white southern lady.[1] Third, they departed from the monolithic southern norm not only in terms of class but also in terms of ethnicity. As a native American, my Grandma Tate was obviously separated from the southern lady stereotype, and because my Grandma Landsbury came from the Ozark foothills, most traditional southern scholars would label her family "mountain folk" rather than "southerners."[2] What is more, millions of other southern women who are black have also been excluded from the term "southern," precisely because of their racial and ethnic background.[3]

Yet the fact that my grandmothers diverged from the norm is not idio-

syncratic; rather, it reflects southern scholars' narrow definition of what
it means to be southern. Although this has been a problem ever since the
South began to perceive itself as a region, it has increasingly become a
problem throughout this century. As the South grows and changes, mod-
ernizes and industrializes, as southern demographics change, making it a
truly multicultural region, and as changing demographics and increased
politicization on the part of minorities and women have led in the South
to the civil rights movement and the birth of the feminist movement,
narrow definitions of what it means to be southern—particularly what
it means to be a southern woman—no longer suffice.

The frustration of trying to understand the complexity and multiplicity of the "southern woman" results not only from male- and white-
dominated scholarship but also from the popular myths of the South
and of southern women that continue to thrive—especially outside the
South. For too long, most southern women's voices have been denied
or obscured; they have not had the means to express themselves and
thus to represent themselves accurately. As poor women—black and
white—they have not had the time to write or to otherwise create nor
have they even had the chance to indulge their imaginations, as Alice
Walker has so memorably pointed out in her landmark essay, "In Search
of Our Mothers' Gardens." Those women who have found the time, education, and support to write have found themselves locked out of the
establishment press or, if published, have found their wares scorned
by a less-than-appreciative New York–controlled literati. In short, the
power of representation has not lain with the multiplicity of women who
constitute the term "southern woman" but with the New York literary
establishment and with Hollywood.

Unfortunately, southern women often define themselves too narrowly
and fail to see beyond the confines of race, ethnicity, and class. While
Lee Smith, for example, moves Appalachian literature in rich new di-
rections, and while she opens a space for voices that have not yet been
heard in southern literature, she consistently denies that she is a southern writer. In an interview with Pat Arnow, Smith asserts that, because
she and other Appalachian writers are not concerned with racial guilt
and because they are not from privileged class backgrounds, they cannot

be categorized as southern writers. Although it is important to acknowledge ethnic, class, and subregional differences that distinguish various writers from each other, it is also important to consider the ways in which these differences are written out of southern literary history. Smith contends that she is not a southern writer because she does not write about upper-middle-class whites from the deep South, but a more expansive definition of "southern" would make room for such differences in race, class, and ethnicity.

In another interview, Smith herself provides a more inclusive type of definition, one that makes possible a richer, less arbitrary notion of what constitutes southern writing. When she argues that southern literature "has something to do often . . . with colloquial voice . . . , with old-style storytelling . . . , with narrative strategy" (qtd. in V. Smith 793), she is less concerned with meeting certain class and ethnic criteria and more concerned with identifying the commonalities that join, rather than divide, southern writers. More inclusive, less discriminatory, this type of definition of southern literature makes room for writers from all subregions south of the Mason-Dixon line, from all races, and from all ethnic backgrounds. Because it seeks to discover points of connection, this type of definition is more accurate and ultimately more useful.

The goal here, of course, is not to obscure difference but to make room for difference. One would not want to argue that there are no differences between those from the deep South and those from Appalachia, between those from the upper middle class and those who have been traditionally labeled "poor whites," or between those who are white and those who are black. By looking for what connects these writers as inhabitants of multiple Souths, one discovers concerns, issues, and priorities that cut across racial, class, and subregional lines. A more inclusive vision of southern literary history would look not only at the proliferation of contemporary southern writers who would have traditionally been obscured by southern studies but also at past writers who have been ignored or devalued because they did not meet strict, elitist views of what constitutes "southern." Unfortunately, the critical foundations for placing southern writers within an appropriately multicultural and inclusive context are almost nonexistent. Traditionally, southern literature has been understood to be that written by white men and, on rare occasions, by white women—and, in almost all cases, by and about white southerners of the upper middle class.[4] Only recently have a handful of scholars begun to write blacks into southern literary history,[5] and almost no attention has been paid to the contributions of southern writers of less privileged class backgrounds.[6] And in many cases, when black or white southerners of less privileged backgrounds do write, they are perceived as not writing about traditionally "southern" subjects (for example, racial guilt, the "burden of history," and southern gothicism). If taken seriously as writers, they are categorized as something other than southern—African-American, Appalachian, poor white, or women—as if these designations could not also denote something southern.

Without erasing or minimalizing difference, southern literary critics need to formulate definitions of southern literature that stress commonality and points of connection among the many voices that make up the wealth of southern literature. Such a revision of traditional definitions necessitates expanding our vision to include works by and about common people, by those outside the deep South, and by black southerners. In discussing the current generation of southern women writers and in tracing one strand of a southern women's literary tradition that anticipates the work of this generation, this study seeks to articulate those cultural characteristics that concern all southern women writers—black and white, the upper middle class as well as the lower classes, deep South and Appalachian. When we rewrite "southern" as an inclusive term, when we focus, as Alice Walker suggests, on "all the sides of the story," we find an expansive, rich tradition of many voices, many stories, many lives mingling together to tell "the whole story." Only when all southern women's voices are heard do we begin to understand the South itself.

As I look at the current literature in the multi-Souths, I am interested in discovering those cultural concerns that are common to southern women from a myriad of backgrounds. In chapter 1, I argue that these points of connection—family, race, history, sense of place, and women's voice—reflect a long-standing tradition in southern women's literature: the emphasis on home and family can contain empowering, liberating, even subversive elements. In tracing a lineage of southern women writers from Kate Chopin and Elizabeth Madox Roberts to Zora Neale Hurston and Eudora Welty, chapter 1 creates an evocative framework for understanding the contemporary generation of southern women writers and illustrates this framework by looking at the role of extended and alternative family in Jill McCorkle's *Tending to Virginia* (1987) and Shay Youngblood's *The Big Mama Stories* (1989). Chapter 2 examines biracial friendships among southern women and considers Ellen Douglas's *Can't Quit You, Baby* (1988), which focuses on the close relationship between a white woman and her black maid, and Dori Sanders's *Clover* (1990), the story of a young black girl raised by her white stepmother. Chapter 3 highlights the South's preoccupation with history, focusing on Rita Mae Brown's *High Hearts* (1986), a Civil War novel that challenges the exclusion of women and blacks from traditional history, and Lee Smith's *Oral History* (1983), which questions the dismissal of Appalachia's lively history. Chapter 4 looks at the southern sense of place, at the relationship between geography and identity, and at the maps of reading embedded in Alice Walker's *The Color Purple* (1982) and Bobbie Ann Mason's *In Country* (1985).

Finally, this study looks at the forces that keep contemporary southern women's writing on the margins of literary discourse. Chapter 5 discusses Steven Spielberg's and Norman Jewison's erasure of the South in their film adaptations of Walker's (1985) and Mason's (1989) novels, respectively, looks at the reasons Spielberg and Jewison fail to read according to the texts' internal systems of reading, and considers the power of white male readers in co-opting southern women's subversive texts. And chapter 6 examines the rise of small, independent presses and their role in providing a vehicle for southern women's voices to be heard. As I examine Linda Beatrice Brown's *Rainbow Roun Mah Shoulder* (1983) and Kaye Gibbons's *A Cure for Dreams* (1991), I consider the subversive quality of southern women's voices and the ways in which southern women use these voices to create empowering female networks in opposition to the totalizing master narratives that seek to define them. While Spielberg and Jewison represent the forces that try to control southern women and to render them invisible, Brown's and Gibbons's novels epitomize southern women's increasingly successful attempts to make themselves heard and to define the terms of their own existence.

Regardless of their ethnic, class, or subregional backgrounds, southern women writers of the 1980s and 1990s are actively redefining what it means to be a woman in the South. As these women carve out new definitions of southern womanhood, they look for ways to retain what is valuable about past conceptions of southern womanhood while seeking to revise and expand these roles. In doing so, they reconsider their relationships to home, family, and other southern women; to issues of race in the South; to women's obscured role in the region's past; and to the southern land itself. Fighting against perceptions of themselves based on myopic male visions, they work to articulate their own visions of themselves. In telling their own stories and the stories of their mothers and grandmothers, these women rewrite southern cultural history and give voice to those who have heretofore been silenced. Through the sheer fact of their existence, these writers create space for women who have previously been excluded from southern culture. In novel after novel, they depict matrices of female empowerment, circles of women who support and nurture one another. As they grow out of an ongoing lineage of southern women writers, and as they reflect an interest in issues that connect southern women writers, past and present, these writers—and those who have gone before them—constitute their own inclusive, empowering, and collectively defined southern weave of women.

ONE

"ALL THE WOMEN":
FAMILY, HOME, AND HEALING
IN THE CHANGING SOUTH

In our young minds houses belonged to women, were their special domain, not as property, but as places where all that truly mattered in life took place—the warmth and comfort of shelter, the feeding of our bodies, the nurturing of our souls.

BELL HOOKS, "Homeplace: A Site of Resistance"

The ancestors and the womb . . . they're one, they're the same.

NANA PEAZANT, *Daughters of the Dust*

*I*n her evocative, lyrical film *Daughters of the Dust* (1991), writer and director Julie Dash tells the story of a Gullah family preparing to migrate from their South Carolina sea island to the mainland at the turn of the century. The film depicts the old matriarch Nana's connection to the Peazant family graveyard and the connection of all the Peazant family women to the natural spaces of their island as emblemized by the picnic site. As natural sanctuaries, these places evocatively fuse domesticated and ritualized space (graveyards, picnic sites) with women's empowering, generative, and creative connection to the land.

Landscape—long held to be feminine in nature[1]—becomes a radical extension of women's domestic space; the graveyard and the picnic site function as the real Peazant family "home," "where all that truly matter[s] in life [takes] place." The women use the island's natural spaces to provide "the warmth and comfort of shelter," to "feed" the "bodies" of their family, and, most important, to "nurture" their "souls." Dash spends little time depicting the actual Peazant family shanty and instead spends most of the film showing the women cooking, caring for children, and tending to the ancestors within natural women-identified space, which marks the family as spiritually "rich," rather than within the constraining walls of the shanty, which marks the family as economically "poor." Appropriately, the film is set on Dahtaw Island ("Dahtaw" being Gullah for "daughter"), underscoring not only Dash's woman-centered vision but also the perfect and easy fusion of the women with the island. The graveyard, the picnic site, and, by extension, the entire island represent the spiritual "home" of the Peazant family, the graveyard representing an especially tangible link between the ancestors and the living family members. As the "home" of the ancestors, the graveyard roots the living members to their past and, with the old matriarch Nana at its center, defines and enacts the matrix of female empowerment. Nana is the mother of all life on Dahtaw Island, the original creator of the matriarchal Peazant clan. In a very literal sense, Nana has brought life to countless children, has brought "seed to blossom," has created "daughters" out of "dust."

Dash's film rewrites home—traditionally seen as restricting and oppressive to women[2]—as liberating, subversive, radical space, and, as bell hooks (an active supporter of the film) has written, as a "site of resistance." What holds this family together—even in the face of impending migration and separation—are the interconnections between the ancestors, the living family members, and the future generations (as symbolized by the unborn child), connections made stronger by the physical and spiritual fact of the graveyard and Dahtaw Island. Dash's ability to reconceive women's space as empowering rather than as constraining comes partially from her position as a woman of the late twentieth century; like many other contemporary southern women writers, Dash looks at previous generations of southern women with new eyes and, as a result, sees herself in new ways. But more important, Dash's vision of women's space as empowering is the natural outgrowth of gardens tilled and tended by previous generations of southern women writers. Dash's film is historical revision that only a granddaughter can undertake: it cherishes the past with an eye to invigorating the present and to envisioning the future. Dash rewrites the traditional conception of women's space and place and shows that the matrix of female empowerment is not new but, rather, has in the past gone unseen and unrecognized.

At the beginning of the twentieth century, the fictional Nana Peazant holds her family together spiritually despite class and racial oppression and the impending separation of economically motivated migration. Around the same time, the real-life Kate Chopin paints literary portraits of Louisiana women who are defined not only by race, class, and gender, but also by their rootedness to a wild natural landscape. Nana Peazant and Kate Chopin may seem, on the surface, an odd pairing. Nana is a "poor" black woman whose family is forced to leave the South Carolina Sea Islands for a "better" future up North; Chopin writes about upper-class and upper-middle-class women, about the tense relationships between black and white women, and about sexual and racial oppression rather than empowering liberation. Nana holds her family together spiritually, inspiring Eula and Yellow Mary to stay on Dahtaw Island rather than moving to the North. Chopin, in her most famous work, depicts a woman who is so unsuccessful in rewriting her societal position that suicide becomes an almost attractive form of liberation from gender oppression. It would seem, on the surface, that there has been much progress from Chopin's bleak feminist critique to Dash's empowering revision of women's history.

But a closer look at Chopin—and her literary heirs—reveals that these writers actually sowed the seeds for Dash's revisionary depiction of women's space and that, like Nana, they gave birth to (literary) daughters out of the dust of patriarchal, racist, and classist oppression. A brief consideration of four paradigmatic texts can provide a foundation for understanding one of the primary strains in the southern women's literary tradition: Kate Chopin's *The Awakening* (1899), Elizabeth Madox Roberts's *The Time of Man* (1926), Zora Neale Hurston's *Their Eyes Were Watching God* (1937), and Eudora Welty's *Delta Wedding* (1946). Each of these texts is infused with a dynamic sense of women's creativity, women's community, women's talk, and women's rootedness to and identity with the natural landscape—all of which are made manifest in the radical creation and extension of women's domestic space. It is not my intention here to discuss fully all of these interconnected aspects of southern women's lives; rather, through discussing women's domestic space, I hope to suggest the importance of these woman-centered concerns and to provide an evocative framework for considering similar issues in fiction by contemporary southern women.

Chopin's *The Awakening* depicts marriage as dehumanizing, southern society as constricting and patriarchal, and the chances for liberation as almost nonexistent; yet it also details a woman's sexual and artistic awakening and the rewriting (and redefining) of domestic space as central to that awakening. As Edna Pontellier leaves her husband's home and moves to a smaller house of her own around the corner, she simultaneously casts off southern and patriarchal convention and redefines the terms of her existence. No longer defined by her status as mother, wife, and homemaker, she now defines herself through her increasingly confident painting, her sexual and romantic relationships with men other than her husband, and her sense of herself as making a life and a place by and for herself:

> The pigeon-house pleased her. It at once assumed the intimate character of a home, while she herself invested it with a charm which it reflected like a warm glow. There was with her a feeling of having descended in the social scale, with a corresponding sense of having risen in the spiritual. Every step which she took toward relieving herself from obligations added to her strength and expansion as an individual. (156)

While ultimately not successful in creating the life she wishes to lead (as Robert withholds his love from her), Edna makes great strides toward liberation, and this liberation—this "strength and expansion"—is symbolized by and enacted through the "pigeon-house." It becomes a tangible marker of her "sense of having risen in the spiritual," and the home is pleasing to her, not only because of the furnishings and comforts she provides, but also because "she herself invested it with a charm which it reflected like a warm glow." Here is Virginia Woolf's "room of one's own"—signally important as Edna recreates her identity and achieves sexual and artistic power.

Also central to understanding Edna's growing sense of self is the network of women's friendships that Chopin suggests in the novel. Not only does Edna talk with Madame Ratignolle and Mademoiselle Reisz, but she also forms crucial bonds with them, coming to Madame Ratignolle's aid during the primal moment of childbirth and looking to Mademoiselle Reisz for artistic and spiritual inspiration. Here, as in her stories, Chopin seems to sense the possibilities of southern women's community and initiates a tradition—however muted—of southern women's talk. Yet her novel focuses primarily on the redefining of one home and of one person in that home and stops short of creating the kind of lively and sustaining women's community evident in work by later southern women writers. Whole and satisfying empowerment in southern patriarchal society is impossible for Edna, and her final liberating moment comes in her submersion into the natural world, rather than in a socially defined moment. Whether read as a bleak indictment of a society that offers suicide as the only viable option for an "expanded" woman like Edna or as an empowering act of choosing and embracing one's own destiny, the novel's final scene is significant in its emphasis on Edna's return to and final merge with the wild, primal, natural element of the water and the sea.

A quarter of a century later Chopin's concerns with women's space, women's culture, and women's identity found fuller treatment in Elizabeth Madox Roberts's *The Time of Man* (1926). The daughter and later the wife of poor tenant tobacco farmers, Ellen Chesser develops an almost artistic sense of personal identity by creating domestic space, tending gardens, singing songs, birthing and raising children, and forging intimate bonds with other women. All of these activities are so well integrated that it is nearly impossible to speak of one without the others. Ellen's early relationship with her friend Tessie, for example, is based on their shared use of houses as a means of dreaming. The rest of the novel traces the development of Ellen's houses throughout the course of her life, from the early tenant house that is dirty and damp and smells of "rats and soot" (10) to the "snug dry room" (240) of the next tenant cabin, from her first house with Jasper to the much larger, four-room house they and their many children share at the end of the novel. No matter how cramped, leaky, or dirty these houses may be, Ellen always transforms the domestic space, carving out her own space within the larger house and making the entire house (and its environs) life-sustaining for the rest of her family. Numerous descriptions of Ellen's "rooms" (for example, her loft in the first house and her locked trunk in the second) are literally womblike, underscoring the connection between woman's body, identity, and domestic space. Roberts describes the second house this way:

> During the first rains of her stay there Ellen felt the snugness of the night, the dark outside, the falling wet, the dry security of the indoors, so that in her room, shut away from the elements, she felt the security to be within herself as if she were detached by the prison-like whiteness of the dry walls from her own memories, to begin her being anew. . . . She would go through the door with a keen rush of sense and, closing the door behind her, she would look at the enclosing walls while a quiver of content would sweep over her nerves and gather deep in her mind. (240–41)

Though the walls "enclose" and are "prison-like," they do not constrict Ellen's experience; instead, they provide the possibility for rebirth (as she "begin[s] her being anew") and a sense of "security" that prompts "content." Here—as in other rooms, other houses—Ellen "gather[s] deep in her mind," makes sense of her external experiences, and nurtures the inner substance of herself.

But Ellen's identity comes not only from her womblike and life-sustaining domestic space but also from her cultivation of gardens, which become extensions of her houses. She plants her first garden during the opening pages of the novel and plants many others as the novel progresses; like Alice Walker's mother, one of the first things Ellen tends to when she moves to a new tenant house is the cultivation of her garden.[3] The gardens, like the houses, become larger and more fertile; by the novel's end, she is growing onions, peas, beets, cabbages, sweet potatoes, cherries, raspberries, and grapes and tending to a rich supply of butter, chickens, and eggs. Tending her garden provides her with another means of "gather[ing] deep in her mind": "Breaking the soil her mind would penetrate the crumbling clod with a question that searched each new-turned lump of earth and pushed always more and more inwardly upon the ground, a lasting question that gathered around some unspoken word such as 'why' or 'how.' Thus until her act of breaking open the clay was itself a search" (362).

Through all of her domestic activity—creating a home, planting a garden, singing songs, sewing garments, cooking food, tending chickens and cows—Ellen gains an increasingly profound sense of herself as a woman and as a creator. On one level, she experiences her creativity through her intense experience of mothering—"Out of me," she says, "come people forever, forever" (333). And it is not until Ellen is herself a mother that she can fully bond with her own mother:

> Going about the small rough farm in the Rock Creek country, her home now, Ellen would remember Nellie, from first to last, a structure which she knew almost entirely in her senses, her deep inner knowledge which lay behind memory. . . . Ellen would merge with Nellie in the long memory she had of her . . . , until her mother's life merged into her own and she could scarcely divide the one from the other, both flowing continuously and mounting. (380–81)

But this connection with her mother and with her own children as well as her domestic activities do not denote a woman bound by biology, constrained by the walls of her house, or oppressed by poverty. Though she is poor, denigrated because of her position as a tenant farmer, and virtually invisible to the rest of "polite" southern society, Ellen Chesser is a strong, bold woman, whose internal life is deep and dangerous.[4]

Even more central to an understanding of the southern women's literary tradition is Zora Neale Hurston's 1937 novel *Their Eyes Were Watching God*. Like nearly all of Hurston's work, *Their Eyes Were Watching God* is set against an evocative backdrop of African-American oral culture, which brings to life not only the sounds of "Mouth-Almighty" —as Hurston termed the community chorus on the porch—but also and more important the sounds of women talking intimately with one another. The novel's frame depicts the just-returned Janie telling her story to her friend Pheoby. "[K]issin'-friends for twenty years" (7), Janie and Pheoby are on such close terms that Pheoby goes in at Janie's "intimate gate" (4), taking with her physical nourishment for her travel-worn friend. After she finishes eating the mulatto rice Pheoby has prepared for her, Janie begins to tell her tale and, in doing so, to provide Pheoby with spiritual sustenance. Telling her story is for Janie a crucial and final act of self-discovery; her need to tell the story stems from "that oldest human longing—self revelation" (6). Janie tells her story to make sense of it, to discover the self she has become through the living of experience, and to make tangible her quest for self-identity. While telling is essential to the development of identity, so is listening; as Janie gets ready to tell her tale, Pheoby is a "hungry" listener (10), and at the close of Janie's story, Pheoby has received spiritual nourishment: "Ah done growed ten feet higher from jus' listenin' tuh you, Janie" (182). Their talk on Janie's back porch, as they sit "in the fresh young darkness close together" (6), rejuvenates both teller and listener.

If *Their Eyes Were Watching God* is about women's need to gain their own voices, it is also about their need to escape oppressive domestic situations and, subsequently, to create alternative, empowering homes. The novel's "inside" story begins with the two homes Janie shares with Nanny: the first, in the backyard of the white family Nanny works for; the second, a house of their own. Janie finds both houses oppressive because Nanny's very presence makes them so. In telling her story to Pheoby, Janie realizes that "her conscious life had commenced at Nanny's gate" (10), symbolized by Johnny Taylor's kiss and Janie's orgasmic vision underneath the pear tree. After this experience, Janie discovers that "[n]othing on the place nor in her grandma's house answered her" (11). Janie moves from Nanny's house to that of Logan Killicks, her first husband. Logan's house is no less oppressive than Nanny's: it "was a lonesome place like a stump in the middle of the woods where nobody had ever been. The house was absent of flavor" (20–21). Still waiting for the house and the horizon she has only dreamt of for herself, Janie runs off with Jody Starks, whose vision of life expands beyond the four walls of a house to a general store, community porch, and an entire African-American town. But, though Jody expands the physical dimensions of her home, Janie discovers that life in Jody's "house" is just as oppressive as it was in the houses she shared with Nanny and Logan. Particularly vexing is Jody's insistence on placing Janie on a pedestal; Jody thinks she should be pleased with the "high chair" he has built her because it allows her to "sit and overlook the world" (58), but Janie finds the "chair" isolating and stultifying and wishes instead to join the other community members on the porch. After she has inherited Jody's property, Janie learns that the physical size of the home and the very fact of property do not in themselves allow a woman to redefine herself. All alone in the "big house," Janie listens as it "creak[s] and crie[s] all night under the weight of lonesomeness" (85).

It is not until Janie falls in love with Tea Cake that she is able to come into her own fully and to create domestic space that is empowering rather than constricting. Ironically, she must leave behind the fine estate she has inherited from Jody and move into a two-room shack on the "muck" to carve out this empowering domestic space. The move from civilized space to the "muck" of the Everglades is crucial: "To Janie's strange eyes, everything in the Everglades was big and new. Big Lake Okechobee, big beans, big cane, big weeds, big everything. . . . Ground so rich that everything went wild" (123). On the muck, Janie finally experiences her full sexuality, the dream of the pear tree at last come true. And on the muck, Janie moves off of the "high stool" and finally joins the other folks in her community. The house she shares with Tea Cake becomes a "magnet, the unauthorized center of the 'job'" (126), and their doorstep is "full of people every night" (127). The group gathered on the doorstep is much like the one that had gathered on the porch of Jody's store, but now Janie gets to participate and, in so doing, gains her voice and a lively sense of herself: "[H]ere, she could listen and laugh and even talk some herself if she wanted to. She got so she could tell big stories herself from listening to the rest" (128). Also important to the empowerment Janie feels in this house is the love she and Tea Cake instill in it. Janie joyfully cooks for Tea Cake, prepares baths for him, and dotes on him in countless other ways; Tea Cake returns the favor by planting and tending a bountiful garden. The spirit of cooperation, love, and community makes this two-room shack a much richer home for Janie than the fine home, store, porch, and "high chair" that Jody gave to her. When she returns to Eatonville, she brings with her a package of Tea Cake's garden seeds and plans to sow them as a "remembrance" to him. Having brought back with her a tangible and organic reminder of Tea Cake and having come back with a "womanish" sense of self and pride in her own voice, Janie will finally be able to remake her inherited estate into a nourishing and sustaining shelter.

A final paradigmatic text—perhaps the text most central to an understanding of this strain of the southern women's literary tradition—is Eudora Welty's *Delta Wedding* (1946). Set in the Mississippi delta, the novel focuses on the week-long series of events leading up to and following the wedding of Dabney Fairchild, one of the many members of the closely knit Fairchild clan. In scene after scene, Welty refers to the many and tangled branches of the Fairchild family tree, which, though never formally "diagrammed" for the reader, is nevertheless felt palpably on every page of the novel. The closeness—sometimes even the cloyishness—of the family is suggested repeatedly, as in this passage: "[B]oys and men, girls and ladies all, the old and the young of the Delta kin— even the dead and the living for Aunt Shannon—were alike—no gap opened between them" (14). Holding the "cousins" together as a "clan" (74) are the "old stories, family stories, Mississippi stories" (191), which, like the implied family tree, permeate every page of the novel.

While the men in the family are certainly important (particularly George), Welty devotes most of her attention to the women in the family, their activities and concerns, and their web of interconnected relationships. The Fairchilds have been termed "a maternally sustained family" (Westling 73) and might even be described as a matriarchy, with Ellen Fairchild functioning as "the mother of them all" (10). Images of feminine fertility abound: Dabney, of course, is getting married and the possibility of a future pregnancy is frequently mentioned; Mary Denis has just delivered a son; Robbie Reid may be pregnant; Ellen is well along in her tenth pregnancy; and numerous scenes, as Louise Westling has shown, depict Dabney, Robbie, and Ellen immersed in eroticized landscapes. The woman-centeredness of the novel is also suggested in the rich and continual references to women's creativity as expressed in domestic activity: Ellen and Laura bake a coconut cake; Aunt Tempe creates pastry cornucopias; Jim Allen spends all of the wedding morning making mints; Aunt Primrose crochets lace mitts for the bridesmaids; Troy's mother, though distant, sends what Westling calls "a womblike sack" of her quilts (81), quilts that Troy hopes will lead to a fertile and happy marriage; and, in the past, Annie Laurie had patched together a cloth doll for her daughter Laura. This sense of women's culture has been carefully preserved and handed down from generation to generation, most notably in Mashula Hines's cookbook and in the diary of the original Fairchild matriarch, Mary Shannon.

In fact, the Fairchild houses are especially associated with the women in the family. Marmion has passed from Annie Laurie to Maureen to Dabney and, in the future, may pass on to Laura; Shellmound is ruled by Ellen, the Fairchild matriarch, and, as Westling argues, can be connected with the Choctaw Indian mound known as "The Great Mother" (72); and the Grove—first built for Mary Shannon and now the residence of the two "old maid" aunts, Primrose and Jim Allen—is an especially important repository of feminine heritage, since "Grandmother's and Great-Grandmother's cherished things were so carefully kept there" (40). The primacy of the women's position in the Fairchild clan is made clear not only in their physical possession of the houses but also in the authority they hold in those houses:

[T]he women always ruled the roost. . . . It was notoriously the women of the Fairchilds who since the Civil War, or—who knew? —since the Indian times, ran the household and had everything at their fingertips—not the men. The women it was who inherited the place—or their brothers, guiltily, handed it over.

In the Delta the land belonged to the women. (144–45)

As this passage makes clear, the Fairchild women's influence extends beyond their houses to the surrounding eroticized landscape—to the fields, bayous, the Yazoo River, and especially to the delta, the very shape of which suggests a woman's Mound of Venus (mons veneris). Closer to home, Ellen's garden is a lush fusion of feminine fertility and creativity. In looking over her garden the morning after the wedding, Ellen thinks to herself, "What would happen to everything if she were not here to watch it . . . , not for the first time when a child was coming. Of all the things she would leave undone, she hated leaving the garden untended— sometimes as much as leaving Bluet [her youngest child], or Battle [her husband]" (226). The mother of a daughter just married and of another child on the way, Ellen finds a creative outlet in the garden that her children and her husband do not afford her. During the final scene of the novel, a family picnic that in some ways anticipates *Daughters of the Dust* (indeed, the entire novel anticipates many of Dash's concerns in the film), Ellen Fairchild experiences a life-affirming moment, which echoes similar moments in Ellen Chesser's life: "The repeating fields, the repeating cycles of season and her own life—there was something in the monotony itself that was beautiful, rewarding—perhaps to what was womanly within her" (Welty 240). *Delta Wedding,* as the story of a boisterous family and the women within it, shows the deep and abiding importance of women's domestic space, women's creativity, women's relationships with each other and with the land, and women's sense of an ongoing and multigenerational matriarchy.

What each of these paradigmatic novels suggests is the pervasive centrality of home and family in the southern women's literary tradition. Southern concerns with home and family—which much scholarly and popular perception has held to be restricting and oppressive to women— appear to be empowering, liberating, even potentially subversive for the women in these novels. Home and family—rewritten as women's dynamic creation of domestic and extradomestic space and as women's intimate and lively relationships with each other—provide a rich backdrop against which to tell southern women's stories. More important, they provide, as bell hooks suggests, a location for empowerment and resistance, a safe and nurturing space for revisionary discourse. In "Homeplace: A Site of Resistance," hooks recognizes the nurturing qualities of her southern grandmother's home as well as its "radical political dimension." She notes that African Americans have historically believed that the

homeplace, however fragile and tenuous (the slave hut, the wooden shack) . . . was the one site where one could freely confront the issue of humanization, where one could resist. . . . [I]t was about the construction of a safe place where black people could affirm one another and by so doing heal the wounds inflicted by racist [and, I would add, patriarchal] domination. ("Homeplace" 42)

Although hooks directs her comments specifically to the construction of safe and subversive domestic space by African-American women, her analysis illuminates the radical potential of domestic space for all southern women, black and white.

"The home place," says Helen Levy, is a recurrent image in American women's fiction, "an ideal pastoral domestic setting" (3), where, as Charlotte Perkins Gilman describes it, there are "no enemies," just "sisters and friends" (qtd. in Levy 3). The idea of the home place is particularly prevalent in southern women's fiction, as women come together to create empowering female networks, to tell stories to one another, to voice their concerns and their triumphs—in short, to give shape and (re)definition to their lives as southern women. The southern woman novelist's emphasis on home—and, correspondingly, on family, women's networks, women's creativity, and women's voices—cuts across racial, class, and subregional lines. While white and black women may construct the idea of family in different ways, while middle-class women and poor women may have differing types of physical space to call home, and while women from different subregional and racial backgrounds may have more or less opportunity to make their voices heard, all of these southern women seek to understand themselves through their relationships with other women in their families and seek to control and redefine notions of home. Rather than being defined by spaces traditionally held to be restrictive, characters in these works gain sustenance and strength from their houses and those of their mothers and grandmothers and use that strength to redefine the terms of their existence in the South. What makes these houses "places . . . that truly matter" (hooks, "Homeplace" 41) are the "weaves of women," the matrices of female empowerment, which give life and shape to southern women's continuing concerns with family, race, history, place, and voice.

As Virginia Woolf said in *A Room of One's Own*, "[W]e think back through our mothers if we are women" (76). Southern women writers,

past and present, think back through their biological mothers and grandmothers—Kate Chopin through her matriarchal upbringing, Eudora
Welty through the sounds of female relatives telling stories, Alice Walker
through her mother's stories and gardens, Julie Dash through the
"[s]craps of memories" that lead us to "know our mothers, grandmothers, and family history. And finally . . . our own selves" (88). Just
as important, southern women writers think back through their literary
mothers—reinvoking, revising, expanding images of women's community, space, creativity, and talk. Teasing out the threads that connect the
multiple generations of southern women writers leads to the discovery
of a rich tradition of woman-centered fiction, a long lineage of literary mothers and daughters who articulate an alternative, empowering,
and sometimes subversive tradition of southern women's community.
And approaching southern women's fiction from a woman-centered perspective and identifying the ways in which southern women inscribe
women's culture and women's community in their texts makes clear that
southern women's fiction is not a defensive or apologetic response to
southern men's fiction but instead an articulation of women's experience
in the South. "The matrix," as Levy argues, "replaces the phallus as the
source of art" (5).

The matrix—as womb, as community, as source of creativity—becomes an apt metaphor for understanding the many layers of southern
women's experience and offers a more positive and empowering vision
of home and family in the South. Two contemporary writers who depict
such southern weaves of women are Jill McCorkle and Shay Youngblood,
whose works illustrate not only continuing concerns with home and
family but also provide a fruitful starting point for the examination of
southern women's culture in the late twentieth century and the ways in
which it is reflected in southern women's texts. Like their literary grandmothers before them, McCorkle and Youngblood celebrate the closeness
and support the family provides, immerse their readers in the sound of
women's talk, and bring to life "the warmth and comfort of shelter, the
feeding of . . . bodies, and the nurturing of . . . souls," the activities that
hooks takes to be central to the women-identified houses of her upbringing ("Homeplace" 41). As empowering accounts of supportive southern

weaves of women, McCorkle's *Tending to Virginia* and Youngblood's *The Big Mama Stories* make clear that these writers—like countless other contemporary southern women writers—are the literary daughters born out of the dust of racist, classist, and patriarchal oppression, the "seed" that previous generations of southern women writers have brought to "blossom."

Jill McCorkle is one of the most prolific and important of the southern literary granddaughters and plays an active role in the Chapel Hill–based resurgence of contemporary southern literature. Her first two novels— *The Cheerleader* and *July 7th*—were published simultaneously in 1984, and her third novel, *Tending to Virginia,* followed in 1987. Her most recent novel, *Ferris Beach,* was published in 1990, and 1992 saw the publication of a collection of her short stories, *Crash Diet.* Each novel is set in a small North Carolina town: *The Cheerleader* and *Ferris Beach* focus on individual protagonists; *July 7th* details a day in the life of a small town; *Tending to Virginia* examines the inter- and intragenerational relationships among the women of the Pearson family. Though McCorkle may express sadness at the fact that "we are progressively losing the extended family" (qtd. in Lesser 58), she takes this opportunity to celebrate its continued, if tenuous, existence. In typical southern style, she focuses not on the conventional nuclear family but on the bond between several generations. Members of a large family clan—Emily, Lena, Hannah, Madge, Cindy, and Virginia—instinctively come together for a week of sharing stories and making confessions, a week of healing and bonding.

Tending to Virginia is a prime example of the traditional extended white southern family continuing into the late twentieth century. Jean E. Friedman's 1985 study, *The Enclosed Garden: Women and Community in the Evangelical South, 1830–1900,* examines the white woman's role in the nineteenth-century southern family and provides a useful way of considering the traditional southern family structure. Friedman's description of rural life in the Victorian South is still very apt in considering small-town interactions in the late twentieth century:

Complex ties of kinship [bind] southern women to each other and
to men. The importance of kinship cannot be underestimated . . . : it
remain[s] the vital connection, the difference between isolation and
security. . . . Southern women's identity, then, may be considered
in the context of familial . . . demand. (3)

Clearly, though the rural dimension has been replaced by the exigencies
of small-town life, the women in *Tending to Virginia* continue to define
themselves in terms of family. Or as Barbara Dixson puts it in her brief
study of contemporary southern women writers, "[A]ll of these characters visit, think about and define themselves in terms of their parents,
grandparents, cousins and aunts" (9).

McCorkle brings life to the matrix of female community in this novel
by populating it with several generations of the Pearson family. Virginia
(or Ginny Sue)[5] and her third cousin Cindy represent the youngest
generation; their mothers (first cousins) Hannah and Madge form the
middle generation; and Virginia's grandmother, Emily (Gram), and her
great-aunt Lena comprise the oldest living generation. Though dead, two
key women provide the family foundation: first, Cindy's grandmother
(and Emily and Lena's sister-in-law), Tessy; and second, the original
matriarch, Virginia Suzanne (Emily and Lena's mother and Virginia's
namesake). The living women span three generations; they are grandmothers, mothers, sisters, aunts, nieces, daughters, cousins. They are
called both by their given names (Emily, Hannah, Cindy) and by their
relational names (Gram, Mama, Aunt Lena), signifying their coming
together both as individual women with their own lives and as members
of a large, though very close, extended family. McCorkle juxtaposes a
fictional family tree with her dedication, composed of her own multigenerational list of female ancestors. Thus, the implied family tree of her
dedication parallels the fictional one, as the first "mother" generates the
tree in which her last "daughter" takes her name:

IN MEMORY OF Claudia Meares Bullington
      With love for:
      Margaret Ann (Annie) Meares Collins
      Melba Collins McCorkle

Jan McCorkle Gane
and
Margaret Ann (Annie) Gane[.]

Where southern women of earlier generations carefully "cultivated" family trees in order "to demonstrate noble ancestry" (Westling 43), McCorkle and her literary sisters, Shay Youngblood and Kaye Gibbons, use family trees to constitute empowering weaves of women. The emphasis shifts from class status to emotional bonding, to core relationships that define women's lives.

Tending to Virginia tells the story of Virginia Turner Ballard's struggle to make the transition from her childhood to her life as wife and mother and the role her extended family plays in supporting her through this transition. Seven months pregnant with her first child, she is the first college-educated person in her family and lives in a North Carolina college town with her husband Mark, an educated northerner. Part of her struggle, then, involves her change in class—from being a member of the rural, lower middle class to being part of a professional, educated, middle-class society—and this struggle, like so many others, is encapsulated in the impending move to Virginia, a commonwealth associated with an American version of the aristocracy, from North Carolina, a state without Virginia's presumed aristocracy. As a woman in the changing South, Virginia must find a way to move ahead economically and socially while still retaining the valuable and empowering qualities of her lower-middle-class background. She must find a way to remain an integral part of her family tree, not in order to maintain aristocratic blood lines but to be sustained by and to perpetuate her family's weave of women. Jill McCorkle shifts our attention from the southern lady who concerned many previous southern women writers to the "average," often invisible southern woman and, in so doing, asks us to consider the deeper concerns that fundamentally define southern women's lives.

Overwhelmed by the changes in her life—marriage, motherhood, education, financial success, and an impending move—Virginia suddenly decides one hot July day to drive to her hometown, Saxapaw, North Carolina. Once there, she visits her grandmother, at whose house she collapses from toxemia, subsequently staying to recover. What follows in the novel are the conversations that take place between the women of the family as they visit Virginia throughout the week of recovery. As in Toni Cade Bambara's *The Salt Eaters* (1980), the healing is both physical and spiritual and comes as a result of the joint efforts of a community of women. These conversations reveal the particular challenges each generation faces; the role of home and family in each of these women's lives, especially the tension between the family allegiances of childhood and those of adulthood; and, most important, the powerful healing these women finally provide for one another, despite their sometimes restrictive southern upbringings. In short, *Tending to Virginia* tells the story of a close-knit group of white southern female relatives.

Forming the first tier of this close-knit family are the old women, Emily and Lena, who are most clearly linked to the traditional rural South and who best exemplify Friedman's depiction of kinship bonds in the old South. Their lives are very much determined by "familial demand"; even more than the younger Pearson women, Emily and Lena define themselves solely through their family. Yet because of their ties to the rapidly fading rural South, Emily and Lena represent a generation fast becoming obsolete: their models of behavior no longer suffice in the modern world. Though they often give wise advice to the younger women, their wisdom is sometimes obscured by the younger generations' inability to grasp their meaning. As Alzheimer's victims, they are prone to making ridiculous comments, providing many laughs for the other family members as well as the reader. Yet Emily and Lena's craziness might be read not only as the product of Alzheimer's-ridden minds but also as emblematic of an old way of life being pushed aside, being made irrelevant and nonsensical. Emily and Lena's obsolescence—indeed, the obsolescence of their entire generation—is further emphasized by the fact that Emily's house (originally the home place of the entire Pearson clan) is destroyed so that a Piggly Wiggly grocery store can be built on the same site. Old notions of home and community are razed to make room for more modern approaches.

Yet the older generation is not the only one facing challenges in the modern South. Indeed, the more difficult challenges may be those the younger women face, particularly Virginia and Cindy. Virginia, for example, has always wanted to be just like Gram and has spent her life trying to behave accordingly. But Gram tells her, "[Y]ou'll have to be more than me; the world will change" (264). Although Virginia will face the same problems as her female ancestors in making the transition from one home to the other, from the parent-centered home of childhood to the husband- and children-centered home of adulthood, she will have to face this particular challenge with the added test that she somehow be more as she makes this transition. Virginia functions very much as a symbol of changing white southern womanhood.

This movement from the old to the new, from the childhood home to the home of adulthood, and the negotiation between the security of the family network and the need to lead an independent and individual life lies at the heart of McCorkle's novel. Like many other southern women writers, McCorkle inextricably fuses ideas of home and family, and to understand her use of one concept is to understand the other. McCorkle frequently refers to geographical detail and repeatedly emphasizes home—that is, the physical manifestation of home. As already mentioned, for example, the replacement of the Pearson family home with the Piggly Wiggly is often invoked as a marker of the destruction of an older way of life. Other places and homes are also frequently mentioned, among them the Saxapaw River, the temporary and far-away housing of Virginia and her husband Mark, and Madge and Raymond's terrifying house. Underlying all these references is yet a deeper level: the down-home, lower-middle-class North Carolina of Virginia's relatives versus the more worldly, educated, middle-class Virginia she and Mark will move to soon. In one of the title's several meanings, then, Virginia is "tending to Virginia," that is, moving tentatively away from North Carolina and toward Virginia. The trick is to find a way to incorporate both states in one life.

Virginia underscores "home as family and people" as opposed to "home as place" when she considers the phenomenon of estate sales. She thinks to herself that a person could buy "tiny silver spoons," "the colander from the kitchen," or even the "door knocker if your initial is the same." Any object purchased, however, would be missing something, for although the buyer might take the object's scents—scents that are "of a family, a home"—to her own home, only the original family could recognize those scents, that is, the spirit of the object. Thus, Virginia stresses the idea that home is defined by the people who constitute it: "Where are the family members? Where are the people who know the scent that is there, the scent that is home, and how can they let it be split and divided and separated?" (132). The "scent that is home," the scent only family members can know, represents the spirit of the place, the idea of "home as family." This construction of home permeates McCorkle's novel so intensely that whenever she or one of the characters invokes the idea of a particular home or a particular place, they simultaneously invoke the idea of the people and family who invest the physical space with the emotional definition of home.

Home looms so important that one of the biggest challenges the older women faced earlier and the younger women now face is the challenge of moving from their childhood homes to their adult homes. Or to put it on another level, each woman must make the transition from her protected role in her childhood family to the vulnerable role of leader in her adult family. Gram describes the lesson this way: "Mama said you gotta know when to let go a little, let go and just leave it there behind you and then go make yourself a plate of biscuits and bleach them shirts of your husband's just as white as they can get and then just let go a little" (277). Although McCorkle devotes some time to exploring the struggles of the older generations, her primary focus is Virginia's attempt to make the same transition, this time in the contemporary world, the world that has changed.

Virginia's struggle is symbolized by her movement from the rented house she shares with Mark to Gram's duplex and back again. Gram's duplex serves as an intensified intersection of the entire family, particularly of the women in the family. Situated within the broader context of home I have already established, Gram's home represents for Virginia all the familiar, comfortable aspects of family—that is, it represents "what she knows" (42). Though now housed in a duplex and not in the old Pearson family house, Gram's home provides a deep, permanent sense of family continuity. The physicality of the duplex differs dramatically from that of the old house, but their spirits are the same: the "heavy dark furniture," the "quilts . . . piled like a mountain," and "the sounds" of "Gram's whispered words" (159) invest the neutral space of the duplex with the history and knowledge of the Pearson clan. Virginia thinks, for example, of her female relatives talking at Gram's duplex: "[T]heir voices, their lives and words and stories are so clear, so familiar as if there have been no changes at all" (34). In short, "[e]verything she knows is there, still at home, just changed and disguised" (35). Like Dash's "scraps of memories," the stories, voices, and quilts allow Virginia to know her "mothers, grandmothers, and family history" and, further, to know herself within a loving context of family history. The graveyard on Dahtaw Island fuses past, present, and future generations, prompting Nana to say that "the ancestors and the womb" are one and the same; likewise, Gram's house becomes an ancestral womb that Virginia grows in, comes to knowledge in, and to which she returns when pregnant with her own child.

Life with Mark and thus in her adult home represents the unknown. "This house and Mark," Virginia feels, "should be familiar" but instead "are so foreign" (34). She feels that Mark is taking "her from her home, already has, slowly, bit by bit, moving further and further from what she knows" (42). Virginia's ultimate fear, however, is that if Gram dies—the primary symbol in her mind of home—she will find herself forever lost in this new world, permanently cut off from what she knows. She imagines getting a call saying that Gram is dead; at that instant, she thinks, she will "turn to face rooms and windows and faces so unfamiliar and she will say: Why? Why am I here this way?" (42). Again, it is not the unfamiliarity of the place that disturbs her; rather, it is the new emotions, the new people, and, most important, the lack of a sense of family Virginia finds threatening. If, in Virginia's mind, Gram embodies home, then Mark symbolizes the unknown, all the threats to family and security awaiting her. When he visits her at Gram's, Virginia feels that he has "overstepped his boundaries, invaded her territory, changed everything" (132). While this movement from childhood to adulthood is common to all the Pearson women, Virginia must make her own transition from one home—or family—to the next. For her, this entails a much greater move geographically, intellectually, and economically than it did for her ancestors. Or as Gram puts it, Virginia will have "to be more than me" (264) to make a successful transition.

To help her with this struggle, all the women of the family spontaneously, almost instinctively, come together for a week of sharing stories and confessions, thereby creating a space in which they can "tend to Virginia" and, to some degree, to Cindy and Madge as well. The novel weaves together numerous scenes indicating the level of intimacy these women share, the tightness of the web connecting them. Stories are shared and remembered. The last section of the novel—which recounts long-ago exchanges between Gram and Tessy—indeed makes clear that the foundation for this storytelling is years and years of prior storytelling and intimate exchanges. Though much of this lore has not been articulated for the present generations, it nevertheless informs their sharing. This intimacy and knowledge is a given, so much so that Virginia confidently banks on its always being there. In running home for security, she depends on "their voices, their lives and words" and their stories "so clear, so familiar" (34). Home, for Virginia, is "where the history and knowledge is solid" (18).

Basking in "faces around her . . . that know everything there is to know about her life" (267), Virginia is clinging to an emotional security blanket. Linda Wagner-Martin accurately describes Virginia's being " 'tended to' by being attended to, by being listened to, thought about, and cared for, not by being protected, smothered, and absorbed" (32). While some women, such as Cindy and Hannah, do at times feel "smothered" and "absorbed," on the whole this southern weave of women is empowering and, importantly, is easily discernible by outsiders. Mark signals the special intimacy of this group when he refers to it as a "secret club": "[T]hat club that meets at your mother's house. All the women. When a man comes in it gets quiet" (74). These women—"all the women" of the "secret club"—are connected to one another not solely by blood but also by the web of intimacy and acceptance they have woven together. Together, in Gram's house, they constitute a circle, a womb of empowerment.

Although this bond is an ancient and ongoing one, the revelations of this particular week are on a new level and represent a shift in and a strengthening of bonds. Hannah, for example, finds herself "trying to pull it all together, this simple simple life, suddenly grown so huge" (244). Madge also comes to terms with the fact that she never knew what went on between her parents, Harv and Tessy, and that consequently she had no real intimate knowledge of her family. In some ways, the weak links between Harv and Tessy, Madge and Raymond, Cindy and her sister Catherine starkly contrast the tighter bonds between Emily and James, Hannah and Ben, Virginia and her brother Robert. Yet all the Pearson women—Emily and Lena, Hannah and Madge, Virginia and Cindy—constitute a strong network of female bonds. It is to these women that Madge confesses her secret and horrific life with Raymond. More important, it is these women who continue to accept and love Madge. Having confessed the murder of Raymond, Madge nervously asks, "What are you going to do with me?" Unconditionally, they reply, "Keep you I reckon" (246). As in Kaye Gibbons's *A Cure for Dreams* and Linda Beatrice Brown's *Rainbow Roun Mah Shoulder,* women band together to protect another who has murdered in response to ongoing brutality and humiliation.

Despite their intimacy on many levels, there is still not complete disclosure among these women. It is not surprising that the older generations tend to remain silent on certain issues. Gram, for example, is particularly fond of saying that "a person ought not to show herself to others" (202), and Madge has built an entire life-style around this command in her perfected ability not to show her pain. Gram and Lena are offended by references to body parts and their functions—"we never discussed such"—while Hannah and Madge are closemouthed about the gritty realities of their lives. But the older generations do not have a monopoly on this characteristic silence. Virginia, for example, is relieved that she is sick and forced to stay at Gram's, for now she has "a reason to stay *without telling the truth*" (119; my emphasis). Likewise, Virginia and Cindy have made a lifetime's practice out of admonishing each other "not to tell" their respective secrets, that is, not to cross generational bounds with their intimacy.

These constraints on emotional disclosure and, in addition, allegiance to one's husband and (immediate) family would seem to severely hamper white southern women's ability to create and maintain true intimacy. In other words, it would be at best difficult to share lives in a culture that dictates "a person ought not to show herself to others" (202). Yet the Pearson women have shared their secrets at least on a limited level throughout their lives and in this intense week on a very deep level. During this week of sharing, the women ask long-overdue questions and articulate their equally overdue answers. The first half of the novel is rife with questions. It emphasizes the younger women's need to know and their strong desire for intimacy and knowledge. The questions are hard ones, and the older women, who have spent lifetimes learning the answers to some and coming to terms with the others, back away for a while. Consequently, during the first half of the novel and, in some cases, throughout its entirety, the older women answer vaguely and evasively. As the novel progresses, however, more answers surface, many to old questions that had never even been articulated. What is sometimes said—but more often remains unsaid—is that it would have helped all these women if the collective wisdom and experience of the group had always been shared. Madge feels this most acutely since her mother Tessy had been particularly closemouthed: "Maybe if she had talked to me, I would have been different" (249).

The Pearson women, however, are learning to share knowledge and wisdom, to confess the realities of their lives. They are able finally to come together at a crucial time and say what needs to be said. Mark is indeed correct in calling this a "secret club" of "all the women," for, though these women love their men, such intimate exchanges could not take place with the men present. The novel is ripe with references to mothering (indeed, Virginia's troubled pregnancy has been the catalyst for their extended visit); to the rhythms of a woman's life, from menstruation and pregnancy to menopause; to her sexuality, however it may be defined; in short, to her blood and physicality. The ancestral womb is felt in the empowering domestic space of Gram's house, in the intimate circle of women's relationships, and in the life-giving blood that joins them.

Mothering—participating in the propagation of the family network—permeates the novel. Virginia has ambivalent feelings toward her unborn child. And though she does not speak of it, Lena profoundly desires children. Tessy is simply described as having "had nine babies" (7). And Gram longs for her mother, especially at her husband's funeral when she wishes she "could grab hold of her own mama and let the tears come" (57). All of these desires speak to the need these women have to mother and to be mothered. As Gram puts it, "Sometimes I feel so alone and what I'm lonely for is my mother" (181). In their sharing and exchanging, these women intuitively discover that they have come together for a week of intense and mutual mothering. In a much earlier time, Virginia Suzanne grieved for a daughter who "wasted away." But despite her grief, despite the pain she could not face, she learned to turn her attention to her surviving children, that is, to "tend to the living." Likewise, during their week of mothering, her surviving children and their descendants learn that they, too, must take care of living family members. Thus, they find themselves sharing, telling stories, listening to confessions, and tending to Madge, Cindy, and, most especially, Virginia.

Shay Youngblood's *The Big Mama Stories* (1989)—her first published full-length work—highlights a closely knit, if largely unrelated, group of women.[6] In this collection of loosely related stories, Youngblood depicts "othermothers," extended "family" connections, symbolic kin references, and shared responsibility for socializing children. She constructs a viable alternative family—a "symbolic kin network." Of African-American and native American descent, the women in these stories create a strong alternative family. Youngblood, like many other contemporary black women writers, as Deborah E. McDowell points out, "tries to reconstruct our notions of what constitutes a family" (qtd. in Fraiman 24).

Like Jill McCorkle, Shay Youngblood envisions a world where women form tight communities to nurture each other. Yet *The Big Mama Stories* begins with a strikingly different dedication than does *Tending to Virginia*. Where McCorkle dedicates her novel to a group of women whose first and last names suggest intergenerational and family connectedness, Youngblood's dedication implies a community of unrelated, if loving, women: "For all my Big Mamas—Luellen, Jennie Mae, Mary Lee, Bessie, Lillian, Nettie Mae, Charlie Mae, Jackie, Maxine, Myrtice, and Mineola." Thus, Youngblood lays the foundation for an alternative vision of family, one in which individual women voluntarily come together to create their own family. Interestingly, the alternative quality of this "family" makes it virtually impossible for Youngblood to include a conventional family tree. The construction of the work itself mirrors this community-as-family: the stories are unrelated and able to stand independently yet gain more when read together as a whole.

From the beginning of slavery, the African-American community attempted—if, perhaps, subconsciously—to preserve aspects of African familial structures and, at the same time, to create new familial patterns to protect and sustain them despite threatening oppression. And, since slavery, African-American families have used similar methods to preserve a sense of community despite economic, classist, racist, and social discrimination. In *The Big Mama Stories,* Youngblood shows these methods at work, depicting women who deliberately come together to form an alternative to the conventional nuclear family. Like their ancestors, they transform old African and African-American methods of nurturing and sustaining one another and create a dynamic and alternative sense of "homeplace" as "a site of resistance."

As Niara Sudarkasa and Wade Nobles have shown, the fluid conception of African kinship structures—which emphasized "the survival of the tribe," "unity, cooperative spirit, mutual responsibility" (Nobles 55) —stood the African slaves in good stead when they arrived in America. As slave families in the United States were divided and family members died, slaves fell back on the African philosophy of cooperation and unity and, as Herbert C. Gutman has shown, began to bestow symbolic kin relationships upon other slaves, binding "unrelated adults to one another" (220) and enhancing "slave group solidarity" (222). Deborah Gray White makes clear that this solidarity was particularly pronounced in slave women, whose strength resided in "what slave women as a group were able to do for one another" (120). In fact, no one "expected the biological mother of a child to fulfill all of that child's needs. Given the circumstances, the responsibilities of motherhood had to be shared, and this required close female cooperation" (127). This system of "female cooperation and interdependence" (124) created a social fabric in which women protected each other "against the depersonalizing regime of plantation work and the general dehumanizing nature of slavery" (131).

Symbolic kin networks and supportive female communities continue to thrive in the contemporary African-American community. In her landmark study, *Black Feminist Thought: Knowledge, Consciousness, and the Politics of Empowerment* (1990), Patricia Hill Collins traces the connections between black women's networks and their empowerment as both individuals and as a group. "As mothers, daughters, sisters, and friends to one another," Collins asserts, "African-American women affirm one another" (96). She delineates three types of "mothers" in the black community: "bloodmothers, othermothers, and women-centered networks" (119). Othermothers are "women who assist bloodmothers by sharing mothering responsibilities" (119), while women-centered networks are made up of bloodmothers and othermothers alike, coming together to form "[o]rganized" and "resilient" alternative families. These bloodmothers, othermothers, and women-centered networks evolved, Collins argues, from the slaves' concept of "themselves as part of an extended family/community consisting of their Black 'brothers' and 'sisters'" (49). Black women—from the slavery era through the late twentieth century—built on this foundation and created a "domestic sphere [that] encompassed a broad range of kin and community relations beyond the nuclear family household" (49).

Youngblood's alternative family closely parallels the symbolic kin network described by these historians and sociologists. In many ways, Youngblood's collection makes a compelling case for the continued existence of this type of network in the urban black community, particularly in the South where ties to rural community structures are stronger than those in the North. Thus, Youngblood's alternative family illustrates what Gutman calls the "transformation of kin obligations into non-kin social obligations" (223). *The Big Mama Stories* also illustrates the "female cooperation and independence" that White highlights in her study of

slave women (especially as this cooperation relates to mothering functions), the sense of "nurturing," "warmth and comfort" that bell hooks
describes, and the "[o]rganized, resilient, women-centered networks of
bloodmothers and othermothers" that Collins examines (119). Though
Toni Cade Bambara's *The Salt Eaters* and Zora Neale Hurston's *Their Eyes
Were Watching God* focus on the healing and nurturing qualities of extra-
familial bonds between women, *The Big Mama Stories* goes even further
in its full depiction of the supportive female community and womb of
female empowerment.

The fictional town of Princeton, Georgia, represents an intermingling
of blacks from a myriad of backgrounds. They come from rural and
urban locales, and many are also of native American descent; but all
have experienced racist and classist oppression. Facing the challenge of
mixed blood of color on one hand and the pressures of urban migration and poverty on the other, many members of this community find
themselves cut off from their families. Just as slave communities were
threatened by slaveowners' disregard for family ties, members of Princeton's black community are similarly threatened by continued economic
and political marginalization, by their position in the invisible under-
class of southern society. Many characters have been disconnected from
their blood families: Maggie is both an orphan and a mother who has
lost or abandoned her children; Miss Rosa, disconnected from a conventional nuclear family, substitutes a menagerie of both live and embalmed
animals; Miss Tom seeks family and love in her unusual relationships
with Miss Juliette and Miss Lily; Uncle Buck's early marriage to Aunt
Hattie is directly and brutally destroyed by the racist and classist prac-
tices of the sawmill at which they work; Miss Blue has lost her son, who
died "years before," and her daughter, whom she claims "slipped through
a crack in the world" (62); and the narrator herself was abandoned by
her mother as a small child and now lives with her brother and their
grandmother, Big Mama.

In the face of economic and social class pressures and racist oppression, the members of this community must discover other ways to support and nurture each other, to create alternative definitions of family.
In several cases, extended family members share the same household,

suggesting the fluid family boundaries of African kinship structures. Another approach is to accept a greater variety of expressions of sexuality, especially as these create a sense of family, as with the lesbian householders, Miss Tom and Miss Lily. The most pervasive attempt at forming alternative family bonds, however, is through creation of community, exemplified by Kin Folks Corner, a "row of shops in the black part of downtown" (79). The narrator explains that many "folks that lived in the city come from the country. When they miss the country they would go to Kin Folks Corner for a piece of home. . . . Kin Folks Corner was a place where you was liable to meet somebody from way back in your past, your family" (79). But certain elements of Kin Folks Corner prey on this community's emotional vulnerability; in other words, this is also the place where you might "get robbed by the flim-flam man" (79). Though the con artists run many scams, a popular one is to "make you think they some kin to you before they take off with your money and disappear" (80). Community members value family connections so highly and miss them so profoundly that they are easily taken in by those claiming to be kin.

This longing for family is most effectively met by the strong network of women the narrator refers to as her "Big Mamas." Their sense of themselves as a "family" and their deep and profound connections to each other have literally been in the making since preslavery days in Africa. To illustrate the process of building alternative families, Youngblood concentrates on the specific development of the adolescent narrator and her gradual initiation into the community. Her search for a mother figure parallels the larger community's search for family and can be seen in three stories. The opening story, "Born with Religion," establishes the narrator's close relationship with her grandmother, Big Mama. "Did My Mama Like To Dance?" shows the narrator's curiosity about her blood-mother and, at the same time, her search for other supportive women in the community. Finally, "They Tell Me . . . Now I Know" portrays her acceptance and understanding of the larger community of women as one big family and, indeed, paints the fullest picture of this family and how it works. Each of these stories illustrates a different component of women's community: the key role that spiritual faith plays in connecting women to one another; the talk and stories that define women's lives; and the web of interconnectedness these women have so carefully woven.

Opening the collection, "Born with Religion" establishes the narrator's relationship with Big Mama as well as a sense of the larger family to which Big Mama belongs and to which the narrator will eventually belong. Though on the surface, "Born with Religion" is the story of the #2 Mission Prayer Circle successfully praying away Aunt Vi's tumor, it relates, like most of the stories in the collection, a deeper tale of the narrator's growing relationship with women in the community, in this case Big Mama. Although not a physically large woman, Big Mama's spirit and faith is nevertheless expansive—and this spirit and faith provides an emotional bedrock for the narrator and for the other women in the community.

The story also, by its very title, makes clear the power of spiritual faith to bind women together. Whether based on Christianity or on an understanding of roots and herbs, these women—like the women in Linda Beatrice Brown's *Rainbow Roun Mah Shoulder*—are linked through their sometimes alternative, sometimes subversive spirituality. They express their spirituality collectively, most notably in their prayer circle, a term that itself suggests collective resistance, the matrix of female empowerment, and their ability to nurture, heal, and sustain one another when acting collectively. Comprised of Big Mama, Miss Mary, Miss Alice, Miss Tom, Miss EmmaLou, Miss Lamama, and Big Mama's sister, Aunt Vi, the #2 Mission Prayer Circle meets at members' homes to pray for the healing of women in the family and to mark special occasions in members' lives. Root and herb work similarly strengthens these women's concept of alternative family and community and underscores the potentially radical uses of black women's spirituality. It is especially interesting to note that in her herbal work Aunt Vi calls upon "ancestor spirits," reinforcing the idea that faith—Christian or nature-oriented—is largely defined by the idea of family and that, as in *The Salt Eaters*, it is most often used to heal and nurture family members.

After the opening story, the narrator begins to make frequent forays into the community, to talk and to listen to other community members, especially the women. As she moves into the community to talk to other

women, the narrator feels the expansiveness of the womb of female empowerment, which is present not only in Big Mama's house and in the
#2 Mission Prayer Circle but also in the community of women at large.
In "Did My Mama Like to Dance?", for example, the narrator gets Miss
Corine, the hairdresser, to "remember my mama to me" (35), since the
women in her blood family find it too difficult to talk about her blood-
mother, Fannie Mae. While this story is important for what it teaches
the narrator about her mother, it is equally important for what it teaches
the reader about the way women in this community nurture each other.
As in the rest of the collection, this story shows not only the simple—
if painful—revelation of Fannie Mae's story but also the workings of
community—particularly women's community—in Princeton, Georgia.
Though her grandmother and aunts cannot face the pain of telling the
story, the narrator finds another community member, a member of her
extended family, who can. Both the hearing and the telling of the story—
though they cause pain—strengthen the narrator, Miss Corine, and the
sense of community between them.

"Did My Mama Like To Dance?" makes clear that the women in this
community take care of each other not only through their expression of
spiritual faith or through their physical support of one another; rather,
the oral tradition—as it builds community and allows women to voice
their own vision of reality—also helps them to construct this alternative
family. Talk predominates in this, as in other, southern women's communities: the women discuss "folks' business, home remedies, and family
problems" (16), Miss Corine and her customers are labeled "walking-
talking-newspapers" (36), and many women in the community have the
gift of storytelling. Yet talk is not simply a way of wiling away the time; it
is also a crucial component in the development of this particular alternative family. Whether she is talking to Miss Corine or learning "the ways
things used to be" from Big Mama (26), the narrator increasingly becomes a part of this community through listening to stories. Illustrating
the power of women's voice to build alternative women's networks, the
stories provide continuity and a sense of history to a threatened community; to a symbolic kin network, in constant need of reinforcement,
the stories provide a sense of connected generations.

The narrator's conversation with Miss Corine in "Did My Mama Like To Dance?" parallels those she increasingly has with other community women: she asks questions and, when the time is right, gets answers. Most important, she is nurtured as a valuable family member. Throughout the collection, the community has wrapped itself protectively around her, an enfolding Youngblood often suggests in the image of the narrator sleeping safely nestled up against Big Mama or Uncle Buck or wrapped in the sounds of Miss Blue's singing. This protectiveness and sense of warm community permeates the collection from the first story, where the #2 Mission Prayer Circle reveals its power to heal one of its own and where Big Mama first assures her granddaughter she has plenty of "Big Mamas." Throughout this discussion of *The Big Mama Stories,* the word "family" has been used to refer to these women, these "Big Mamas," not simply because they are very closely knit but because they consciously perceive themselves as a family. In "Snuff Dippers," for example, the narrator says that "Big Mama *raised me* in the company of wise old Black women like herself" (19; my emphasis), suggesting that these women are not just incidental neighbors but consciously chosen parent figures who help Big Mama raise the narrator.

Nowhere does Youngblood make this idea of community-as-family more explicit, however, than in the last story, "They Tell Me . . . Now I Know." In this story, the narrator gets her period, her "blood," for the first time, and she knows her initiation into the family will soon take place. She says, "When I was a lil girl I knew the day was coming when I would join the circle of women" (101). Significantly, it is the coming of "blood" that allows the narrator to become part of this circle. Previously nurtured by the womb of female empowerment, she now literally and tangibly becomes a part of this womb. Again, it is clear that this is not just a tightly knit group of friends. Big Mama's assertion that "*the women in the family* [will] take her to a secret place for the crossing over" (102; my emphasis) shows that these women have constructed an alternative to the nuclear family. The narrator further underscores this idea by referring to these women as "all my Big Mamas" (103, 104) and by claiming that "[t]hese women were my mamas. They had always been there to give me whatever I thought I needed" (106). As a living, breathing organism, the nurturing womb of women grows and changes as it gives birth to and makes room for a new young woman.

Here Youngblood makes an interesting shift. Blacks have traditionally used "Big Mama" as a name for grandmothers (see, for example, Fanny's "Big Mama Celie" in Walker's *The Temple of My Familiar*), and though the narrator herself has used the term in this way, Youngblood moves the epithet from pure denotation to evocative connotation. "Big Mamas," in these stories, are women who open themselves up to new daughters, motherless children who need to become part of the family. Thus, Youngblood invokes the idea of using terms of blood relation to refer to symbolic kin bonds. This shift in the use of the term "Big Mama"— and in general, the use of the term "Mama"—suggests the narrator's growing understanding and appreciation of these women as mamas, as she moves from a childlike faith in Big Mama, to a curiosity about her bloodmother, to a search for other mother figures (especially in "Maggie Agatha Christmas St. Clair"), to the final story when she understands these women as a collective mama or alternative family.

Most important, in the last story the narrator is initiated into the community and, significantly, given a name (Rita). Though nameless throughout the book, in the final story she moves from anonymity to particularity, thereby achieving distinction as a woman. She tells of the event: "Standing in that circle of light behind the Eighth Street Baptist Church on a clear September night I was given my name and invited into the circle of women, no longer a lil girl. I was a woman now" (106). Her big mamas have played the most important part in her movement toward womanhood. They have answered her questions, watched and waited for her to gain her "blood" and to achieve readiness for womanhood, and defined the ritual, the "crossing over" which makes her part of their community. Most important, they have shared stories with her. As she spends "time alone with my Big Mamas" (103) in preparation for this rite of passage, they talk and share with her: "All the stories they had told me were gifts, all the love more precious than gold. They tell me . . . now I know" (106). Once again, the power of women's stories is crucial in shaping women's identity. A resilient matrix of female empowerment, the circle of big mamas have effectively fought the dehumanizing effects of classist and racist oppression and have given spiritual birth to one of their own.

These women have voluntarily—and consciously—come together to form an alternative to the conventional nuclear family. Historically thwarted by the white South in their attempts to form and maintain bonds with immediate family members—a form of oppression that persists today due to social and economic pressures—the women in this community transform old African and African-American methods of nurturing and supporting one another. The narrator's search for a mother —that is, for family—is rewarded when she takes the time to listen to the stories and ask careful questions. Youngblood, like bell hooks, Julie Dash, Jill McCorkle, and their literary grandmothers, focuses on the positive role of family and challenges conventional definitions of that word. In the face of racist, classist, and patriarchal oppression, women are often disappointed when they look solely to immediate—or even extended blood—family for support and nurturing. When they begin to re-create notions of family, when they create matrices of female empowerment, however, new possibilities for strong bonds and sustaining connections emerge.

TWO

RACE AND REGION:
BLACK AND WHITE SISTERS
OF THE NOW SOUTH

What we have in the South are two cultures in symbiosis, each
constantly taking from the other. . . . White culture feeds off of
black and grows and changes, and black culture feeds from white and
grows and changes. Finally, it is possible to speak of two cultures, one
white and the other black, but it is also proper to speak of a fusion of
cultures. This fusion . . . is the substantial beginning of the oneness of
modern Southern life. It is why black people and white people in similar
situations perform very much alike. It is why they share many of the
same values. It is why they can . . . sometimes relate to one another with
great intensity and understanding.

JOEL WILLIAMSON, *The Crucible of Race*

*T*he *Three Faces of Eve* (1957) is psychologists Corbett H. Thigpen's
and Hervey M. Cleckley's report of an actual southern woman who
suffered from a multiple personality disorder. "Eve," a twenty-five-year-
old white Baptist homemaker from Georgia, exhibits two distinct, but
diametrically opposed, personalities. "Eve White," who emerges most
frequently in Eve's day-to-day life, epitomizes the southern lady, while
"Eve Black" is "provocative and, in every nuance of voice and manner, flaunt[s] sexual challenge and promise" (Thigpen and Cleckley 83).
Although Joel Williamson sees *The Three Faces of Eve* as "a nearly perfect
allegory for the mind of the white South in race relations" (495), that is,
although he sees in Eve's struggle the history of white treatment of and
relationship to blacks, I believe Eve's story can more strikingly be seen
as an allegory of southern womanhood's split into two halves, white
and black, which while inextricably connected nevertheless cannot meet
and fuse successfully into a whole ideal of southern womanhood. As

Williamson himself states, "Eve was wholly white racially, visibly she was thoroughly female, but she had difficulty being totally good. If she could not be totally good, she would be totally bad. In the South, a 'good woman' (white) cannot be a little bit bad . . . anymore than she can be a little bit black" (497).

Thus, Eve—in her dual manifestation as Eve White and Eve Black— embodies the schizophrenic existence of white and black women in the South who have historically occupied necessarily opposite sexual and social space. But as Eve's story ultimately suggests, it is possible for white and black women in the South to fuse new ideals of southern womanhood that eschew the labels "white" and "black." At the end of Eve's story, Jane, a new and balanced personality, emerges as Eve White and Eve Black finally die. The struggle to create healthy friendships between Eve Whites and Eve Blacks and in doing so to bring life to Janes all over the South lies at the heart of Ellen Douglas's *Can't Quit You, Baby* (1988) and Dori Sanders's *Clover* (1990).

Above all, the South is set aside and made distinct by its peculiar racial relations. The issue of race, in fact, has been the defining factor of the South since its inception as a region apart. Though some legitimately argue that the North has practiced and continues to practice its own heinous forms of racial discrimination, the South has been the locus of pervasive violence against blacks, and the white South has been blatant and outspoken in its attempts to create and maintain a segregated society. Though the social climate may be changing for southern blacks, and while this may partially explain recent black immigration to the South, the rest of the country still perceives the South—deservedly or not—as a haven for white racists.

Such a view precludes an understanding of the multicultural South and hampers us from examining how the southern white and black communities influence and inform each other. Nowhere is the "great intensity and understanding" between whites and blacks seen more fully than in the connections between white and black southern women. As Minrose Gwin argues, "[B]lack and white women . . . mirror the paradox of the South. Their bonds are often deep and strong. Yet they are those of victim and oppressor, and they are cemented by suffering" (16). Gwin's excellent 1985 study, *Black and White Women of the Old South: The Peculiar Sisterhood in American Literature,* examines in great depth and detail the provocative relationship between southern black and white women.

The prevailing image of the white southern woman has been that of the aristocratic lady who reigns precariously on her pedestal and whose position is defined by the intersection of her class and racial status. As Williamson points out, though "upper-class women in [nineteenth-century] Western civilization generally were being pedestalized, in the South the pedestal was higher and rising" (31). The white southern lady was expected to be, as Anne Goodwyn Jones describes her, "physically pure, fragile, and beautiful, socially dignified, cultured, and gracious, within the family sacrificial and submissive, yet, if the occasion required, intelligent and brave" (xi).

Balancing the white lady on her pedestal was her black "sister"—often literally her half-sister. As Gwin argues, "[T]he patriarchy of the Old South seems to have firmly assisted its ladies up onto the pedestal, that emblem of chastity and powerlessness, just as surely as it forced black women into the dark corners of the Big House to be used as vessels of sexual pleasure or to breed new property" (4). Although some white women understood the mutual oppression they shared with their black sisters,[1] most white women of this period (as reflected in their auto-biographies) had "extremely ambivalent feelings toward black women" (Gwin 82). Gwin notes that "one constant" exists in nineteenth-century white southern women's articulation of their experience: they "rarely perceive[d] or acknowledge[d] . . . the humanity of their black sisters" (5); instead, "[t]hey beat black women, nurture[d] them, sentimental-ize[d] them, despise[d] them—but they seldom [saw] them as individuals with selves commensurate to their own" (5). Black women were kept in their places not only by race but also by their social and economic dis-enfranchisement. Though both the white woman and the black woman were treated as property, the white woman—the china doll—was far better off financially than her black sister, who ranked no higher than the cattle and horses sold at auction.

So obscured was white women's view of black women in the nineteenth-century South that they were forced to categorize their black sisters as "Eve Black." In other words, as Gwin argues, white women saw "black women as a color, as servants, as children, as adjuncts, as sexual competition, as dark sides of their own sexual selves—as black Other" (5). Gwin goes so far as to assert white women's understanding of black women as "the darker side of a repressed self, her own id" (49). The peculiar tenseness that existed between southern blacks and whites, but particularly between black and white southern women, comprises what Lillian Smith called the "race-sex-sin spiral" (121). Smith focuses on southern race relations of the first half of the twentieth century in her landmark memoir, *Killers of the Dream* (1949; rev. 1961). Compelling in its examination of the interconnections between the southern brands of racism, sexism, and Protestantism, Smith notes that although she "realize[s] this is a personal memoir," she also believes that "in another sense, it is Every Southerner's memoir" (21), speaking to the pervasiveness and commonality of the problem she addresses.

Smith traces the historical development of this southern neurosis from the white master's sexual exploitation of his female slaves—a practice that, Smith claims, would have had to have been seen as bestiality, given their prior premise that blacks were "animals" and thus legitimately enslaved (120). "The white man's role as slaveholder and Christian and puritan," Smith argues, "were exacting far more than the strength of his mind could sustain. Each time he found the back-yard temptation irresistible, his conscience split more deeply from his acts and his mind from things as they are" (120–21). But the "race-sex-sin spiral" did not end with slavery; instead it continued to perpetuate itself well into the twentieth century. So profoundly did "[g]uilt, shame, fear, [and] lust" "weave in and out of southern life" (121) that even small children felt the threatening connection between them. Smith writes, "[W]hen we as small children crept over the race line and ate and played with Negroes or broke other segregation customs known to us, we felt the same dread fear of consequences, the same overwhelming guilt we felt when we crept over the sex line and played with our body" (84). This connection between race and sex also stimulated the white South's sadistic—even erotic—response to the lynchings and castrations of black men.

Out of the race-sex-sin spiral grew a complex system of interactions between black and white southern women. The pattern for these interactions initially formed during slavery, which "demanded moral superiority from white women and sexual availability from black [women]," while all the time expecting "mistress and slave woman to live and work in intimate physical proximity" (Gwin 45–46). Gwin terms them "obverse images in the popular mind"—"the chaste belle and the lustful female slave" (46). Given the "intimate physical proximity" these women shared—the "kitchen, boudoir, and Big House," as Gwin says (46)—the natural question arises: did these women also share emotional bonds? Although a few scholars believe they did not,[2] many other writers suggest there were occasional moments of bonding and emotional response between black and white women in the old South. Gwin asserts that although there are some instances of bonding between slave and mistress, and although "[f]rom both white and black female perspectives [there] emerge moments of real closeness in the face of common suffering" (12), such bonding took place at a high price. Many white women, says Gwin, " 'love[d]' their female slaves or servants only when the black women assume[d] a demeanor of inferiority and powerlessness" (11), while black women who felt affection for their white mistresses often did so, Gwin suggests, because they sought in them "the natural nurturance that circumstance [and, I might add, the patriarchal oppression of chattel slavery] ha[d] denied them in their real mothers" (12). Though some "cross-racial relationships" existed due to "a shared sense of societal demands which placed them in opposite but mutually dependent roles" (11), more often "color lines blinded white women to the humanity of their black sisters and built in black women massive layers of hatred for those fair ladies who would not, or could not, see their suffering" (109). These women, then, "were both drawn to and repelled by their racial female Other" (11). Whether or not black and white women shared close emotional bonds, one thing remains clear: they had a charged relationship. As Gwin argues, "Each is only one half of a self. What is so terribly ironic is that the missing piece so fervently desired by one race of women seems to have caused so much suffering for the other" (11).[3]

The tense relationship between white and black southern women did not end with the Civil War but instead continued throughout Reconstruction, the first half of the twentieth century, the civil rights movement, and into the late twentieth century. Such works as Margaret Walker's *Jubilee* (1966), Grace King's *Monsieur Motte* (1888), and Kate Chopin's collection of short stories, *Bayou Folk* (1894), suggest that black and white women continued to interact with each other much as they had before the Civil War. Black women continued to work for white women, usually as domestic workers, while well-to-do white women continued to lead "sheltered lives," to borrow Ellen Glasgow's term. White and black women continued to be defined not only by their racial differences but also by their economic and class relationship to each other: upper-class white women were still to be pampered and lower-class black women were still the ones expected to do the pampering. Such a world was constantly defined by what Smith calls "the edgy blackness and whiteness of things" (12).

This tense connection between southern blacks and whites continued to dominate southern social and political structures, finally resulting in the civil rights movement. Early relationships between black women participating in the Montgomery bus boycott and their sometimes sympathetic white female employers are captured in the film *The Long Walk Home* (1991), although documents from the sixties suggest that the relationships between black and white women involved in the movement continued to be strained with mutual fear as well as mutual attraction. Though some white women claimed to have found new role models in the black women they met ("For the first time," said one white woman, "I had role models I could really respect" [qtd. in Evans 51]), others had to confront their fears. When asked if she sensed any hostility from black women, one white woman replied, "Oh! tons and tons. I was very afraid of black women, very afraid" (qtd. in Evans 81). And as a black southern woman involved in the movement asserted, "If white women had a problem in SNCC (Student Nonviolent Coordinating Committee) it was not just a male/woman problem . . . it was also a black woman/ white woman problem. It was a race problem rather than a woman's problem" (qtd. in Evans 81).

Despite resentment on both sides, some white women began to see, as had their foremothers in the nineteenth century, that black and white southern women shared a mutual oppression. This growing realization prompted what Sara Evans asserts was the "earliest feminist response" in America during this era. In her 1979 study, *Personal Politics: The Roots of Women's Liberation in the Civil Rights Movement and the New Left*, Evans argues that the feminist movement of the 1960s and 1970s arose in large part from the efforts of southern women involved in the civil rights movement and was fostered primarily by a "network of southern women"—Casey Hayden, Mary King, Jane Stembridge, and others (57).[4] The central participation of these women in redefining women's position in the South and elsewhere laid the foundation for the generation of southern women, artists, and writers to follow who would continue and build upon this process of redefinition. The empowerment of women via alternative female networks and via the voicing of women's concerns—empowerment central to the understanding of contemporary southern women's fiction—started with the work of southern women in the civil rights movement. The recent resurgence in literature by African Americans and other peoples of color can also be attributed to this same movement.

In 1964, an anonymous paper entitled "The Position of Women in SNCC" was circulated at a movement conference and was erroneously assumed to have been written by Ruby Doris Smith Robinson, an outspoken southern black woman. Because black women were beginning to hold positions of power in SNCC, many white women in the movement "believed that if anyone could be expected to write such a paper, it would be black women" (Evans 88). Yet importantly, this paper— the first explicit statement about sexism in the movement and, more significant, the first real articulation of what would soon become the feminist movement—was not written by Robinson but rather by two southern white women, Casey Hayden and Mary King.[5] As the "spiritual daughters" of the Grimké sisters (Evans 101), Hayden, King, and other southern white women began to see the connection between southern blacks' oppression (against which they were fighting in the civil rights movement) and their own oppression as women. Hayden and King, in a 1965 "kind of memo" to which they did sign their names, wrote that women, like blacks,

> seem to be caught up in a common-law caste system that operates, sometimes subtly, forcing them to work around or outside hierarchical structures of power which may exclude them. Women seem to be placed in the same position of assumed subordination in personal situations too. It is a caste system which, at its worst, uses and exploits women. (qtd. in Evans 98–99)

Though both black and white women were beginning to understand that they needed to band together in reaction against the southern patriarchy, and though this understanding would soon make a very large contribution to the women's liberation movement, the shift in thinking was particularly galvanizing for southern white women. As Dorothy Burlage points out, southern white women began to see that the civil rights movement was "a key to pulling down all the fascist notions and mythologies and institutions in the South . . . , notions about white women and repression" (qtd. in Evans 58). As they began to recognize and resist the race-sex-sin spiral, these women began "to forge a new sense of themselves, to redefine the meaning of being a woman quite apart from the flawed image they had inherited" (Evans 57).

Perhaps now that the civil rights and women's liberation movements have played themselves out in the South, now that blacks are beginning to move back to the historical region of oppression, and now that many southern women are beginning to articulate new ideals of southern womanhood, perhaps only now can white and black southern women envision new friendships between themselves, to break through the edgy tension that exists between them, and to achieve the previously elusive resolution. Perhaps only now Jane can emerge from the fragments of Eve White and Eve Black. Both Ellen Douglas's *Can't Quit You, Baby* (1988) and Dori Sanders's *Clover* (1990) depict black and white women forming intimate bonds with one another and trace their emergence from the rigid categories of Eve White and Eve Black that have defined the relationships between southern white and black women for so long. They may not yet have emerged as Janes, and they may not yet have formed perfect friendships, but they have taken the important first steps. Gwin's assertion that "the southern racial experience is ultimately ambiguous" (16) will probably continue to be accurate for a long time to come, and certainly, as Catherine Clinton points out in her study on the plantation mistress, we will hear the "rattling of the chains" for many years (231). The point, it seems to me, is to acknowledge the debt of slavery and racism in the South and to create new ways for black and white women to share more than mutual oppression. As Gwin puts it, "What lies in the hidden past, and this is particularly true of the southern past, lives within many of us whether we know it or not, whether we wish it or not" (9).

Ellen Douglas (a pseudonym for Josephine Haxton) began writing in the early sixties. *A Family's Affairs*, awarded the Houghton Mifflin Fellowship Award, was published in 1962 and was followed by *Black Cloud, White Cloud* (1963), *Where the Dreams Cross* (1968), *Apostles of Light* (1973), *The Rock Cried Out* (1979), *A Lifetime Burning* (1982), and *Can't Quit You, Baby* (1988). But Douglas's progressive interest in contemporary issues, particularly southern race relations, her narrative experimentation, and the vitality of her recent fiction place her in the spirit of the contemporary generation.

Douglas grew out of a society with strict notions of racial relations, but she also grew up in a protected and rarefied well-to-do white southern world. Her background as "an upper middle class Southern girl from an unusually pious radically sheltering family" ("Faulkner in Time" 290) has led her to deal closely and deeply with issues of race in nearly all her novels, most recently in *Can't Quit You, Baby*. In this novel, she tells the story of the friendship between Cornelia O'Kelly, a white woman, and Julia "Tweet" Carrier, her black servant. Set against the backdrop of racially defined Mississippi, *Can't Quit You, Baby* looks at the barriers that separate black and white women, at the unacknowledged bonds that develop between them, and the painful process both sides must undergo as they attempt to build meaningful friendships with one another. Ultimately, Cornelia and Tweet find ways to acknowledge their friendship as well as their bitterness and anger toward one another. Yet Douglas's novel suggests they are still somewhat defined as Eve White and Eve Black, though such rigid categories are blurring in their lives.

The novel's opening scene sets the stage for our consideration of Tweet and Cornelia's peculiar relationship:

> The two women are sitting at right angles to each other at the kitchen table on a sunny July morning in the nineteen-sixties. On the stove behind them a pot of boiling syrup scents the air with cloves and cinnamon. They are making preserves. . . .
>
> Of all the preserves they make together, the two agree that figs are the most delicious, the most aesthetically pleasing. . . . Separately their mothers or grandmothers must have taught them this recipe, for they did not know each other until they were grown. (3–4)

This scene suggests that these women have a long and ongoing, if often unacknowledged, bond. Significantly, their bonding takes place in the kitchen, a room that simultaneously suggests their creativity, their mutual oppression, and their relationship as servant and mistress. Just as important, this novel is set in the 1960s—the period in which black and white women in the South were actively redefining the terms of their existence as women in the South and in which they were beginning to realize their mutual oppression. This opening scene sets the novel's defining tensions in motion: the women share a creative bond but are also placed against each other. Despite the affection that emerges in subsequent pages, Tweet remains Cornelia's servant, Cornelia remains Tweet's boss. To reinforce these class-defined roles, Tweet calls Cornelia "Mrs. O'Kelly" while Cornelia calls Tweet "Julia" and her husband "Mr. Carrier," unable to bring herself to call them by their nicknames, Tweet and Nig.

As Douglas tells the story of a particular white woman and her black servant and of their oppositional relationship, she does so with a decidedly metafictional narrative approach. The novel's narrator—almost a character in her own right—tells Cornelia's story and reports Cornelia's thoughts and, in the narrator's own identification as a white woman, presumably has a great deal of insight into Cornelia's thoughts and actions. Tweet's story, however, comes to us via the narrator's report of Tweet's narrative so that the reader remains one step removed from Tweet's own telling of her story. Most interesting, perhaps, is Douglas's creation of the enigmatic narrator, presumably a stand-in for the author herself. The narrator frequently calls attention to herself, her storytelling, her attitudes, and the ways these attitudes affect her storytelling. Douglas's metafictional novel foregrounds not only the tangled bond between Tweet and Cornelia but also the difficulty of rendering that tale accurately and completely. The narrator, then, constantly complicates her narrative, calling attention, for example, not only to the racial divisions between Tweet and Cornelia but also to the difficulty of distinguishing racial divisions. As she attempts to understand Cornelia and Tweet's snarled relationship, she considers over and over again "the crushing together of lives" (214) and considers, for example, Cornelia's viewing of many paintings in a museum, which suggests that all "lives and deaths, no matter that no one knows why, must be entangled beyond extricating" (215).

Tweet's and Cornelia's entangled lives result from the oppositional relationship all southern black and white women share, Tweet's perilous position as sexual chattel held in tension by Cornelia's precarious perch on the pedestal. Tweet's vulnerability as sexual chattel for the white male community directly results from her status as a black woman. Douglas paints a damning portrait of the white community's paternalistic treatment of blacks most fully in those sections focusing on Tweet, her grandfather, and their land. Tweet first comprehends her lack of power in the larger community when she realizes that, as a black woman, especially as a black fifteen-year-old, her suspicions of her father's murder of her grandfather will be dismissed. Moreover, because no one pays attention to the word of a black person, much less a young black woman, Tweet's efforts to claim her inheritance of land result not only in a fight with her father but also in manipulation by Mr. Lord as well. These moves by the white community were protocol for the time period: "[S]uch transactions, through which small farms owned by black people became part of larger farms owned by white people, were routine—to everyone's advantage. The land would be more economical to work and the Negroes could move to Chicago" (112). Tweet's story of her robbed inheritance not only echoes a similar occurrence in Alice Walker's *The Color Purple* (1982) but also graphically illustrates southern blacks' lack of control over their legal or financial—and thus, their social—destinies. It is clear that their social position is defined not only by racial discrimination but also by class constraints.

Although the entire black community was deeply affected by the social structure that actively oppressed them, southern black women were forced to play perhaps the most peculiar role in the "peculiar institution" and its latter-day equivalents. If white men were to place their wives and daughters on pedestals and revere them as chaste, they needed to balance that perception by putting other women in the role of sexual chattel. Situated within this framework, then, the opening scene in which Tweet tells Cornelia of Wayne Jones's sexual harassment of her takes on profound resonance. Cornelia has just told Tweet of the death of Jones, Tweet's former boss and a white man. As Tweet tells Cornelia of her sexual vulnerability at the hands of a socially and economically powerful white man, she details not only the horror of her position in relation to his but also her decision to tell his wife about the situation. As a black woman, Tweet oversteps prescribed boundaries by being so frank in her revelations to her white employer and by detailing to a southern white woman her position as sexual chattel of the southern white man. And as a white woman, Cornelia feels forced to uphold the status quo position on the issue of forced concubinage and ultimately ignores the implications of Tweet's story.

If this scene foregrounds Tweet's position as possible sexual chattel, the entire novel not only indicates Cornelia's position on the pedestal but also complicates it as well. Douglas's depiction of the pedestal involves the recurring image of Cornelia's elopement from her tower bedroom. Cornelia epitomizes the southern white woman. As Tweet puts it, she is "reserve" (60) and so polite that, like Tweet's landlady, she "[m]akes an excuse if she ax you to wait on her" (102). She is almost regal in her carriage: "Do you notice that she stands slightly swayback, as if she's lifted her shoulders like a queen ready to receive the heavy, ermine-trimmed mantle she must wear to the coronation?" (39). If she is a queen, she is the queen of her kitchen, where she "prefers to hold court": "Cornelia is an accomplished cook and the kitchen is her throne room" (6). All her life she has maintained a certain aloofness to those around her, both to her employees and to her family. In her position as one of the "sheltered" women, she not only maintains this aloofness to others but also maintains an aloofness to her own inner self.

Cornelia complicates her destiny as a proper southern white woman by eloping with a socially unacceptable Irish-Catholic army air corpsman. Appropriately enough, Cornelia escapes from her tower bedroom in which her mother has locked her. The tower—which Douglas refers to in *A Family's Affairs* as a "Rapunzel's tower" (384)—functions as a tangible image of the pedestal. Though romantic ("What could be more romantic than the sight of a young girl sitting in the morning sunshine in her tower bedroom brushing her hair?" [72]), the tower is also isolating: boys do not come by to see her, and she is removed from the normal social interactions of her peers. When she meets and falls in love with John, the tower becomes something she must escape, since her frantic mother has now literally locked her there. When John discovers Cornelia's imprisonment, he asks her, "Will you come down? . . . Or shall I climb up?" (90). Significantly, Cornelia decides to come down and apparently to step off the pedestal. She easily achieves this initial, apparent move off the pedestal: she "ease[s] herself off the ledge," "dangl[es] thirty feet above the yard, high over the yellow carpet of ginkgo leaves," "[t]he limbs shake, leaves fall around her in a golden shower, and John draws her steadily across" (92–93).

Yet Cornelia's early elopement from the tower—despite its symbolic resonance—does not ultimately signal a real and profound move off the pedestal. If anything, John simply becomes a substitute for her mother. As he dotes on her, reveres her, and insulates her from the real world, he perpetuates her position on the pedestal. They have a happy life together, their love for each other grows rather than diminishes, and they have two perfect children and a successful business. Cornelia's refusal to consider both what she gains while remaining perched and what she surrenders marks her throughout the bulk of the novel.

Ultimately Cornelia is forced off the pedestal. She discovers that her son has been living out of wedlock with a lower-class divorcée with two children, and as she lashes out in anger not only at this but also at the knowledge that her husband and children have kept many secrets from her over the years, her husband has a sudden stroke and dies. The pain of these events and the realization of her insulated, protected status sends Cornelia over the edge of her pedestal. She initially sinks and falls; she has a nervous breakdown and finally goes to New York to pull herself together. But as she makes love to a stranger, she consciously decides to step off the pedestal rather than fall off it. The movement from the pedestal she had begun so long ago at the age of seventeen is finally completed, a prerequisite to her friendship with Tweet.

Although Cornelia and Tweet are placed in diametric opposition, they—like many other black and white southern women before them—forge an unacknowledged bond. Their oppositional status, in fact, joins them: because they are both oppressed by the still-dominant southern white patriarchy, they must implicitly look to each other for support. They rarely, if ever, articulate their affection, though their actions suggest the bond they feel. They come to each other's aid when their relatives die and in other moments of crisis. Most significant, Tweet has expressed her affection to Cornelia during their years together by sharing numerous stories, revealing herself, bringing Cornelia into her life by telling of her painful past. But Cornelia, who is hard-of-hearing, often pretends not to hear, implicitly rejecting Tweet's offer of friendship. At other times, she listens out of apparent politeness and condescension. Yet the quality of Tweet's narratives and Cornelia's reciprocated affection during key moments in Tweet's life foreshadow Cornelia's realization of Tweet's importance in her life. Though she may believe she listens to Tweet because she has an obligation to do so, the reader suspects she listens because she is drawn to Tweet and needs to learn her lessons.

Later in the novel, as Cornelia imagines conversations with Tweet in New York, she hears Tweet finally admonishing her for her pretense at listening:

Listen to *me,* she says. I'm too polite to say, but I notice you don't hardly ever ax a question, and sometimes *seems* like you're listening—you put on listening—but you ain't. Seems like you think you don't need to ax, don't need to listen, you already got answers, or else you don't want to hear none. But where are all them words, if you don't ax, don't tell, don't answer? (194)

As Cornelia confronts the implications of her nonlistening and of her noninvolvement with the world, she keeps remembering Tweet's statement about listening for her grandfather's voice in the cypress brake: "I'm afraid. Nevertheless I go. I make myself strong to listen" (206). Finally, Cornelia has learned one of Tweet's most important lessons: she needs to make herself "strong to listen," to hear all of what Tweet has to tell her, to listen to her own inner conscience, to break through the willful deafness that has separated her from others. Lessons learned, Cornelia returns home to care for Tweet in her illness and attempts to heal Tweet by returning the favor—by talking.

Cornelia's realization of her willful deafness and of the need to be a much more active and committed listener *and* talker is paramount to her realization of Tweet's significance in her life. Her imagined and remembered conversations with Tweet reveal not only the caring that has gone unacknowledged but also the anger, hatred, and repulsion. As she remembers moments of affection as well as moments of anger, Cornelia works toward a much fuller understanding of her complex link to Tweet and of her own need to take a deliberate step off the pedestal in order to join the real world and to forge a true friendship with Tweet.

Upon her return to Mississippi to care for Tweet, Cornelia immediately establishes a therapy of talk and massage:

Cornelia keeps one hand on Tweet's arm, skin touching skin. . . . Cornelia squeezes Tweet's hand. I'm coming to see you every day, she says. . . . We can talk. I have some things to tell you, to talk to you about. You don't know it yet, but you've . . . you've been *with* me—I mean in New York. . . . I *heard* you. Like you used to say your grandpa talked to you—remember? (237–38)

In this poignant scene, Cornelia reaches out to Tweet as fully and honestly as she can. But though Cornelia has acknowledged her coolness toward Tweet and her family, her love for Tweet, and her need to move fully off the pedestal in order to shape a new and meaningful relationship with Tweet, she has characteristically—both for herself individually and for southern white women in general—forgotten to take into account one crucial element: Tweet's own feelings about the situation.

Though Cornelia is ready to repair her relationship with Tweet, Tweet herself is still angry with Cornelia. At one point, Tweet shoots Cornelia "a look of such rage and hatred" that "it ran through the air like fire through a wick, joined their eyes together, pierced hers [Cornelia's] like a fork of lightning" (238). Ultimately, Cornelia decides to use Tweet's anger as a motivation to rejoin the world. As she helps Tweet "sing" her way back to speech, Cornelia also encourages Tweet to express her anger at her. Tweet's rage is twofold. She resents Cornelia first because, as a white woman, she represents a group of people who have actively—if sometimes unwittingly—oppressed her. To remind herself of this symbolic anger, Tweet has stolen one of Cornelia's barrettes and now keeps it in a bowl in her living room. As Tweet says, "Sometimes I forget" (254). On a more personal level, Tweet resents Cornelia's willingness to forget the painful past she shares with Tweet and her presumptuous decision to form a sudden and new friendship with Tweet. Here begins Cornelia and Tweet's hardest fight, as Cornelia pushes her to "come back into the world," and as Tweet comes back into that world by actively expressing her anger at Cornelia.

Finally, Tweet accepts Cornelia's invitation to friendship. As they engage in one final round of angry words, the bowl holding Tweet's jewelry and the stolen barrette clatters to the floor. They get down on the floor together, "picking up the strings of beads, the plastic doubloons" (255). Tweet picks up the barrette and hands it to Cornelia, who significantly "drops it back in the bowl" (255). The symbol of Tweet's relationship to white women, the symbol of her need to remind herself that she must, by definition, hate Cornelia, the symbol ultimately of the barrier that must always divide her from her best friend, is returned to her bowl. Cornelia can no more take back the barrette and dissolve the barrier between them than Tweet can forget that she hates Cornelia for what she represents. It is at this moment when Tweet and Cornelia acknowledge the eternal barrier that divides them but also the deep bond that connects them:

> Well, Tweet says. She reaches out, touches Cornelia's hand. Lord, what I'm talking all that foolishness [about being mad], she says.
> Cornelia laughs. What can we do, she says, when we've shot somebody? Look around? See where we're headed? That's all I can see to do after you shoot somebody. (255–56)

Tweet and Cornelia have formed a new kind of relationship between southern black and white women, based both on now-acknowledged bonds as well as on an essential consciousness of the patriarchally imposed barriers that divide them. Douglas's novel marks an important step in the developing relationship between the black and white communities in the South, particularly between black and white women, but it is no mere utopian fiction. Cornelia and Tweet's relationship grows out of a centuries-long bond between white women and black women in the South, especially between wealthy white women and their black slaves or servants. The acknowledgment of the bond and the concurrent realization that the barriers will continue to exist represent a new era in biracial friendships among women, but Douglas suggests that with determination and love, black and white women can shape new patterns of relating to one another if they wish.

Throughout the novel, Tweet, true to her name, has sung several songs, including the Willie Dixon tune, "Can't Quit You, Baby." She sings this song often as she thinks of her husband, Nig: "Can't quit you, baby, but I got to put you down a little while. I love you, baby, but I sure do hate your ways." Though this song lyric provides both the title and the epigraph for the novel, its true significance does not become clear until the final pages. Having just fought out their anger and resentment and having just resolved the particular moment by putting the barrette back into Tweet's jewelry bowl, Tweet and Cornelia finally separate for the day:

> Cornelia is leaving now, walking down the sidewalk toward her car. She turns, looks at Tweet, who is standing on the front porch,

watching her go. Tweet sings out suddenly: Oh, I love you, baby, but I sure do hate your ways. She's laughing and singing at the same time. I say, I love you, darlin, but I hate your treacherous low down ways.

That's how the song goes, she calls to Cornelia. (256)

Both Tweet and Cornelia have learned that that is indeed "how the song goes." They "can't quit" each other—they are too inextricably bound up in each other's lives—but they have to put each other down "a little while"; they must allow themselves to experience their anger as well as their love for one another. Only when southern women acknowledge all the complexities of the peculiarly fraught relationship between southern black and white women, that is, only when they acknowledge the edgy tension that lies beneath the surface of proper black-white, servant-mistress relations, can true friendships between them be forged.

If Ellen Douglas grew up in a stereotypical racially defined southern world, Dori Sanders grew up in a world in which racial and class prescriptions were not nearly so rigid. Her father, the principal of a segregated elementary school, also possessed one of the oldest black-owned farms in York County, South Carolina, thus breaking the pervasive class barriers that confront most southern blacks. Sanders writes, "As a schoolteacher and a landowner, who very early on purchased additional land for his sons, my father enjoyed a certain status in both the black and the white farm communities" (*Ideal Land* [4]). More important, such a situation meant that Mr. Sanders was not placed into the "sharecropper-type relationship that some blacks . . . had with white landowners. There was no one to say, 'Boy, plow the cotton today. Y'hear?'" ([4]). As with Douglas, Sanders's upbringing shapes her attitude toward and narrative of southern relationships between the races, as evidenced in her novels, *Clover* (1990) and *Her Own Place* (1993). And like much of Douglas's work, *Clover* looks at developing friendships and bonds between black and white southern women.

Clover portrays the interaction of two distinct and separate southern communities: the white South and the black South. College-educated and middle-class Gaten Hill, the principal of an integrated school, is a black widower with a ten-year-old daughter, Clover. Gaten shocks his community of Round Hill when he marries Sara Kate, a white woman. Just hours after the wedding, Gaten dies in an automobile accident, leaving Sara Kate to raise Clover. The novel focuses on Sara Kate's developing relationship with the Round Hill community, with Gaten's extended family, and, most important, with her new stepdaughter. In its depiction of the biracial mother-daughter bond, Sanders's novel makes a bold departure because it avoids the economically and socially dominant pattern of the white woman and her maid. As Clover, Sara Kate, and Clover's aunt Everleen work toward new relationships between black and white women, they do so in an innovative way. For instead of the black women having to make overtures into the white community, the white woman must come into the black community and put herself on the line to forge these biracial bonds. Ultimately, Sanders's vision of black-white relationships in the South may be more optimistic as well as more radical: it posits a deep, significant, ongoing bond between black and white communities in the South and articulates a new vision of integrated southern community. It gives tangible life to Williamson's argument that the fusion of black and white cultures in the South "is the substantial beginning of the oneness of modern Southern life" (39).

Told in a series of flashbacks, *Clover* is at once the story of a young black girl's coming of age in the 1980s as well as a parable of black-white relationships. Sanders highlights her interest in racial interactions through several graphic black-white images in the novel. The novel begins, for example, with Clover saying, "They dressed me in white for my daddy's funeral. White from my head to my toes" (1), underscoring not only the vast cultural differences between Clover and her new stepmother (Sara Kate, says Clover, does not "know any better" in asking Clover to wear white, not black, at her father's funeral) but also graphically reversing cultural and symbolic expectations. Long before the reader knows the novel will focus on black-white relations, Sanders overturns her expectations for the proper positioning of "black" (funeral colors) and "white" (wedding colors). Clover notices other black-white contrasts at her father's funeral: "Sara Kate is wedged between me and Uncle Jim Ed, squeezed in between us on the crowded bench like vanilla cream between dark chocolate cookies. My daddy is dead. . . . And all I can think of is an Oreo cookie. An Oreo cookie" (22–23). As Clover grapples with her father's death and her new white stepmother, she continues to be hyperaware of other black-white contrasts, describing a group of black children, for example, as having "[b]ig wide eyes [that] pop out from faces like big white cotton balls on a blackboard" (15–16) and calling attention to the fact that the black school janitor, Mr. Jackson, is an albino (22). Repeatedly, Sanders calls upon black and white visual images to underscore the racial tension that informs most of the novel.

Virtually all of this novel about black-white relationships is set in the black community of Round Hill. In many ways, this rural community mirrors the more urban community portrayed in Shay Youngblood's *The Big Mama Stories*. Although Youngblood's alternative family depends on an extensive symbolic kin network, its primary focus is on the strong bonds between the community's children and their elders. The same is true of *Clover*. Though her mother died when she was young, Clover has enjoyed, like Douglas's Tweet, a close relationship with her grandfather (83–84) and an especially close bond with her father, Gaten. In addition, her Aunt Everleen functions as a substitute mother figure. Indeed, one of Clover's early descriptions of Everleen echoes the narrator's description of her Big Mama in Youngblood's work: "I buried my face against her sweaty arm, glad there was the sweat so she couldn't feel the tears streaming down my face. Her hot, sweaty smell, coated with Avon talcum powder, filled my nose. It was her own special smell. I felt safe" (7).

Into this close-knit family and community comes Sara Kate, the educated white textile designer who, by virtue of her skin color and class difference, could not be further removed from the cultural prescripts of Round Hill. Interestingly, Sanders delays the knowledge that Sara Kate is white: not until page 16 (after her description of the accident that kills her father and the subsequent funeral) does Clover finally tell us that

Sara Kate "is a white woman, a stranger to Round Hill" (16). In fact, only Clover's hyperawareness of black-white visual images indicates her struggle with a new hierarchy of meanings between the colors black and white.

Though Sanders does not always explicitly refer to difference in skin color, she constantly reveals the black and white communities' cultural and class differences. She exposes Sara Kate's distance from black customs in two early events: the family reunion at which Gaten introduces her to his family, and Gaten's funeral. At the family reunion, Sara Kate tries at all costs to fit in with Gaten's family. This comes through in her attempt to eat all the food they have prepared despite its strangeness to her. Clover says,

> Deep down in my heart I knew before that day was over Sara Kate was going to be sick, sick. I could tell from the look on her face when she saw that boiling grease in that big black iron washpot. She had never seen fish cooked like that in her life. Still, whenever someone brought her a piece she ate it. (37)

In addition, she eats "the ham Gideon cooked, even after everybody tried to warn her it came from a boar" (37). Food in this scene—as in many others throughout the novel—signifies Sara Kate's cultural and class distance from the black community. Clover marvels, for example, that Sara Kate "doesn't even know what mountain oysters are" (37–38). Not surprisingly, Sara Kate becomes sick as Clover had predicted: "People are starting to leave. Sara Kate is sitting all alone at the end of a long table. What little lipstick she had on is all gone. She is as white as a sheet. She looks as sick as a dog" (53). Here, though Sara Kate has tried valiantly to fit in with Gaten's family, she has removed herself even further from them, accentuating her racial difference by becoming "white as a sheet."

The family reunion reveals the hostile response Sara Kate receives from the Round Hill community in general and from Gaten's family in particular. Sanders makes this especially clear in her depiction of the black women's response to Sara Kate. One family member—representative of the entire community—calls her Gaten's "fancy lady friend" (41) and says that she sure "cramps his style" (41), while Everleen feels put upon as she is forced to deal with her new sister-in-law, referring to her as "some fancy woman" (5) and as "Miss Uppity-class" (6). Here, as in the following passage where several of the women in the family discuss Sara Kate at length, the women refer to her class and cultural differences as a way of veiling their unspoken distrust of her racial position:

> "Can't you just die from all that beige and taupe she's wearing?"
> "Girl, them some Gloria Vanderbilt's pants."
> "Aw shucks now, go on, girl."
> "Wonder what's wrong with her?"
> "I don't know, but there is something that's caused her to be rejected by her own men."
> . . . "I say she's an epileptic. . . . It's the way her eyes get that blank stare. You can be talking to her, but she's not there."
> "She could be in a deep study about something."
> "Well, something's wrong with her. Why else would she take up with a black dude?" (42)

In fact, as Clover points out, "There was hardly a woman there who could stand Sara Kate" (40), and Clover conjectures that what really upsets the women and makes "them so jealous and hopping mad" is her class (and, by extension, racial) background: "You can look at the woman and see she is certainly not poor trash" (42).

But the cultural differences between the black and white communities come out most clearly at Gaten's funeral. Sara Kate makes several cultural missteps: she does not dress totally in black (1); does not understand the custom of having someone stay at home during a funeral or of stopping the clock at the time of the loved one's death (14–15); refuses to allow the custom that dictates that the deceased's body be laid out in the home (15); removes the plastic flowers Gaten's family members and friends have placed on his grave (142); and, most offensive to the black community, does not cry at the wake or funeral (67). But as Clover realizes after some time, Sara Kate makes these mistakes not because she wishes to fly in the face of convention but because "she just plain doesn't know any better" (1).

The misunderstanding does not occur solely on Sara Kate's side, however; because she does not cry or otherwise express her feelings in a public manner, many community members assume she is unfeeling. As Clover says,

> If Sara Kate had done some of all the crying she's doing now at Gaten's funeral, she wouldn't have seemed so curious. There wouldn't have been so much talk about how easy she took her husband's death, either. Everleen says white folks don't cry and carry on like we do when somebody dies. They don't love as hard as we do. (67)

The reader, of course, can see from Clover's report that Sara Kate does "love as hard as" the black community does but does so differently. Her mourning goes unnoticed by everyone but Clover and, even then, is misunderstood. Clover states:

> After the funeral she lit a candle and sat alone in the dark. I haven't been able to quite figure out why. People I know in Round Hill don't light candles when folks die. I didn't ask Sara Kate about the candle. I didn't even tell Everleen about it, either. I guess, in a strange sort of way, I don't want anybody thinking like, well, that Sara Kate was strange and everything. (67)

Both communities have ways of expressing grief, but Sara Kate's more private ritual marks the difference between her and the rest of the Round Hill community. Though "Sara Kate is very proper and truly smart," Clover says, there are still "things she doesn't know" (142).

The family reunion, the funeral, and numerous day-to-day events make clear that Sara Kate's position as a white woman starkly contrasts with the black womanhood that thrives in Round Hill. Though Everleen can proudly say, "The blacker the berry, the sweeter the juice" (78), Sara Kate is literally thin-skinned, uptight, and restrained. At the funeral, her "body is as straight as a cornstalk" (23), and when she feels deep emotion—whether because things happen she does not like or because she is deeply in love with Gaten—"[h]er face shows her true feelings straight out" (24). Clover and the rest of the Round Hill community see Sara Kate through a filter of their own misperceptions of white women.

They believe that "most of them have been sheltered and petted all their lives," that "[t]he least little thing just tears them up" (64), and that they need constant reinforcement from the black community. Clover, for example, says,

> It blows me away that [Sara Kate] calls sitting down in a cool air-conditioned house, drawing and painting designs, hard work. What my aunt Everleen does is hard work, picking peaches in the hot sun, and then hanging around that hot peach shed all day trying to sell them. (154–55)

Given all of these misperceptions based on race and class differences and given her own inability to reach out to the community, Sara Kate struggles for quite some time to be accepted by the Round Hill community and especially by Gaten's brother Jim Ed and his wife Everleen. As she settles into the community and takes on the duty of being Clover's stepmother, Sara Kate must forge close and meaningful relationships with Jim Ed and Everleen. Having served as Clover's surrogate mother for quite some time, Everleen feels especially threatened by Sara Kate's intrusion into her family and by the new relationships that will emerge as Sara Kate becomes part of the family. Her initially hostile response to Sara Kate results from the threat she poses to the family, not only as a newcomer to their family circle but also as a well-to-do white woman wholly unfamiliar with their culture, customs, and relationships. In fact, Everleen takes personal offense at Sara Kate's well-intentioned attempts to become part of the family. For example, when Sara Kate suggests to Everleen that Clover's leg pain may be psychosomatic, Everleen replies, "What you trying to say in a nice fancy way is, the child ain't got right good sense. I don't go for *some outsider* coming in and trying to cook up that kind of mess" (147; my emphasis). Here, as elsewhere, Everleen and other members of Gaten's extended family express their distrust of the intrusive white woman who threatens to disrupt their family, defined as it is by racial, cultural, and class hegemony.

Most important, Clover, too, initially responds quite negatively to her new stepmother. Though the community and family resentment may make Sara Kate's life unpleasant, Clover's less than enthusiastic reaction causes Sara Kate much more pain. Clover, like Everleen and Jim Ed, resents Sara Kate for what she represents in her life:

> To this day I can't see how Gaten could think that his bringing a woman I'd never laid eyes on in my life could possibly be a surprise for me. Especially a woman that might become my stepmother. . . . I didn't want a stepmother. Even if I had to have one, I sure wouldn't pick one like Sara Kate. (33)

Clover realizes early in the novel that the stepmother/stepdaughter relationship is, by definition, tense: "All I had heard my daddy say about her meant absolutely nothing to me. I still did not know the woman. To me she was a total stranger. How could I know her? It takes time to learn a person" (13). Unfortunately, Sara Kate and Clover are thrown together long before they have had time to "learn" each other. At Gaten's funeral, they sit "side by side as stiff as painted leaves on a painted tree" (23), and in fact, though Jim Ed places his hand on Sara Kate's arm, Clover and Sara Kate do not touch. But their problematic relationship goes beyond their inability to touch: Clover says, "We didn't set horses from the start" (31). They fight and bicker frequently, often over food, which can mark cultural differences deeply and divisively. Clover stakes out food and meals as her battling terrain, telling Sara Kate in one instance, "You sure can't cook grits" (64) and, in another, "[Y]ou didn't ask me if I wanted this nasty lunch" (154). Such explosions from Clover hurt Sara Kate: "I could see the red hurt under her skin. She's got the thinnest skin I've ever seen" (64).

Eventually, however, Sara Kate is accepted warmly into the Round Hill community and into Gaten's family, and this acceptance results when Sara Kate and Clover themselves begin to form a loving bond. Their first step in creating a friendship comes in their awareness that they share a bond of sadness. As Clover says midway through the novel, "I hope Sara Kate is not sad she got tied up with Gaten and ended up with me. I hate it when she is sad like that. It's really hard on me. Because, you see, a lot of the time, actually, most of the time, I'm sad also. Really sad" (104). And in another instance, she says, "There is a lot of sadness sewed up in Sara Kate, a sadness I can't figure out. . . . Sometimes I believe she really loved my daddy. It doesn't make me love her more, though. Still, something in me wants to like her—to have her like me too" (66).

In addition to the sadness they share over Gaten's death, Clover and Sara Kate are drawn closer together simply through being together. As Clover says, "[W]hen you live with someone and they aren't mean or nothing they kind of grow on you" (140). Or as she says a few pages earlier,

> They say when two people live together, they start to look alike. Well, Sara Kate and I have been living together for a long time and there is no way we will ever look alike.
>
> But in strange little ways, we are starting to kind of act alike. Things like the way she helped me out with the fried pies at Miss Katie's house. And little by little, a part of me is slowly beginning to change towards Sara Kate. Even the picture of her face that shed no tears at my daddy's funeral looks different in my mind now. Maybe it's because now I know it wasn't that Sara Kate didn't cry because she didn't care. She didn't because she couldn't. . . .
>
> Anyway, things are shaping up pretty good between us. (130–31)

Now that they have lived together and spent time together, they share more than a bond of sadness: "If Sara Kate and I ever forget who we are, and sometimes we do, then we are at ease with each other and we have a pretty good little time together. Sometimes we even laugh" (100).

The final ingredient in Sara Kate and Clover's developing bond is Clover's realization that she has a great deal to learn from Sara Kate. She begins to perceive her not as a white woman but as an adult who can teach her about the world. She learns that "in spite of her curious ways, she might want to be my friend—that in some small way, she might even like me" (101). But more than that she also begins to realize Sara Kate's rules and ideas are good so that "[a] part of me was little by little starting to obey and care for Sara Kate without my even knowing it" (163). In one late scene, Clover, who relishes mutilating insects, starts to kill a big spider but then finds herself unable to do so: "That was the first time something like that happened to me. Sara Kate's thinking is rubbing off on me for sure" (162).

This relationship—built on shared sadness and occasional moments of laughter, on living and spending time together, and on Clover's burgeoning sense of Sara Kate as an adult from whom she can learn—finally develops into a real mother-daughter bond. At first this bond is tenuous. Clover states,

> At a glance the house seems to be just a warm, ordinary household. Like the kind you see on television, a house filled with pretty things and a happy family. But after a little while what is real sweeps through. . . .
>
> It becomes real that there is something about our house that is not all that happy. It kind of reminds me of a thick morning fog. It's there, you can see it, yet you can't put your finger on it. Like the fog, a strange, uneasy feeling has filled the house, and settled down upon us.
>
> There is just the two of us. A stepmother and child. Two people in a house. Together, yet apart. Aside from the music, the house is too quiet. We move about in separate ways. We are like peaches. Peaches picked from the same tree, but put in separate baskets. (99–100)

Later, as the stepmother and child relationship becomes stronger, Clover makes the important realization that Sara Kate takes her mothering role very seriously. When Sara Kate takes Clover to the doctor to have her leg examined, the doctor says, "Your daughter likely tore a ligament in the beginning and doubtless kept hurting the same leg over and over." The doctor's casual use of the word "daughter" stuns Clover: "He called me her daughter. Sara Kate had called me her daughter. She kept saying it. . . . Now that was really something" (160). What surprises Clover is Sara Kate's willingness to acknowledge her connection to Clover in the racially defined South. She is similarly surprised when she goes to a cookout with Sara Kate and her friend Chase Porter: "I got too many curious questioning stares when I walked about between the two of them with Sara Kate holding my hand" (174). Yet though Sara Kate may be ready to let the world know about her caring relationship with Clover, she also realizes it will take time to solidify their new mother-daughter bond. Thus, when Chase Porter asks her to marry him, she replies, "I think for now . . . loving each other is all Clover and I can handle" (175).

Clover's developing bond with Sara Kate paves the way for Sara Kate's acceptance into the larger Round Hill community. She saves Jim Ed's life when a swarm of yellow jackets attacks him; this seals her acceptance into the community: "I think the people in Round Hill will talk about what she did for the rest of their lives" (179). More important, she is finally warmly welcomed into the Hill family. Though Everleen resented her initially because as a white woman she represented a potential threat to her family, a part of Everleen wants to accept Sara Kate regardless of her racial background: "People need to be accepted and judged," says Everleen, "by the kind of person they are inside, not on the basis of the color of their skin" (97). Yet Everleen cannot put this egalitarian belief into action until some more tangible bond arises between her and Sara Kate. Eventually that bond takes the form of Clover's upbringing. When Sara Kate and Clover fight once again over a meal, Sara Kate decides to talk it over with Everleen, who is outraged at Clover's inappropriate behavior. Because Everleen supports Sara Kate in her fight with Clover, Clover says, "I think just having Everleen not dump on her, plus take her side, did her all the good in the world" (157). As Clover points out, the fight over the meal proved fortuitous, because it paved the way for Sara Kate and Everleen to become better friends:

> Maybe in the way things turned out, it all happened for the good. Because, you see, after that very day, Everleen and Sara Kate became closer. All because they were both siding with each other against me. I say that about them, but secretly I'm kind of glad that they both care enough about me to make me do the right thing. (177)

Just as Sara Kate and Clover develop a real mother-daughter relationship, so Sara Kate and Gaten's family forge true family bonds. Everleen, says Clover, "has started bragging about her a little bit. My sister-in-law did such and such, she'll say. Sara Kate takes up for her" (182). On the last page of the novel, a truly new community of integration emerges, one that Sara Kate, Gaten's family, and the entire Round Hill community have formed together:

> Even things at home are going good. People are starting to drop by. People other than Jim Ed and Everleen. After the yellow jacket thing, they walk over almost every evening after we close the peach shed. They sit out under the big oaks in the front yard and talk until dark.
>
> Gaten's hammock is still stretched between two of the trees. Sometimes Jim Ed will rest there until it's time to go home. It's almost like old times. (183)

The close and intimate community Gaten Hill shared with his extended family and with his neighbors was disrupted not only by his death but also and more important by the addition of his new widow, an educated white woman. Initially met with hostility and distrust, Sara Kate discovers that over a period of time, with love and good will and a sincere desire to become part of the family and community, even racial and cultural barriers can be overcome. Sanders believes, in fact, that racial, cultural, class, and culinary differences are simply that: differences. They are "obstacles to be overcome, rather than unbreachable barriers" (Kastor F9). Such a vision—though quiet and simple—is also radical and provocative. In a coup of simplicity and starkness of vision, Sanders revises the traditional notion of black-white relations in the South. Significantly, she chooses the most intimate and potentially volatile of bonds—that of mothers and daughters—as her battleground for the development of truly strong and meaningful bonds between black and white southern women.

The bonds between Cornelia and Tweet and between Clover and Sara Kate are defined by centuries of race relations in the South. As women in the 1960s, Cornelia and Tweet continue to enact the aloof surface relationship between the nineteenth-century plantation mistress and slave, while also feeling the same unacknowledged bond that existed between many slave mistresses and their slaves. Though Clover and Sara Kate are also defined by centuries of race relations in the South, their relationship is wholly different as Sara Kate, the white woman, becomes part of Clover's black community. In choosing to act on what connects them—their position as women in the patriarchal South—rather than on the racial and class differences that separate them, Cornelia and Tweet and Clover and Sara Kate take a bold step toward the creation of an alternative southern female network that cuts across racial and class boundaries. Together, they have the potential to give birth to southern Janes, whole women emerging from the fragments of Eve White and Eve Black.

THREE

REVISIONING THE BACKWARD GLANCE:
NEW VIEWS OF SOUTHERN HISTORY

[M]y "history" starts not with the taking of lands, or the births, battles, and deaths of Great Men, but with one woman asking another for her underwear.

ALICE WALKER, "Writing *The Color Purple*"

*I*n her book on the American Civil War (most recently published as *Mary Chesnut's Civil War*), Mary Boykin Chesnut, the wife of a Confederate general, describes a woman seeking a pardon for her husband:

> She was strong, and her way of telling her story was hard and cold enough. She told it simply, but over and over again, with slight variations as to words—never as to facts.
> She seemed afraid we would forget. (610–11)

This passage is but one of many in the book that signals Chesnut's desire to tell the story of the South during the Civil War. This impulse to record the past is part of what would become in the twentieth century an even larger southern concern with history, which Allen Tate labeled the "backward glance."[1] In this passage, Chesnut indicates her own concerns in glancing at the past: to document history so that her readers won't "forget" and to record more than just the facts of history, by telling her story over and over again artfully. In reworking her diary for publication in the 1880s, Chesnut deleted and moved sections, added dialogue and other novellike detail to create a hybrid genre of diary, memoir, autobiography, and, even to some extent, novel. She weaves together accounts of her own experiences with stories that others have told her and creates an anthology of anecdotes about members of the Confederate society, a crazy quilt of Civil War lore. Chesnut both records history and tells a story, presents both the "facts" and the lives behind the facts. As a southern woman, she realizes that her role as historian is not an easy one. She needs also to capture the drama beyond the facts, to go "behind the scenes," and to do that she found that she needed to expand her genre as far as it could go—indeed, to take it into an almost fictional realm. Her book, then, becomes much more than just history or just literature; it becomes *histoire*.

In exploding the boundaries of genre, Chesnut left a text that historians and literary critics still battle over in their attempts to own and label it, to fix and control it. Perhaps what makes scholars uncomfortable is Chesnut's refusal to confine herself to traditional history—what C. Vann Woodward, the editor of the 1981 edition of the book, would elsewhere refer to as "the public and external forces that go to make up the collective experience and give shape to the group character of a people" (xi). Although Chesnut certainly does include many references to the public dimensions of the Confederacy, she devotes considerably more attention to what Woodward deems the "private and the individual" (ix), those aspects of the past that as a male historian he deems less significant and that as a woman writer she deems essential to an understanding of Confederate life as it was lived. Chesnut tells us repeatedly that there is more to history than just facts: "History reveals men's deeds—their outward characters but not themselves. There is a secret self that hath its own life 'rounded by a dream'—unpenetrated, unguessed" (799).[2]

The "secret self" that is "unpenetrated, unguessed" by the white male world has been at the heart of many southern women's tales of the past. In *Gone with the Wind* (1936), for example, Margaret Mitchell emphasized the private and the individual as symptomatic of the public and external. By painting the paradoxical conflict and bond between the self-sacrificing, honorable Ashley Wilkes and Melanie Hamilton, on the one hand, and the strong-willed, opportunistic Scarlett O'Hara and Rhett Butler, on the other, Mitchell illustrated the tensions between the Old and New Souths. Elizabeth Madox Roberts also linked the private and individual to the public and external in *The Great Meadow* (1930), which depicted the pioneer period in Kentucky history. Diony Hall's husbands—Evan Muir and Berk Jarvis—represent the two veins of pioneer strength: the perseverance that aided the steady construction of a new life in a new land and the more violent, more confrontative, more restless spirit of adventure and dominance. Ellen Glasgow wrote of nostalgia for a fading era in *The Sheltered Life* (1932), again connecting the two realms of experience. Young Jenny Blair tries to reconcile, on the one hand, what she has learned about Eva Birdsong, the ideal personification of the passing "age of make believe," and, on the other, what she begins to learn about her poorer neighbors, harbingers of the new industrialized age. And in one of the grandest southern epics of the century, *Jubilee* (1966), Margaret Walker used the private and individual to express collective history. The story of Vyry's move from slavery to the tenuous creation of a new life for herself and her family parallels the story of southern blacks in the late nineteenth century.

In addition to the above-named authors, a counter female historical tradition authorizes oral ways of understanding the past, a tradition that collapses the distinction between the "private and individual" and the "public and external." Eudora Welty's *Losing Battles* (1970) describes a lively family reunion and, like her earlier novel, *Delta Wedding* (1946), depicts the family celebration as a place where group members exchange stories, anecdotes, and remembrances. Although Welty's narrative technique is traditional in its linearity and dependence on an omniscient narrator, she emphasizes the talk and storytelling among family and community members and the knowing of history through tales and imagination. Among black women writers, Zora Neale Hurston's work with folklore creates a truly living sense of history, which Alice Walker understands better after she passes Hurston's stories on to her relatives:

> No matter how they read the stories Zora had collected, no matter how much distance they tried to maintain between themselves, as new sophisticates, and the lives their parents and grandparents lived, no matter how they tried to remain cool toward all Zora revealed, in the end they could not hold back the smiles, the laughter, the joy over who she was showing them to be: descendants of an inventive, joyous, courageous, and outrageous people. (Walker, "Zora Neale Hurston" 85)

As Hurston helps her readers to appreciate their ancestors, she necessarily creates a sense of community history. Though Welty and Hurston are fundamentally concerned with the "forces that go to make up the collective experience and give shape to the group character of a people" (Woodward xi), their work has not been thought of as particularly "historical." This is precisely because their histories maintain a distinct distance from the "public and external."

Several contemporary southern women writers have continued the traditions of women's alternative history. Alice Walker brings the historical into the domestic sphere in *The Color Purple* (1982). Public and external events—world wars, the movement of African Americans back to Africa, the destruction of the African bush, the emergence of the automobile—form the background for the experiences of southern black women in the first half of the twentieth century, experiences not perceived as deserving attention, even by black men. The events that shape the collective experience—that is, the history—of these women are rarely articulated and then often only among black women themselves: Celie's repeated rape by her stepfather and her abusive relationship with her husband; Sophia's humiliation as the mayor's maid; Shug's early life experiences; Nettie's true relationship to Adam and Olivia; and so on. The novel begins with letters addressed to "God," letters that never reach their intended recipient because they are intercepted by an abusive and oppressive husband, and continues with whispered stories and delayed telegrams. But the novel ends with a strong sense of communication: some letters do get to their intended recipients and there is a stronger, bolder telling of stories. Thus, Walker shows how black women's experiences are pushed to the margins and how they can recover those experiences by building stronger bonds between themselves. The intimacy of "one woman asking another for her underwear" makes it possible for two women to share not just their underwear but the stories of past experience as well.

Bobbie Ann Mason also carefully considers the role of history in the contemporary South. She frequently portrays characters who have lost a historical feeling for their region and their world and who consequently develop a sense of meaninglessness. For example, Leroy, the main character of "Shiloh," realizes that "[h]e is leaving out the insides of history" (16). Although Mason's characters begin to get glimmerings of their loss of connection to the past, they find it more difficult to go the next step and recover that connection. But as Robert H. Brinkmeyer, Jr., notes, Mason believes this step is "crucial to achieving perspective and growth" ("Finding One's History" 31).

A strong connection to the past as a step in self-understanding forms the core of the historical novels of Rita Mae Brown and Lee Smith, whether this connection is to women's past or to an entire community's past. Although Brown is probably most often associated with lesbian writing for her watershed novel *Rubyfruit Jungle* (1973), she is probably as much—if not more—concerned with southern history as with lesbianism. Although she has continued to include lesbian characters, sexual orientation as a major textual issue has faded from her work as her interest in southern history has grown. *Six of One* (1978), *Southern Discomfort* (1982), and, most recently, *Bingo* (1988) address the issue of southern history to varying degrees, but *High Hearts* (1986) is her most historical novel to date. Set during the Civil War, it tells the story of Geneva Chatfield Nash, who disguises herself as a man and joins the cavalry. Framed on either end by historical documents, references, and discussions of the importance of women's history, this novel clearly sets as its main agenda the reclaiming of the past of women and slaves.

Lee Smith is best known for her writing about life in the Appalachian mountains. Whereas Brown puts a new twist on the public and external, including women in the larger, collective, historical experience, Smith gives a voice and a place to the private, the individual, and the family— especially as these relate to people rarely included in previous southern literature. Her novels often deal with many generations of one mountain family and take as their main topic the tension between the lively mountain culture of the past and the encroachments of modern, industrialized civilization. *Family Linen* (1985), *Fair and Tender Ladies* (1988), and *The Devil's Dream* (1992), for example, all deal to some degree with these issues. Smith's use of history and historical concerns is most clearly seen, however, in her best-known novel, *Oral History* (1983). In this book, the history of the Cantrell family parallels the history of the culture and the region. Here Smith uses the oral tradition in much the same way other contemporary ethnic writers do. That is, she argues that the ability to share the old stories—whether by telling or by actively listening—is key to the community's survival.

Although Brown revises history so that her readers will not forget it and paints particular characters as emblematic of the collective, public experience, Smith records not the external facts of history but the artful renderings of legend that ultimately make up the foundation of our known collective experience. If Brown opens spaces for women in the public realm, Smith concentrates more on creating spaces for the entire marginalized Appalachian community. Although each author has a different focal point, they share one primary goal: both argue implicitly that southern women must understand their past—their families' past, their culture's past, their region's past, women's past in general—in order to achieve greater self-understanding and self-redefinition. Re-presenting history, according to Brown and Smith, may lead women and other marginalized figures in the South to a better understanding of their cultural past and may allow them to find better and more satisfying places for themselves in the contemporary South.

Over a century and a quarter after the Battle of Atlanta, the downtown of that city looks today much more like a sprawling metropolis of tomorrow than a city that has seen tremendous defeat. As an outsider, it is a strange experience to walk the streets of this emerging city. One expects to find numerous plaques and monuments to famous events in the city's history, to see parks commemorating skirmishes and battles, to encounter native Atlantans pointing with pride to famous buildings—or, because most buildings were burned in the battle, to legendary roads. When this does occur, however, it is the exception rather than the rule. Instead, the visitor finds numerous vacant lots where speculators have razed old buildings; many non-native transplants who know little of the city's past; and only a handful of historic landmarks, designated primarily as commercial tourist attractions. The defeat of the Civil War is a distant, vague memory; certainly, it does not capture the Atlantan's imagination as one might expect to find in the largest city of a region supposedly preoccupied with its past.

A couple of counties to the north, however, the peculiar spirit of "The Lost Cause" proudly lives on. There, on a Saturday night, one may find patrons of Dawsonville's Lantern Inn singing a slow, mournful "Dixie," waving banners with hands placed over hearts and dabbing handkerchiefs at tearful eyes. There, also, one may find a resolute determination to live a "pure" life, untainted by notions from the liberal North. This is most typified by nearby Forsyth County's longtime persistence as all-white. Here, the implicit appeal is to the region's past, not as a genuine desire to return to a more agrarian life-style, but rather as a justification for a peculiar mind-set that distrusts any and all outsiders. These folks seem to feel that the war is not yet over and that the loss of the mythical Dixie is still palpably with them. As the slogan to *Blue and Gray Magazine* puts it, they are "those who still hear the guns."

These contradictions in southern perceptions of the past create a decided challenge for the contemporary southern historical novelist, particularly for someone intent on writing revisionist history. The South, of course, is not a monolith, and north Georgia is far different from Rita Mae Brown's piedmont Virginia, which, as Brown asserts, "nurses its own peculiar vision of world events" (xii). But whatever the subregion of the larger South, writer after writer bemoans this generation's lack of historical consciousness. Southerners—native or transplanted—do not remember, often do not know, what happened here. If they do remember, or think they do, they often tend to perpetuate an oversimplified, Dixie version of that history.

High Hearts is an ambitious, if sometimes failed, attempt to correct both these trends. Brown tries to bring the Civil War to life and, in so doing, to revise our understanding of the public and external forces that shaped our collective past. For Brown, these public and external forces cannot be defined simply as the actions of white men. Rather, the roles that women and blacks played in the shaping of collective experience must be considered. As she looks at the role of women and blacks, however, Brown sometimes seems dangerously close herself to falling into an oversimplified Dixie version of history. Though her portrayal of woman warriors is exciting and long overdue, her portrayal of slaves and of their relationships with their owners suffers from a lack of sensitivity and of careful research. Most disturbing, however, is not Brown's factual errors but rather her failure to approach her revision of history with the sophistication and sense of complexity that a reader might desire.

Of course, Rita Mae Brown is not pretending to be a disciplined historian, but her desire to correct and revise our understanding of Civil War history—and to do that from a decidedly southern viewpoint—is made clear in her preface and foreword. Brown's South is Virginia, and she clearly wants to give voice to the Confederate experience: "While I admire a novel that attempts to explain both sides of a story," she writes, "that was not my intention" (xii). To highlight her concern with history, Brown uses traditional historical materials and includes numerous statements on the importance of history. Her historical materials include an exhaustive acknowledgments section, suggesting the breadth of her research; a lengthy foreword, in which she sketches out the basic points of her novel; an epilogue providing enlistment and death records for all soldiers in Albemarle County (whose citizens she follows throughout the war); a glossary of Confederate military units; and a substantial bibliography of primary and secondary sources.

Brown uses her sources carefully and gives a detailed sense of daily life during the war. She worked with weather reports and Episcopal Church almanacs from those years. Thus, the reader is led to believe in the novel's concrete historical foundation. If Lutie reads a biblical lesson on a certain day, the reader knows that all Episcopalians were indeed reading this lesson on that particular day. In addition to these supporting materials, Brown also gives the illusion of authentic history by dividing the novel itself, not into chapters, but into narratives for particular days throughout the war. The bulk of the novel takes place between the dates of April 11, 1861, and August 24, 1862, although Brown includes one last entry for June 11, 1910, in which she recounts Geneva's talk with her soon-to-be-married granddaughter. Here, Geneva summarizes the events after the war and reflects on the meaning of the war.

Brown further underscores her concern with history by making editorial statements on the importance of understanding the past. Many of these appear in her foreword and in supplementary sections of the novel. Brown, as in her previous books, is enthusiastic about her cause. She is adamant that her readers not forget what happened because, like Chesnut and Mason, she feels that remembering and understanding the past leads to self-understanding. She notes in her foreword, "[M]uch of what vexes you today was clearly expressed then," and she lists among these vexations questions of local autonomy, rights to free trade, questions of the quality of life (industry vs. agriculture), and environmental issues (xv). But on a deeper level, Brown implicitly argues that the purpose of her novel is to create better models and legends for those who were previously left out of southern history. Her targets are white women and blacks in the South, whose self-perception has rested on the belief that they were victimized by an oppressive, patriarchal, paternal institution perpetrated by white men. Brown believes that, if women can view themselves as descendants of brave women who fought for their beliefs, and if blacks can see themselves as people with a "rare spiritual courage" (xiii), they will then better understand themselves as strong and confident people.

Brown reinforces her historical concern through the speeches of various characters. Although comments from Lutie, Geneva, and other characters sometimes read like mini-essays by Rita Mae Brown, thereby rendering *High Hearts* rather two-dimensional, these speeches illuminate her positions on history and on the Civil War. Lutie, for example, wonders if those who come after her will remember what their ancestors went through. "One hundred years from now," she thinks,

> every person in church today will be dead. Will anyone remember us? Even my own blood kin? Will my great-grandchildren and great-great-grandchildren know who I was or care what I did? . . . We'll be shadows, shadows dispensed with their sunlight, their problems, their triumphs. They won't believe that we loved, fought, sung, cried, and died nor will they care. (339)

Here Brown insists that contemporary southerners need to remember what happened in the Civil War. If they do not, Brown warns, many people will have died and suffered to no avail. In this passage, Lutie anticipates contemporary Atlantans and other southerners who have busily gone about the business of building a skyscraper future, indifferently destroying the past as they go.

But as Atlanta's neighbors two counties away show us, many are obsessed with history or caught up in it for the wrong reasons. Geneva tells her granddaughter, "You're alive now. Make the most of it. When people tell about their war experiences, it sounds exciting. It was, but, honey, I saw things I'll never forget" (405). Finally, through Geneva's thoughts at the end of the novel, Brown provides an overview of the war:

> She did not believe in lost loves or lost causes. The rest of the South could wrap themselves in their imagined chivalry, but it was over. The dead numbered in the hundreds of thousands. What started out as a classic war became something new, something ugly, something that twisted everyone. No one was safe at the end. We all live in the dark shadow of Sherman, she thought. (412)

Geneva—and Brown through her—argues that we need to remember the past as it was, not as we wish it had been.

Brown's strong need to remember the past not only led her to conduct the research for *High Hearts* but also to dedicate it as a monument to the people who inspired the novel:

> To the best of my knowledge, there is not one monument in the South to commemorate the sacrifice of our women nor is there even so much as a plaque paying tribute to the slaves for their contribution. . . . Some paid with their lives, all paid with their worldly goods, many paid with their health, and no one, no one was ever the same again. Until such time as we correct this oversight, let this book stand as their monument. (xvi–xvii)

Brown uses the story of the Chatfield family to construct this narrative memorial. Lutie and Henley have been married for many years. One son, James Chatfield, is dead; another, Sumner, joins the war in its earliest stages; and their daughter, Geneva, widely known as an expert horsewoman, marries Nash Hart three days before the war begins. Black members of the household include Sin-Sin, Lutie's valued slave and close friend; Di-Peachy, a slave about the same age as Geneva and daughter of Henley Chatfield; and Ernie June, head cook and Sin-Sin's rival. Soon after the novel opens and the men have gone off to war, Geneva, distraught over Nash's absence, decides to disguise herself and join his cavalry unit, renaming herself Jimmy Chatfield. The rest of the novel alternates between Geneva/Jimmy and Nash's military unit, Lutie's work at home and in Charlottesville and Richmond nursing wounded soldiers, and Henley's role as a senior officer. This alternation between the public and official world of the battlefront and the private domain of the home, between the makeshift hospitals and the war offices of the Confederacy, creates the feeling that all of these domains are legitimate parts of history. That is, where Woodward might only recognize the battlefront and the war offices as legitimate war theaters, Brown acknowledges the home and the hospital as equally valid historical sites. This intermingling equalizes these different experiences and suggests that what happened in each location was as important as the others.

Just as Brown valorizes all fronts on which the Civil War was fought, so too she upholds the contributions of all Confederate supporters. She particularly stresses the contributions of women. Geneva, of course, transforms herself physically by taking on the guise of a soldier but also transforms herself psychologically, increasingly becoming a warrior in spirit as well as in deed. But Brown shows other women in the novel becoming warriors as well—if not physically as soldiers, then psychologically and spiritually as stalwarts of the Cause. She highlights the concept of woman-as-warrior in two key scenes. In the first, Henley and Lutie are chatting about their children and the pride they feel in them. Henley, who tells Lutie, "We spawned two warriors," considers Geneva to be as much a warrior as Sumner. But Lutie also numbers Henley among the family's warriors because "you did your duty." When Henley responds that he did so because "I am a Chatfield," Lutie replies, "So am I," a statement which leads Henley to conclude that the family has "Four warriors then" (287). Brown continues the idea of women warriors a few scenes later. Mars Vickers, Geneva's commanding officer, tells his unit the legend of the Valkyries, "twelve female warriors from Valhalla, the Teutonic heaven" (319). These mythical warriors, Mars tells his men, are "[t]he fiercest warriors in Teutonic mythology" (319).

Both scenes depict male characters misreading the women warriors around them. Although Henley readily accepts Geneva as a warrior—and here as elsewhere in the novel Brown uses this term in the psychological sense as much as, if not more so than, the physical one—he is slow to realize that his wife is a warrior in her own right. Similarly, though Mars admires Geneva/Jimmy more than any other "man" in his unit, and though he values the concept of a woman warrior (at least as an abstract idea), he is unable to read the signs around him that point to Geneva's true sex. Later, as her second husband, he reconciles his respect for Geneva as a soldier and his love for her as a woman. Though Henley and Mars both work toward an understanding of Lutie and Geneva as warriors, their initial resistance and misperceptions are quite interesting. Brown may be suggesting in both these scenes that a great deal of misreading occurred during the Civil War, misreading that clearly led to our lack of information today. More important, these parallel scenes allow Brown to align both Geneva and Lutie (and by extension other women in the novel and in the actual past) with the concept of the woman warrior, or Valkyrie. Such a woman is not only physically strong—whether capable of fighting in the cavalry or of nursing in appalling surroundings—but also psychologically and spiritually strong.

Although it is only mildly surprising that the young and headstrong Geneva goes into active military service, Lutie's achievements as she becomes a nurse are more astonishing. Depicting Confederate women as nurses is not, of course, a new phenomenon. Margaret Mitchell, for example, described the iron will of women such as Scarlett O'Hara and Melanie Hamilton, as they were transformed from women of leisure into women literally up to their elbows in blood and gore. Despite these literary antecedents, however, it is still difficult to imagine wealthy plantation women—particularly stereotypical southern ladies—putting themselves in such grueling positions. To Brown's credit, the main character she chooses to represent these women is not one who already understood her own strength or who already had a sense of her inner resources. Instead, at the novel's beginning, Lutie Chatfield appears to have none of the characteristics needed to survive the impending war. Distraught for many years over the death of her young son James, she suffers from mental illness, particularly from depression and hysteria. In her position as the sheltered, fragile, "hysterical" lady, Lutie is the epitome of the white southern lady on the pedestal. But as the narrative progresses, Lutie gathers strength. In the end, her strength rivals that of her daughter's.

As she works in Charlottesville and Richmond among wounded soldiers, Lutie contemplates the horrors of the war, thinking of

the women from the icy coasts of Maine to the sticky swamps of Florida. . . . Two nations were weeping for their dead, for what was lost, and for what would never be.

Carefully she put the toe of her shoe into the churned earth. "I won't weep," she vowed. "I've been down this road before, and I won't weep. I'll fight!" She was determined to bear the yoke Fate laid on her back. (231)

In this scene, more than vaguely reminiscent of that earlier warrior, Scarlett O'Hara, and her vow never to go hungry again, Lutie begins to regain her power. Yet Lutie's power comes not just from being "determined to bear the yoke Fate laid on her back"; rather, her power also comes from her understanding that the problem she faces is a problem every woman in the country faces.

As Lutie gains power and strength, she transfers it to her work with the wounded soldiers. The military officers and surgeons have low expectations of Lutie and the other women successfully performing their duties in such horrible surroundings. Brown describes Major Bullette's thinking about these women:

They performed well but he thought these high-born women would get tired of the daily drudgery of nursing soon enough. Their life of opulence and luxury did not equip them for hard labor. Once these two women grew tired of being useful the others would follow like glamorous sheep. (298–99)

Lutie proves Major Bullette wrong. Her strength, determination, and
dedication to her country make her capable of what surprises even the
reader. She explains her work to Colonel Jeffrey Windsor: "I'm a soldier
in the shadow army of the Confederacy. . . . But I don't have the sash of
an officer. I get to tie an apron around my waist instead. . . . I think of the
women of Virginia as a shadow army. You have your duties, and we have
ours" (300). This passage comes only a few pages after Henley's recognition of Lutie as a warrior, and Brown's tight linking of these scenes
underscores her argument that many Confederate women were warriors
in their own right. Although early in the novel Lutie says that the war
makes her "feel pulled around backwards" (4), the war, ironically, allows
her to come into her own.

If Lutie and other women become warriors in the shadow army,
Geneva becomes a leading warrior in the more conventional sense. It is
not surprising that Geneva decides to join the fight. She is desperately in
love with her husband; she feels a great passion for defending the South;
and by her own admission she is not well suited for more traditional
female roles. She takes very quickly to military life. Descriptions of her
are those of a woman who has found her niche: "The only time she was
happy was on horseback. Then her skill weighed more than her sex, her
family name, her family wealth" (76). But being a soldier is more than a
way for Geneva to excel athletically; it also gives her the chance to fight
for her beliefs:

> She was a good citizen; she was even willing to die for her coun-
> try. . . . She had come for love of her husband, but when she saw
> those thousands in uniform, amassed for the deliverance of their
> nation, she realized she was part of that great purpose. For the first
> time in her life, Geneva had a goal outside her own self. She felt
> magnified, important, useful. (95)

Geneva has made the transition from a woman whose primary passion
is her husband to a woman whose passion is her engagement with the
world. In the reader's mind, this scene—as do so many others—links
Geneva to the mythical Valkyries.

But Geneva does not achieve the fullness of her warriorhood easily.

Although Brown often blurs gender, race, and class distinctions, she never pretends that such blurring is painless. In this novel, as in her others, she describes the character's conflict as she breaks through these artificial boundaries. Here, she shows the tension Geneva feels as she gains strength, ability, and spirit as a warrior while Nash simultaneously becomes a pacifist. When Nash bears "the grueling pace with no complaint," Geneva is "thrilled" (145); when his teeth chatter with fear, Geneva, "heart pounding, [feels] only the urge to go forward, to fight" (148). Both lovers feel their relationship slipping away: the growing space in their relationship frustrates Nash, saddens Geneva. Nash never reconciles himself to the changes in their relationship, and consequently his frustration never really diminishes. Geneva, however, grows in self-knowledge, particularly in terms of her differences from Nash. This self-knowledge leads her to more careful self-definition. As she defends her choice to her father, she says, "It's asking a lot of me to flounce around in starched petticoats. I'm a good soldier. . . . If I can stand, I can fight. And if I die, well, I won't know about it, will I? I found something, and I won't ever give it up! . . . I found myself" (307). Like Lutie, Geneva suffers great losses due to the war, but the war also gives her unequalled opportunities for achieving self-knowledge.

In the end, Geneva's pursuit of her own destiny and her insistence on continuing to fight serves her well. When she stays at the Warrenton Hotel, she decides to be "grand and put her name in the register," and as she does so, she signs, "Master Sergeant James Chatfield, First Virginia Cavalry" (396). Here Brown points to the final gender barrier facing Geneva and presumably other women who fought in the Confederate Army. Although Geneva has achieved a great deal as a cavalry "man," she cannot take credit for these accomplishments herself. This moment— which should truly be one of the "grandest" in Geneva's life— actually works to obscure her contribution to the war. This scene implicitly asks how many Confederate women might actually have recorded their contributions in the same manner. Her novel, then, at least in regards to white women, begins to set the record straight and to give long overdue credit for accomplishments that have heretofore gone unnoted. Whether Brown focuses on the public and external forces or on behind-the-scenes activities, then, her enthusiastic descriptions of southern Valkyries such as Geneva and Lutie give voice to the actual women who made such contributions and at the same time create new models for contemporary southern white women.

But Brown's purpose in *High Hearts* was not only to "commemorate the sacrifice of [southern white] women"; it was also to pay "tribute to the slaves for their contributions" (xvi) to the Confederate cause. Though her portrayal of white women's role in the war is largely successful, her rendering of slaves and their relationships with their owners, though admirable in its intent, is nevertheless problematic. Through her portrayal of Sin-Sin, Di-Peachy, and Ernie June, Brown attempts to suggest the complexity of the slave woman's experience. The entire Chatfield household—both white Chatfields and black "Chatfields"—comprises a larger "family." While the white antebellum South liked to believe that the plantation constituted one big happy family, that emphasis on family—and its rejection by slaves—was apparently even more pronounced in the relationships between house slaves and their owners. At the same time, house slaves might have had more frequent opportunities for close interactions with their owners, particularly with white women, and thus may have also felt strong affection for the women with whom they spent most of their lives.

Not surprisingly, the Chatfield household operates under a similar aporia of tensions. The whites, for example, are unclear as to the status of the slaves in their "family." On the one hand, close bonds exist between Lutie and Sin-Sin and between Geneva and Di-Peachy. All of the women attest to the friendship that exists between them. On the other hand, even though Lutie may be somewhat enlightened, she nevertheless believes in the benevolence of slavery as an institution since "these people [can't] think for themselves" (109). This family arrangement causes predictably greater turmoil for the slaves. The black women, for example, insist on the importance of their relationship to the family—as evidenced by their position as house slaves as opposed to the position of the other slaves as field hands. In addition, only Sin-Sin and Di-Peachy (Geneva's unacknowledged half-sister) feel particularly strong and close ties to the Chatfields, suggesting that their relationships exist not only because they have worked with and for these women for so long but also because they share certain sensibilities. Both Sin-Sin and Di-Peachy realize, as Di-Peachy puts it, that "we're bound by ties of love" (348). Sin-Sin agrees, saying, "I could no more break my invisible chains than fly." But such a realization is not an easy one to make, nor is it a short time in coming; as Sin-Sin says, "[I]t take a long, long time to develop mother wit" (348).

Despite the close bonds of love that Brown depicts between these women, the "peculiar institution" of slavery still manages to make itself felt. Di-Peachy particularly resents that she cannot get an education, and, though she dreams of being free, going to college, and coming home to "teach my people," she also does not foresee such an opportunity, even with the impending freedom of slaves. As she tells Geneva, "[I]t seems to me that whether you win this war or whether you lose it, the fate of my people, of me, is going to be one thunderstorm after another. I don't see any rainbows" (310). Di-Peachy's despair is undercut by Geneva's firm belief that "[y]our fate is with Chatfield. We're sisters; we rise or we fall together!" (310). Such a scene is typical of the world Brown paints: though black and white women can feel bonds of friendship, the white women cannot always cross the racial and institutional boundaries that divide them from their friends, obscuring for them the true experiences of the black women. Di-Peachy's relationship with Mercer Hackett, a white soldier, creates similar tension in her friendship with Geneva, who, though happy that Di-Peachy is in love, is nevertheless profoundly uncomfortable with the idea of an interracial relationship. Brown turns the spotlight less often on black experience in this novel, but when she does she begins to explore the complex emotions at the center of this experience.

Though Brown does address to some degree the conflicted relationships between black and white women, she falls short in key areas, particularly in the problematic stereotype of the "happy darky" she seems dangerously close to invoking and in terms of the questionable methods she uses to construct her historical revision. Although she constructs credible revisions of white Confederate women, she is much less successful at creating believable black characters who are "curious, caring, and filled with a rare perspective due to their phenomenal experience" (xiii). Brown's failure to realize fully her stated intent stems from two problems: an inability to imagine slave life more fully and a failure to draw from better sources.

First, Brown is unable to imagine the lives of slaves as fully as she imagined the lives of white women. To paint strong and credible portraits of Lutie and Geneva, for example, Brown's imagination infused those characterizations, not by constructing distortions of their types, but by actively imagining what it might have been like for white women in the patriarchal South who were suddenly given a chance to break beyond prescribed boundaries. Perhaps, due to her own background, it was easier for Brown to make this leap of imagination in depicting white women. But she also drew heavily from works by authors who had visualized the lives of white Confederate women—such as Margaret Mitchell's *Gone with the Wind,* Mary Chesnut's Civil War diary, and *Kate: The Journal of a Confederate Nurse* (ed. Richard B. Harwell). Since Brown apparently (and not surprisingly) found it more difficult to imagine the lives of black women as creatively and sensitively as she had the lives of white women, the reader might expect her to have gone to similar works by black women in constructing her depiction of slaves.

This expectation leads to the second root cause of Brown's weak characterization of slaves. Although she cites heavy dependence on the WPA interviews of ex-slaves,[3] she also admits using records written by slave-owners. This in itself is problematic, since, as Harriet Jacobs and other authors of slave narratives have shown, slaveholders frequently painted false pictures of slave attitudes. Although Brown took a strong first step in using the WPA interviews, this was not enough. In particular, she might have drawn from the substantial number of extant slave narratives, rather than relying solely on the work of Frederick Douglass.[4] More important, Margaret Walker's *Jubilee* (1966) could have provided a feel for slave attitudes similar to the feel for white women's attitudes that Mitchell's novel provides. A more carefully constructed revision of slave contributions to the Confederacy would have drawn more fully from extant slave narratives and fictional accounts such as *Jubilee.* What results instead is a dangerous tightrope walk between an intriguing replay of slaves as genuinely and understandably loving and forgiving, on the one side, and a recapitulation of the myth of the "happy darky," on the other.

Despite her flawed portrayal of slaves, Brown's novel goes a long way toward revising traditional notions of southern history. In *High Hearts*, Brown set herself a difficult task: to tell undocumented, untold stories. She is to be applauded for her exciting and believable characterizations of white women as warriors. But her problematic treatment of black women and her failure to problematize her re-creation of history leaves the reader wishing she had acknowledged more openly the questions that still exist, the black holes of women's history to which we may never have the answers. The reader is left longing for an admission from Brown that, despite her carefully documented historical research, painstaking detail of weather and church devotional records, and knowledge of military units and parlance, her revision of Civil War history is only a necessary first step toward imagining the way things might have been.

The role of oral culture in a community's survival has increasingly been a focus for minority writers. In *Brown Girl, Brownstones* (1959), for example, Paule Marshall focuses on "the wordshop of the kitchen," a term she uses to describe the times when "the poets in the kitchen"—her mother and her mother's friends—shared stories. According to Marshall, these women, who worked as domestic laborers, used talk as therapy, as recovery from "bargaining over their labor" and from "the humiliations of the work-day" ("The Making of a Writer" 6); as an outlet for creative expression; as a refuge from a foreign culture; and as a "weapon" against "their invisibility, their powerlessness" (7). Likewise, Leslie Marmon Silko examines the healing power of words in *Ceremony* (1977): stories, she asserts, "aren't just entertainment. . . . They are all we have . . . to fight off illness and death" (3). Louise Erdrich also emphasizes the role of storytelling in native American culture. In *Tracks* (1988), for example, Nanapush says, "I saved myself by starting a story. . . . I got well by talking" (46). Many other minority group writers work from this premise, among them Maxine Hong Kingston, N. Scott Momaday, and

Toni Morrison. Each weaves together elements from the oral tradition, such as ceremonies, rituals, legends, stories, magic words, names, and songs. As Jay Clayton argues in "The Narrative Turn in Minority Fiction," many contemporary ethnic novelists "believe that the act of telling a story can be empowering" (379) and that narrative can even be put to "subversive uses" (379). Narrative—the simple act of telling a story—is aligned "with unauthorized forms of knowledge" (378), what Morrison calls "discredited" knowledge (qtd. in McKay 428). Overwhelmingly, contemporary ethnic writers link a marginalized community's ability to recover and survive as a community to its ability to reclaim and make vital its oral tradition.

Although the people Lee Smith writes about are white, they have nevertheless been marginalized. Many Americans—northerners and southerners alike—have traditionally perceived mountain people as "backward" and "anachronistic"; "primitive, romantic, violent, and retarded"; "underprivileged, uneducated"; as a "peculiar people" who inhabit a "strange land"; as victims of "crass ignorance" and "in-breeding"; and as "ignorant, isolated hillbillies, poor, shiftless, and easily provoked."[5] A number of scholars, however, have attempted to provide more accurate portrayals of the mountaineers; they point out that most were originally farmers who later became miners and millhands and that, although certain elements of their lives have lent truth to the cruel stereotype, they nevertheless form proud and close-knit families and communities. Although they have not been nearly as isolated as mainstream America has believed, white mountaineers have been thought to live in a separate country, in but not of America, and have been relegated to a decidedly inferior status. The stereotype has continued late into the twentieth century, most popularly captured in the television program *The Beverly Hillbillies* and in the film *Deliverance* (1972).

Such misperceptions of Appalachia have relegated it to a third world status in relation to the rest of America. In an insightful essay assessing Appalachia's position as "a negativity," "a gap," Rodger Cunningham argues that while the South may be labeled "Other" by the North, Appalachia becomes the "Other's Other—a region marked by double otherness which complicates its very sense of its own being."[6] And while Appalachia's status as a third world entity has shaped economic and political policies, Cunningham notes, it is only with the recent Appalachian Renaissance that these concerns have been expressed in cultural and literary terms. The Renaissance—an emergence in the 1970s and 1980s of poetry and fiction by and about Appalachians—includes such writers as Jim Wayne Miller, Wendell Berry, Fred Chappell, Gurney Norman, Jayne Anne Phillips, Meredith Sue Willis, Breece D'J Pancake, Pinckney Benedict, and, of course, Lee Smith, who stands as one of the best and most prominent writers of this group.[7] This move to cultural expression, according to Cunningham, creates "an expanding framework of possibilities" and opens up "a creative space."

Clearly, Lee Smith agrees. Having grown up in Grundy, Virginia, Smith was part of the town community but "still had all these deep mountain experiences, these talks with my older relatives" (qtd. in Bourne 51). Her perception as both insider and outsider and her frequent trips back home have allowed Smith to assess the development and destruction of the Appalachian community over a period of time. She states, "Appalachia is changing. In fifty years or a hundred years, everything will have changed drastically. Even now there are these dishes where people are getting T.V. reception in the most remote hollers and coves. So I do feel a sense of trying to catch it before it goes" (qtd. in Bourne 47). But Smith does not stop with "trying to catch" the culture before it goes; she goes one step further to argue for the preservation of this largely oral culture so that it will not disappear. Like Marshall, Silko, Erdrich, Kingston, Momaday, and Morrison, Smith believes that the ability of an ethnic people to tell stories and to listen to them appreciatively, coupled with their ability to preserve a sense of history as a collaborative, dynamic enterprise, are keys to the community's survival.

In arguing for the connection between oral traditions and a shared sense of community, Smith focuses on the Appalachian community's ability to preserve a sense of the past, to construct an alternative view of its own history. Like Rita Mae Brown, Smith lets her readers know that her primary concern in *Oral History* is the construction and epistemology of history. She begins with an "Author's Note" in which she lists the books she used to create her story, leading books on Appalachian culture: Horace Kephart's *Our Southern Highlanders* (1922), John C. Campbell's *The Southern Highlander and His Homeland* (1921), and the popular *Foxfire* series. In addition, she lists several collections of stories, legends, and folklore as sources for some of the stories in her novel. In keeping with the concept of oral history, she also credits a number of people who passed along to her "songs, tales and stories, ideas for sources, [and] good lines" (n.p.). And to give her novel a truly authentic feel, she uses real names; the primary family in the novel, for example, are the "Cantrells," a family name common in Smith's home county (qtd. in Bourne 51).

The novel is divided into six sections. The "outside" frame of the novel consists of very short, italicized sections that tell the story happening in the present—Jennifer Bingham's visit to Hoot Owl Holler. The "inside" of the novel includes four much longer sections that tell the heart of the Cantrell family story. These sections may include accounts from a number of different people—both community members and outsiders. Each of these "inside" sections is introduced with a family tree, done in an old-time, handwritten script. As the story progresses and the reader learns more about the Cantrell family history, the family tree grows, until the names of most of the important "family" members have been added to the tree at the novel's end. The tree that introduces the novel's first major section lists only "Almarine Cantrell" and his birthdate, but successive versions add more and more marriages, births, and deaths leading to the last tree, which includes twenty different family members. Interestingly, these successive versions leave out key characters, particularly those whom the family wants to forget. Richard Burlage, for example, whose love affair with Dory Cantrell leaves her with twin daughters Pearl and Maggie, is not included in the family tree. Rather, Little Luther Wade is shown as the father of these children because he married Dory and took responsibility for them. Although the family tree is intended as a quasi-historical document telling a family's complete story, this revered document is, in fact, a falsification of the actual events. And although this is purported to be a family tree, many of the people on the tree are not blood relatives at all. Mountain families take on each other's children and conceal extramarital relationships when necessary. Therefore, the pseudopublic document is not likely to contain completely accurate information regarding each person's ancestors. This written version of history, then, is questionable—a recurring phenomenon in the novel.[8]

The novel's final "historical" element is Richard Burlage's memoirs. Two portions of the novel are attributed to Richard. The first, entitled "Richard Burlage: His Journal, Fall, 1923," traces in diary form his few months in the area, with particular attention to his affair with Dory Cantrell. Appearing much later, the second section, "Richard Burlage Discourses Upon the Circumstances Concerning His Collection of Appalachian Photographs, c. 1934," contains Richard's ruminations on his photography tour of the area eleven years after his brief earlier life there. Although Richard is the character with the least knowledge of the area, his chronicle of events gains the most credibility in the outside world. With tongue in cheek, Smith concludes Richard's story by saying that he "will write his memoirs and they will be published, to universal if somewhat limited acclaim, by LSU Press" (291).

These written documents—bibliography of sources, replicated family trees, and academic memoirs—are the standard ingredients in traditional linear history. But by its very title, *Oral History* challenges the reader to consider the relationship between written and oral accounts of the past. It is easy to create a sense of traditional history through written documents; it is more difficult, even paradoxical, to give a sense of oral history in a novel. Smith does this in one way by weaving a number of narratives from expert storytellers throughout her novel. But she also creates a sense of oral history through her positioning of these narratives. Smith wrote *Oral History* originally as a story of the same name, a story which, as Smith describes it, "was just about the girl coming to tape the relatives and leaving the tape running and somebody going back to get it" (qtd. in Arnold 249). As she wrote the novel, "filling in what would be on the tape" (249), what resulted were many more layers and perspectives that together tell the whole *oral* history. Her novel consists of the brief opening and closing italicized sections that tell the surface story of Jennifer and her trip to the mountains. Between the italicized sections, however, several community members tell their own versions of the Cantrell family's past.

Beginning with Granny Younger's story and ending with Sally's much more recent story, the "inside" of the novel challenges the reader to consider the effect of each teller's viewpoint and agenda. Often, the narratives contradict each other, and it quickly becomes clear that no one narrator in this novel is privy to the whole story and that the speaker's own personal agenda may color his or her interpretation of the "facts." History in this novel, then, becomes a collaborative, dynamic process, rather than a static endeavor undertaken by one person. Smith's creation of a narrative structure that plays many competing voices off of one another mirrors the way oral history actually works. Unlike a traditional linear text told from the point of view of an omniscient narrator, *Oral History* demonstrates the vitality and complexity of storytelling from multiple perspectives. As Smith herself puts it, "I guess I see some sort of central mystery at the center of the past, of any past, that you can't, no matter what a good attempt you make at understanding how it was, you never can quite get at it" (qtd. in Arnold 246). This complex narrative technique makes it difficult to privilege one text over another or to reach any easy conclusions about Smith's intentions in this novel. "Life is complicated and muddy," she says, "and so is good fiction" (qtd. in Bourne 41).

While Smith's novel is not a simplistic reification of oral traditions, it does pit written, academic treatments by outsiders (known as "foreigners" in Appalachian parlance) against oral narratives by community members—and, when taken in toto, the oral narratives are clearly those Smith values more highly. Richard Burlage and his granddaughter Jennifer Bingham epitomize the first approach; as "foreigners," they come to Appalachia with preconceived ideas about the community and with their own agendas for personal and professional fulfillment. Smith repeatedly shows the limitations in Richard's and Jennifer's approach and the misreadings that result. Juxtaposed against Richard's and Jennifer's texts are the narratives of community members themselves—most frequently written in the first person, as with Granny Younger, Rose Hibbitts, Little Luther Wade, Ludie Davenport, Jink Cantrell, Ora Mae, and Sally, but sometimes written in the limited third-person perspective, as with Pricey Jane, Almarine, and Justine Poole. While these narratives often contradict each other, and while they almost always show the inability of one particular person to know the whole story, they nevertheless provide a rich and compelling opposition to the totalizing and obscuring discourse of Richard and Jennifer. While there are certainly limitations attached even to oral attempts to understand the past, the community narratives taken as a whole show the importance of history as an ongoing collaboration that creates by its very existence a sense of community.

If oral narrative, as Clayton argues, is "subversive," if it is "discredited," as Morrison posits, it is so because of its relation to the privileged discourse of traditional history. Oral knowledge created by the community is obscured and devalued, and thus the Appalachian community as it defines itself is rendered invisible; written and academic knowledge is reified and privileged, and hence the misperceptions outsiders construct about Appalachia are perceived as the truth. Misreadings become official readings. Richard's attitude toward the mountain people is a prime example of this phenomenon. He begins his sojourn in the area with an early journal entry that illustrates his unrealistic and naive expectations: "I intend for this journal to be a valid record of what I regard as essentially a pilgrimage, a simple geographical pilgrimage, yes, but also a pilgrimage back through time, a pilgrimage to a simpler era, back—dare I hope it—to the very roots of consciousness and belief" (93). While Richard recognizes that the mountain community still works on some primal level that the civilized society of Richmond does not, his assumptions about mountain culture—that living in it will take him back through time, that it is "simpler," that it represents the "very roots of consciousness and belief"—obscure a clear view of the mountain culture.

Richard's "tendency . . . to catalog a thing to death" (96) is a key aspect of the traditional linear history account, the approach that tries to classify and compartmentalize events and the participants in events. In fact, it is tied to the assumption that we can look at the past and discern distinct "events." This way of looking at the world is directly opposed to that of the people of Hoot Owl Holler, who understand the world by talking through "events" and experiences, who spin stories and legends about the past, and who resist overrationalization. Consequently, Richard has a difficult time in Hoot Owl Holler. Appropriately enough, Richard's position as the schoolteacher highlights his role as the irrelevant academician in a world that has little patience with "book-larnin'."

Richard's problems with overrationalization are best seen in his peculiar method of trying to understand his relationship with Dory. His first journal entry about their relationship begins with a quote from Marlowe, and then, as Dory's image fills his mind, he says, "The words seem to dance in the air! I begin to think that I myself may begin to write" (122). Richard cannot enjoy Dory for herself but rather must transform her into a springboard for intellectual activity. Later, as he tries to determine whether or not to continue his affair with her, he makes lists: "Reasons for pursuing Miss Dory Cantrell" and "Reasons to forget Miss Cantrell entirely" (134). These lists are followed by other lists: "I therefore resolve" and "Notes on the state of my soul" (135). The last reason Richard lists for forgetting Dory—"Her father and her brothers would kill me" (135)—is the first one that occurs to the reader and underscores the great gap in understanding between Richard and the mountain community.

When events do come to a head and Richard is forced to leave town, he reacts—as with his list making—by taking an overly formal position. Instead of talking to Dory, Richard sends a note asking her to leave with him. In this instance, the written word causes particular damage: it ultimately destroys a life. For, as the reader learns later, Dory's older "sister" Ora Mae keeps the note from her, leaving Dory to assume that Richard ran off without her. This assumption contributes to her suicide fourteen years later. When Dory does not leave with him, Richard reverts to his love of overrationalization. He vows that he will return to get Dory someday but immediately after says, "I shall never marry, I shall become an artist, I will transform all of this into a novel" (166). This impulse to transform his experiences into written language is not merely pompous. Rather, the violence of the written word in this community—here symbolized by the breakdown of communication caused by the interception of the note—leads not only to Dory's eventual self-mutilation but also to the destruction of the Appalachian community as a whole. As Suzanne W. Jones argues, "Smith suggests an academic exploitation of the hills which, though different from that of the loggers, miners, and mill owners who invaded Appalachia earlier in this century, is still abusive" (104).

Further academic exploitation is evident in Richard's second section, in which he describes the photographs he takes on a return trip to the area eleven years later. Although he writes that he comes back "different from the boy who had left here ten years back" (222), he does not seem to be much changed—or if so, only in degree. If anything, he is even more of a pedant than before. Where once he had gone about the town writing down his observations, now he walks and drives about, taking photographs of the inhabitants, certain that he is capturing the essence of mountain life. Against a photograph of a young, tubercular mother, for example, he writes, "[H]er lips parted slightly as if to utter something she cannot articulate, something which I feel I captured, nonetheless, in this photograph" (224). As usual, Richard cannot define this "something" but feels he has "captured" it. Similarly, when he goes to see Dory, he does not speak to her or stay very long with her; rather, he takes a picture and leaves. Seeing his great love after years of separation suggests not only his disappointment at the changes in her but also reinforces his inability to see the mountain community clearly. His entire description of Dory reads, "She was reduced to an indistinct, stooped shape, the posture of an older woman—they age so fast in those mountains anyway— or perhaps it was simply the angle of her head and the way she stood at the door, her head a mere bright blur. Even when I blew it up, there was nothing there" (234). Once again, when Richard has the opportunity to take even a small leap into the gritty world of mountain poverty, he steps back and objectifies any sadness, regret, or guilt he might be feeling. Dory becomes a photograph and part of a memoir like the other mountain folk. In Richard's memoirs, the violence of the written word is expanded to include the violence of other academic epistemologies. Though Richard does not use a gun, he might as well, as he stops his car and "lean[s] out for a couple of quick *shots*" (233; my emphasis). Although he believes that "a frame, a photograph, can illumine and enlarge one's vision rather than limit it" (228), it is clear that Smith feels just the opposite; Richard's tendency to frame his experiences, whether through lists, memoirs, or photographs, always leads him to limit his vision.

Richard's approach to this community and its culture not only falls short in what it can actually teach him but also works to destroy that community. Another person guilty of this limiting and destructive approach is Richard's granddaughter, Jennifer Bingham. Like Richard, Jennifer does not see the mountain culture as it is and fails to construct appropriate strategies for reading this community. Jennifer comes to Hoot Owl Holler not only with stereotypes that will obscure her vision but also with her own personal and academic agenda; she has come there not so much in an effort to get in touch with her roots but with a desire to impress her professor and to pat herself on the back for her willingness to confront her family. Her biggest misreading comes from her lack of knowledge regarding her "blood" relatives. The novel opens and closes with the account of her visit to the people she erroneously believes are her grandparents. Yet as the novel progresses, the reader discovers that, although Ora Mae and Little Luther Wade are part of the family system from which Jennifer is descended, they are not actually her grandparents. In addition, although Jennifer is ostensibly part of this mountain family and likewise part of the mountain culture, it is possible that she has only one-eighth mountain blood, rather than the one-half she believes she has. Here the problems with falsified family trees become clear. Though the family tree tells her that Little Luther Wade is her grandfather, and though her lack of family history leads her to believe Ora Mae is her grandmother, in reality her grandparents are Richard Burlage and Dory Cantrell. Moreover, Dory's mother, Pricey Jane, is of unknown ancestry, but it is possible—even probable—that she did not come from mountain stock at all. Jennifer is only loosely related to these people, but no one bothers to tell her this. Rather, they watch her come and go on this visit, knowing that she does not understand them or their culture. At the same time, she is unable, unwilling, or afraid to ask appropriate and penetrating questions. As a foreigner whose vision is obscured by her own preconceptions and agenda and whose access to the Cantrells is denied by their distrust and disdain for her and other outsiders, Jennifer leaves with a text of the mountains as inaccurate as the one Richard takes away.

Jennifer's flawed methods of reading lead directly to her failed construction of a text of this community. If Smith criticizes Richard for seeing the mountains through a pedantic filter, she criticizes Jennifer for expecting shortcuts to knowledge about "her people." True knowing takes a lifetime for people like Ora Mae and Little Luther Wade, and they are unlikely to share what they have learned and the pain they have experienced with an outsider—even with someone who is ostensibly part of their family. Yet Jennifer thinks it is as easy as taking the appropriate college course, driving up to the mountain, setting up her tape recorder, and jotting down a few impressions. Her visit to the mountain ends violently as Al Cantrell "rapes" her with his tongue:

> [W]hen he opens the door of the Toyota for her, just before she can get in, her uncle Al grabs her right up off her feet and kisses her so hard that stars smash in front of her eyes. Al sticks his tongue inside her mouth. Then before Jennifer can even think what is happening to her, Al lets go of her and she drops back against the open door. (290)

After some thought, however, she sees the visit in a good light: "[B]y the time she gets back to the college, Jennifer has stopped crying and gotten a hold on herself. She has changed it all around in her head" (290). Just as her grandfather Burlage was ready to "transform all of this [his mountain experiences] into a novel," so Jennifer is able to change her visit "all around in her head."

Misreadings, limited vision, and condescension are at the heart of academic, written, outside approaches to the Appalachian community. The misreadings result because outsiders cannot understand the value of alternative approaches to history, cannot hear the songs and stories that constitute knowledge in this community. As an oppositional text to standard histories and sociological studies about Appalachia, Smith's novel foregrounds Appalachian oral culture and makes clear that the oral tradition has the power to preserve the entire community. The way one comes to know this culture is through talking, exchanging stories, and singing. The following discussion of the novel's "first" Cantrell, Alma-rine, and the ultimate result of his passionate affair with the "witch," Red Emmy, typifies the way knowledge is created in this community:

> "I tell you he kilt her," the eldest said. "You was there too and you seed him come back. You seed the blood."
>
> "I don't know if I seed it or not," the youngest said.
>
> "Well, you was right there as sure as you're a-living," the eldest yelled out. "What ails you, boy?"
>
> "Never kilt her," another one said. "Bill Horn has seed her in West Virginia on the streets of Williamson, I tell you, right out on the street a-whoring. And he said she looked pretty good."
>
> "Ast Almarine iffen he kilt her or not, an' you credit me," the eldest said, but the others said, "Hoo! Not me!" and "I'll not ast Almarine nothin'!" (85)

Because the men are unwilling to ask Almarine what happened, they work toward knowledge through talk, gossip, and the like, its conduits in this community. An event happens, people talk, and the verbal construction takes on a life of its own. In time, the legend gains legitimacy over the actual event. As the Methodist minister Aldous Rife explains, "[S]omebody could have started up a tale about her [Rose Hibbitts] . . . only she started up a tale about Almarine instead. And once it starts, it just goes on by itself, it takes on a life of its own no matter who may be hurt in the process" (186–87). History, then, as it is understood in this culture, is not the actual event. Rather, the legend constructed around that event takes its place as the history of the community. This is precisely why it is difficult for outsiders to write the community's history. Traditional historical accounts will not work because discrete events are difficult to discern and categorize, agreements about past events difficult to reach.

Although Rife criticizes these tales, he has been in Black Rock "writing a kind of 'history' of this region" for thirty years (142). Though he is also writing, his version of history is different from Richard's. Although problems arise because he is an outsider, Rife understands that the folktales of this community are its history. At crucial moments, he is able to tell appropriate stories. For example, to illustrate his point that Richard is in danger of being killed by Dory's father and brothers, Rife tells him the story of the Baisden brothers, legendary for coming to town and killing people. "When was this?" asks Richard. "Twenty, thirty years ago," Rife replies. "The time doesn't really matter." "Of course it matters," answers Richard. "This could be a fact of history, or it could be a county myth, a folk tale. . . . I know you collect them, and you know it too. I suspect you make some of them up." But Richard misses the essential point: the myths are the history. Even if they do not contain actual "facts of history," they encapsulate an attitude, a way of being, a knowledge about the culture. As Rife explains to him, "It doesn't matter. . . . Nothing ever changes that much" (150–51).

Cultural knowledge and a sense of collective history is also passed along through songs. Although many marginalized communities use songs as one form for passing down oral tradition, as in Toni Morrison's *Song of Solomon* (1977), Appalachian music has had particular power. Contemporary country music—which largely derives from mountain music[9]—is now enjoyed primarily for its entertainment value; but the original—if often unconscious—purpose of songs, like folktales, was to transmit mountain lore, stories of individual people, and a tight sense of culture and community. Smith makes this particularly clear in *The Devil's Dream* (1992), which simultaneously tells the story of a multi-generational singing and recording family of Appalachia and of the development of mountain and country music as a whole. While mountain music is not the central focus of *Oral History* as it is in *The Devil's Dream,* it nevertheless plays a key role. For example, Little Luther Wade's song about the mining disaster of 1933, "Buried Alive," continues to be sung fifty years later and to be the primary means by which the community remembers that event (248). Smith emphasizes the importance of mountain music by taking the novel's epigraph from the song "Fair and Tender Ladies," which is also the title of one of her novels. She weaves many other songs throughout the novel as well, including "Mighty Lak a Rose," "Fox on the Run," "Mama, Don't Whup Little Buford," "Wildwood Flower," "Wise County Jail," "Barbary Allen," and "Down in the Valley."

In countless scenes, characters sing, clog, and play guitars, dulcimers, and fiddles; the careful reader hears music on every page, music that is an integral part of the daily fabric of this community.

Smith alerts the reader to the centrality of music by opening the novel with a description of Little Luther Wade, the novel's most adept songwriter and musician, sitting on his son's porch and strumming his dulcimer while his wife Ora Mae is making an afghan. This opening immediately immerses the reader in Appalachian culture and signals the importance of Little Luther's song about Dory that appears later in the novel. Where Richard Burlage is unable in seventy-four pages to reach a full understanding of his relationship with Dory, Little Luther encapsulates in a short song not only the events leading up to Richard's departure but also the likely impact of these events on his and Dory's lives. Smith places the short section containing Little Luther's song immediately after Richard's section, thereby sharpening the contrast between Richard's long-winded pomposity and Little Luther's brief, evocative treatment of the event. Although Little Luther expects that he will "never sing it to nobody, least of all to her" (175), his ability to present his experience so concisely yet so powerfully is impressive—especially after the reader observes Richard's inability to say much of anything in seventy-four pages. Little Luther is one of the novel's true artists and, therefore, one of its primary historians. Little Luther's approach, rendered in a simple song, strikingly undercuts Richard's inappropriate approach to reading and writing this community.

Unfortunately, though the songs sung by Little Luther and his like have been preserved somewhat in contemporary country music, this music has been exploited and weakened to the point that its origins as mountain music are often unidentifiable. Smith herself ties this exploitation of mountain music to the parallel exploitation of the Appalachian area itself (Arnold 247). When the songs are still played—as when Little Luther continues to play in the 1980s on his front porch—the youngest generation cannot hear it: Little Luther's grandchildren turn up the television so that his singing will not drown out "Magnum, P.I." Yet the constant presence of this music in the background (underneath "Magnum") may yet seep into the subconscious of these young Appalachians.

For even Little Luther's despicable son Al and his wife Debra sing and clog to the music, showing that even those members of the community who are exploiting and rejecting it still almost unconsciously appreciate the oral tradition that is so much a part of that community.

But Smith's emphasis in this novel is not on individual songs or folktales but on the collective, collaborative sense of history that the sharing of songs and tales creates. It is crucial to consider not only the discrete bits of folklore she revives in her novel—whether Luther's song "The Ring-a-ding-a-doo" or Parrot's story about the witch woman—but to look also at the larger tales of this particular community that are created when these individual narratives are woven together. To see this larger intricate fabric created by the oral tradition, the reader must be willing—as Richard and Jennifer are not—to see the construction of history as an ongoing, collaborative effort, which requires active participation on the part of the teller and the listener, roles that all members of the community—in order to keep the oral tradition alive—must play at different times. As Clayton describes it, oral narrative "creates interdependence, an intersubjectivity that exists not only among but also within every member of the community" (387). This narrative interdependence becomes subversive as it allows the community to define itself rather than to be defined by outsiders.

Two storytellers whose larger visions give shape to the dynamic history of this family are Granny Younger and Sally, who together represent the movement from the oldest generation of the novel to the youngest. Granny Younger's narrative opens the inside of the novel and sets the story of the Cantrell family in motion. Although not a Cantrell herself, Granny Younger is in many ways a symbolic member of the family, serving as the community's midwife and medicine woman and ultimately being buried in the Cantrell family plot on top of Hoot Owl Mountain. Her power as a preserver of oral culture comes through both in her role as a healer and in her role as a chronicler of community history. As the medicine woman, Granny Younger intimately understands the healing power of words. Her description of her healing techniques also speaks to the power of women's voice and of the knowledge passed from generation to generation via the women of the community:

The next thing I done was what my mama showed me and which I
am knowed for everywhere in these parts, what I do to stop bleeding. They will call me anytime, day or night, and when I hear who
it is I start saying the words even afore I get my bonnet on, I start
saying the words which I know by heart from my mama, and when
I get there, most times, the bleeding's already stopped. (20)

The process of healing and of preserving oral culture continues to be
passed along to other generations, as Granny Younger prepares Rhoda
Hibbitts (later Granny Hibbitts) to take her place. Such discredited approaches to healing are threatened, however, when Ora Mae—who has
the "gift"—refuses to let Granny Hibbitts train her to make full use of it.
Still, Ora Mae is an important, if reluctant, repositor of community lore,
and like Granny Younger, Granny Hibbitts, and Rose Hibbitts she states
the unsettling truth more plainly than most listeners would like. All of
these women pay a price for their "foolish notions," as their community
often perceives them as "[c]razy old wom[e]n" (49).

If she is important in her community as a medicine woman, Granny
Younger is crucial to the novel as a key storyteller. She tells the beginning of the story—the relationship between Almarine and Red Emmy
and his later marriage to Pricey Jane—and, in doing so, uses many of
the devices of a veteran storyteller. She takes her own time spinning
her yarn, assuring her listener that "I'll tell it all directly" (27). Granny
Younger knows what's important in the story—not the facts, but the
essence:

Iffen twas my story, I never would tell it at all. There's tales I'll tell,
and tales I won't. And iffen twas my story, why I'd be all hemmed
in by the facts of it like Hoot Owl Holler is hemmed in by them
three mountains. . . . I said I know moren you know and mought be
I'll tell you moren you want to hear. I'll tell you a story that's truer
than true, and nothing so true is so pretty. It's blood on the moon,
as I said. The way I tell a story is the way I want to, and iffen you
mislike it, you don't have to hear. (28)

Granny Younger's story is not something Richard or Jennifer would be
comfortable hearing. It would not correspond to Richard's desire for "a

simpler era," and it is difficult to imagine it corroborating Jennifer's "new appreciation of these colorful, interesting folk." Not only does Granny Younger tell "a story that's truer than true"; she also forces her listener to confront painful reality: "mought be I'll tell you moren you want to hear."

With Granny Younger's narrative, Smith introduces not only the vitality of the rich oral culture but also alerts the reader to the limitations of even this approach to the past. For Granny Younger, like many in her community, mistakenly believes that Red Emmy is a witch. And it seems likely that her persistence in this belief is less a result of her belief in the supernatural (although that is a factor) and more a result of her intolerance for Red Emmy's divergence from community standards for appropriate female appearance and behavior. Rodger Cunningham argues that Granny Younger's inaccurate portrayal of Red Emmy deconstructs the oral tradition as a preferable method to written, academic history. He claims that the novel "does not idealize [Appalachian] culture . . . but rather presents its mechanical 'folk'-solidarity as the first of the master-discourses that obscure the facts of domination." Granny Younger, he continues, "is not a repository of timeless folk-wisdom . . . , but rather is the first of the voices of that history against which the human souls of the characters are locked in struggle." While Granny Younger's narrative is not completely reliable, and while the community does work together to erase any accurate representation of Red Emmy, it would be dangerous to conclude, as Cunningham does, that the novel devalues oral approaches to the past. Granny Younger's narrative may include some inaccuracies and in some ways be unreliable, but its importance as a key oral text comes when it is taken in toto with the narratives of other community and family members.

Granny Younger and the other narrators participate in creating a dynamic, collaborative, living sense of the past, a sense most strikingly emphasized in the narrative by the youngest storyteller, Sally, who with Granny Younger brackets either side of the family history. Sally and her second husband Roy are blessed with the rare ability to truly enjoy life. Sally has lived through her share of pain, especially in her mother Dory's suicide when Sally was thirteen and later in her first marriage. Despite these tragedies, Sally has a real love of life and an abiding sense of humor. She opens her section by saying: "There's two things I like to do better than anything else in this world, even at my age—and one of them is talk. You all can guess what the other one is" (237). Her section, like Granny Younger's, written in the first person, addresses an implied audience. Sally tells this audience a story she had told Roy when he was ill, suggesting literally the healing and nurturing power of words. Moreover, her first husband did not allow her to talk and she languished; getting back the power to talk not only heals those around her but also allows her to regain a strong sense of herself.

Though she loves to talk, Sally admits that telling the story is not easy: "'Listen,' I said, and I got him [Roy] a beer, 'I'll start at the beginning,' I said, which I did, and although I told it the best I could, I'm still not sure I got it straight. It took me a day to tell the whole thing" (239–40). A few pages later, after having told the story of her early family life, she says, "I can see I'll have to start again. It's hard, you know, to find the beginning. This is not it either, of course—nothing ever is—but this is where we'll start" (250). In the telling she quickens her pace for certain parts, sometimes because events are painful, sometimes because she must go back to work.

Like Granny Younger, Sally is a sensitive storyteller. She knows that beginnings are never easy to discern, if they exist at all; stories cause pain and, more often, ambivalent feelings ("that part . . . *is* funny, even though it is also bad" [280]); listeners are eager to get through the background and to arrive at the heart of the story. Most important, Sally knows the complexity of stories. She recognizes the limitations of knowing the past. At one point, for example, she says: "Is that true? I thought. My problem is, I can't decide, looking back, what is true and what's not" (270). She also emphasizes the importance of the sense of what happened (as opposed to the actual facts). For example, she relates the events of her mother's death very quickly: "She died in 1937, when I was thirteen years old. She fell—or laid down—on the spur line, and the train cut off her head. // Everybody knows that" (249). Then, she proceeds to a much fuller discussion of the impact of that death on her family. Details such as the actual death, the year it happened, how old she was, and the way it happened are easily dismissed. That is, she satisfies Richard's need for the "actual facts of history" very quickly. It is the sense of what happened, the emotions, the enduring quality of that event, that is harder to capture and that deserves more of the story-teller's effort and time. "Everybody knows that" is Sally's favorite refrain; in story after story she relays the "actual facts of history" very quickly, then backs up to tell the deeper "real" story at work.

Consequently, Sally, unlike her niece Jennifer, feels no need to take shortcuts in getting to the truth. She may speed up parts of the story but only to get at the deeper underlying structures of the story that are harder to articulate. Unlike her brother Al, who builds an amuse-ment park out of the haunted family homestead, she does not value the commercial possibilities of her family's legend. Indeed, she resents the fact that, after her mother's death, her home becomes a "tourist attrac-tion" (250). Finally, unlike Richard, Sally does not understand the world through cataloging "facts of history"; rather her enduring sense of her-self, her place in her community, her sense of her community's place in the world—all keys to survival—come through her intuitive knowledge that, as Aldous Rife put it, "Nothing ever changes that much" (150–51).

It is not surprising that when Smith ends the novel by quickly listing what each of the character's lives will bring, she states that it is Sally and Roy who "will continue to live out their long and happy lives" (291), for Sally and Roy understand the key to survival in this community. Yet even though people like Sally and Roy can still be found in the current generation, that is, though there are some who still appreciate the cul-ture and work in their own way to preserve it, others of this generation, those, like Al, who want to capitalize on their culture, appear at this point to be winning. The novel ends with a full discussion of Al Can-trell's destiny: his climb to the top of AmWay, his election as president of the Junior Toastmasters Club, and his investment in Ghostland. The last half-page of the novel is devoted to a description of the ultimate outcome of the Cantrell family story:

Ghostland, designed by a Nashville architect, will be the prettiest theme park east of Opryland itself, its rides and amusements ter-raced up and down the steep holler, its skylift zooming up and down from the burial ground where the cafeteria is. And the old homeplace still stands, smack in the middle of Ghostland, untouched. Vines grow up through the porch where the rocking chair sits, and the south wall of the house has fallen in. It's surrounded by a chain link fence, fronted by the observation deck with redwood benches which fill up every summer night at sunset with those who have paid the extra $4.50 to be here, to sit in this cool misty hush while the shadows lengthen from the three mountains—Hoot Owl, Snowman, and Hurricane—while the night settles in, to be here when dark comes and the wind and the laughter start, to see it with their own eyes when that rocking chair starts rocking and rocks like crazy the whole night long. (292)

Here Smith encapsulates the artifacts of this family's past—not the memoirs Richard publishes with LSU Press nor the living tales that Sally tells—but the tourist attraction the family homestead has become. This would seem to be an unrelentingly pessimistic ending: Al sells his family's land, commercializes their memories and legends, and, what is worse, exposes their pain to the outside world's ridicule. But a glimmer of hope, of optimism remains: "the old homeplace still stands . . . untouched." Smith suggests in this one fleeting image that Appalachian culture has a chance of surviving, that it is not necessarily destined to disappear.

Any hope for survival remains with those members of the Appalachian community who can maintain or recuperate a lively, shared interest in the oral traditions of this community—the tales, the songs, the collaborative and dynamic approach to the culture's past. Although even Sally's narrative is limited by her sometimes inaccurate knowledge of the past (she knows nothing, for example, about her mother's affair with Richard Burlage), she nevertheless relishes the old tales and is willing to tell them over and over again, creating as she does a strong sense of herself and of her community. Toni Morrison has said, "People *crave* narration. . . . That's the way they learn things" (qtd. in Bakerman 58; Morrison's emphasis). Satisfying our collective craving for narration and the integral need for the recovery of Appalachian culture are Smith and all of the other participants in the Appalachian Renaissance, who understand, along with other contemporary ethnic writers, that sharing stories builds community.

Like Mary Chesnut, both Rita Mae Brown and Lee Smith seek to give voice to the "secret self," the experience of women and minorities that goes "unpenetrated, unguessed." Each of these writers understands that telling stories is not only empowering but also subversive. The act of telling one's own story, these writers suggest, challenges the myopic traditional histories of public and external events that render women and minorities invisible and unimportant. When women and minorities give voice to the experiences that have shaped them, they expand our very notions of what constitutes history and point the way for other women and minorities to lay claim to this redefined vision of the past, this revisioned "backward glance."

FOUR

NO PLACE LIKE HOME:
LEARNING TO READ TWO WRITERS' MAPS

> The feeling reminds her of her aerobics instructor . . . when they did the
> pelvic tilt in gym last year. A row of girls with their asses reaching for
> heaven. "Squeeze your butt-*ox*. Squeeze tight, girls," she would say, and
> they would grit their teeth and flex their butts, and hold for a count of
> five, and then she would say, "Now squeeze one layer deeper." That is
> what the new feeling is like: you know something as well as you can and
> then you squeeze one layer deeper and something more is there.
>
> SAMANTHA, *In Country*

*I*n *The Color Purple* (1982) and *In Country* (1985), Alice Walker and
Bobbie Ann Mason argue the primacy of their texts' own internal systems of reading over externally imposed master narratives. Walker does
so in two ways: first, by questioning traditional definitions of art and,
implicitly, ways of seeing texts; and second, by creating in Celie a model
reader and writer who illustrates the active process all must undergo
in understanding any text. In her essays, stories, and novels (especially
"In Search of Our Mothers' Gardens" and "Everyday Use"), Walker challenges the ways the white patriarchy determines political and social
definitions of art. Walker presents quilts and gardens as legitimate works
of art made by women who, like their Appalachian counterparts, stand
outside the dominant, patriarchal society that defines art, creativity,
imagination, and knowledge. Because white men cannot read quilts and
gardens as works of art, they render these texts invisible. Walker's second
novel, *Meridian* (1977), exposes the ways the academy (and, by extension, the literary establishment) controls "bright young black women"
by assimilating them into a dominant white culture. Such a move makes
powerless their dangerous position on the sidelines of culture.

But if Walker argues against the limitations of perception and the move to contain potentially subversive elements, that is, if she argues against the ways black women are read and defined by the white male power establishment, she also provides a more productive way to approach black women's texts. By foregrounding in *The Color Purple* a poor black southern woman's creation of her own text and, thus, her active interpretation of her own experience, Walker posits black women's need to seize control over the defining process by creating their own systems of reading. Hence, if a reader wants to approach black women's texts more fruitfully, Walker argues, he or she will use the very model of interpretation Celie engages. The novel's epistolary form forces the reader to become an active participant in creating meaning out of daily fragments of experience: Celie's letters allow her to interpret her world and gain greater self-understanding but at the same time provide the reader with a method of reading the text.

Though some readers will follow Walker's rhetorical cues, and though Celie-as-reader successfully reaches a coherent and fluent interpretation of the world-as-text, many readers will misinterpret Walker's cues and hence her novel, just as many characters in the novel misunderstand each other. As Wendy Wall argues in her discussion of Walker's systems of reading, the pervasive instances of miscommunication in the novel— of "[c]riss-crossed letters, letters written to an absence, letters received from the dead, hidden and confiscated letters"—"call attention to the inherent problems within the processes of reading, writing, and interpretation" (94). Moreover, various interruptions in the text—Albert's confiscation of Nettie's letters to Celie and Celie's decision to write to God, "who, as a white male listener, is ill-equipped to hear what she has to say" (Tucker 82)—point to the ways black women's texts are appropriated and co-opted by those in positions of power.

Similarly, Bobbie Ann Mason implicitly addresses the misreadings her work provokes. Though she is quite popular, Mason's sparseness and bare-bones prose style is frequently attacked. Those who find her minimalist approach annoying complain of her "numbing use of the present tense" (DePietro 620), of her "K-Mart realism," and of her superficial treatment of serious subjects. In reviewing *Shiloh and Other Stories,* Mona Molarsky sums up the despair of many readers: Mason "seems content to detail a way of life and then trail off. Would a reader really be greedy in asking for something more, some broader perspective or deeper understanding?" (58).

Molarsky misses Mason's point entirely. Mason's work does go beyond the superficial to a "broader perspective," but she requires the reader to play an active part in reaching that perspective. Though she does not foreground this process as Walker does, her early reference to "squeezing" to another layer of meaning suggests an embedded system of reading. In "Minimalism and the American Dream," Barbara Henning examines the role of minimalism in Mason's fiction, with particular emphasis on the reader's role in creating meaning. Henning argues:

> Without a reader, minimalist fiction is a static product of contempo-
> rary American life. With a responding reader, however, it becomes a
> powerful reaction to and interpretation of daily life. The minimalist
> writer, a writer shaped by the society she lives in, asks the reader
> to do her part, to make connections, bring insight and resolution,
> provide the reasoning, question, revise, accept. (698)

Clearly, the reader would indeed be too greedy in asking Mason to make all the leaps of reasoning. Mason does not make connections explicit nor lay the meaning out on the table. She creates a thin surface layer of meaning—a surface level all too many readers take as *the* meaning of the text. But we are not to take this as the heart of the novel; rather, like Samantha in *In Country,* we too must "squeeze one layer deeper." Though we might believe we "know [Mason] as well as [we] can," if we "squeeze one layer deeper" we will find that "something more is there." Like Walker, then, Mason portrays her main character as the ideal reader who actively engages with each potential part of the world-as-text, who looks beyond the surface of what she sees and experiences, and who also importantly recognizes the limitations of her reading and of her ability to empathize and thus interpret experience radically different from her own.

A consideration of Walker's *The Color Purple* and Mason's *In Country* and, in chapter 5, the readings they foster, can illustrate Walker's and Mason's own approaches to interpretation and reading. At the heart of each of these novels is the examination of the connection between place (the South) and identity (the role of women within the South). To gain a clear understanding of their connection, it is necessary to read according to the interpretive maps Walker and Mason provide. The model readers at the center of their texts—Celie and Sam—teach us to read their interpretive maps correctly and to join them on their journeys in search of the South and of themselves as women in the South.

While many readers argue that *The Color Purple* fails as the realistic novel it was intended to be,[1] and while a few other readers astutely link it instead to the romance and fairy tale traditions,[2] Walker's novel refuses to fall neatly into specific genre categories. The blurring of genre conventions indicates her noncompliance with the social contract between writer and reader. Walker's conflicting signals in this regard—on the one hand, for example, her use of the realistic convention of the epistolary novel, and on the other, her choice of the novel's original subtitle, *A Moral Tale*—suggest not that she was unable finally to fix on a particular literary tradition out of which to write. Rather, these conflicting signals indicate her wish to foreground issues of reading and interpretation and, at the same time, to place her text deliberately on the margins of discourse. By refusing to adhere to one set of generic conventions, she also refuses to be placed at the center of a particular genre; hence, she attempts to disengage herself from the totalizing discourse that would see her solely as a realistic writer or solely as a romance artist.

Playing with these various genre conventions, Alice Walker transforms Celie's individual story into an allegory of the black southern struggle for spiritual liberation and for reconciliation to a homeland. Thus, her work is both realistic and grounded in a specific sociocultural, historical moment and, at the same time, is magical or mythic, signifying beyond the particular moment in time and place it represents. Walker's mythic story—which she retells in almost all of her work (fiction, poetry, and essays)—is that of the movement from the South to the North and back to the South again. Though other African-American writers have highlighted this movement, and though a few have returned their characters to the South, Walker remains the preeminent example of a writer who assertively and consistently argues for the South as a black homeland. She makes a radical and subversive argument: blacks need to make peace with the region of oppression and to reclaim that which is rightfully theirs.

Walker's South-North-South pattern grows out of a long-standing African-American literary tradition of movement. In countless slave narratives, the North epitomizes liberation. *Narrative of the Life of Frederick Douglass* (1845) ends with Douglass's successful migration to the North, suggesting that he has achieved freedom. But as later narratives show, such as Douglass's own *My Bondage and My Freedom* (1855) and Harriet Jacobs's *Incidents in the Life of a Slave Girl* (1861), movement North did not fulfill the promise of liberation. Both Douglass and Jacobs find themselves frustrated by the northern white community's attempts at restricting their speech and by the obstacles they encounter as they try to provide the authority for their own narratives.

At the same time, however, the South often implicitly symbolized home and a nurturing black community. Both Douglass and Jacobs, for example, construct what Houston Baker calls the "prior unity" of initially warm and satisfying relationships with the South via the loving homes of their grandmothers. The move to the alienating North allows the former slaves to achieve freedom from chattel slavery but also renders them homeless. Douglass realizes that "I was not only free from slavery, but I was free from home, as well" (*Bondage* 207). The slave narratives fit within the African-American literary tradition Robert Stepto terms the "ascent narrative," in which the black quester may achieve a modicum of freedom but may also experience alienation. Other twentieth-century narratives, including Ralph Ellison's *Invisible Man* (1952) and Richard Wright's *Native Son* (1940), fall within this "ascent" narrative as well.

Stepto further notes the move to a second African-American tradition, that of the "immersion narrative." Here, the quester goes on "a ritualized journey into a symbolic South" in an attempt to become whole; the end of a typical immersion narrative finds the quester "located in or near the narrative's most oppressive social structure" but paradoxically "free" as

he gains "newfound balms of group identity" (167). Such a pattern replicates black demographics, indicating as it does that while many blacks
continued to move North, others either stayed in the South or eventually
returned there. Twentieth-century examples of the immersion narrative
include Jean Toomer's *Cane* (1923) and Ernest Gaines's mythohistorical novel, *The Autobiography of Miss Jane Pittman* (1971). Likewise, Toni
Morrison's characters, though positioned in the Midwest, are constantly
informed by this sense of regional motion. In *Song of Solomon* (1977),
Milkman, like his father and aunt before him, is a sojourner, moving
back and forth between the North and the South.

This South-North-South pattern permeates Walker's first three novels;
her short stories, such as "Everyday Use"; her poems, such as "South: The
Name of Home" and "Burial"; and her essays, in which she documents
this struggle in her own life. Walker fully describes this South-North-
South movement in her first novel, *The Third Life of Grange Copeland*
(1970). Grange Copeland moves from the oppression of the sharecrop-
per South to the failed promise of the North and, finally, back to the
South where he achieves redemption. The vision of Grange Copeland's
first life in the South is the only one many readers can accept: that of
the South as "a place of terrible entrapment which destroys family life
and enslaves blacks to an endless cycle of physical and spiritual poverty"
(Butler 70). Though he goes north seeking social and economic liberation, Grange eventually discovers that the North is "a cruel hoax" (Butler
71). Finally, Grange realizes that the only redemption he will find is in
making peace with the South. Such redemption does not come because
he loves the South as a particular place but because he finally creates a
safe space for himself there. Most important, Grange's journey represents
not only a pattern of South-North-South movement many individual
African-Americans have made, but it also—and more significant—encapsulates the historical movement of blacks from southern slavery to
the industrial North and the return to the South, which, in Grange's
case, is an economically triumphant return as well.

This emphasis on mythohistoricism also informs *The Color Purple* on
every level, in both content and form. Indeed, Walker based the character of Celie on her great-grandmother, a slave raped by her owner at

age twelve. By transforming her great-grandmother's story into one of ultimate redemption and reconciliation, Walker says that she "liberated her from her own history" (qtd. in Anello and Abramson 67). The earliest portions of the novel parallel slavery, establishing a mythohistorical account of the lives of Walker's great-grandmother and countless other slave women. The novel's long middle section parallels the black community's lengthy sojourn in the region imposed upon them by slave owners and continued in the twentieth century by oppressive institutions such as sharecropping. Celie's eventual move to Memphis symbolically marks the black community's twentieth-century migration to the North, with an emphasis both on the economic liberation the North provides as well as the threats it presents to black cultural identity. It is important to note that, although even Celie knows that "Memphis, Tennessee ain't North" (110), Walker nevertheless uses it symbolically in this novel to represent the North much as Richard Wright did in his autobiography, *Black Boy* (1945). Grady, for example, who is from Memphis, tries "to talk like somebody from the North" (110); when Squeak announces she is going to Memphis with Celie and Shug, she says "I'm going North" (183); and when Mr. _____ tries to discourage Celie from going to Memphis, he says, "Nothing up North for nobody like you" (186). In her repeated emphasis on the alienation Celie and others experience in Memphis, it is clear that Walker wants to use Memphis as a stand-in for the urban North. This is not, of course, to ignore Memphis's rich identification with the blues, with Elvis, with the delta—all powerful images of southern culture, black and white; rather, it is only to suggest that the geographical pattern indicated by Celie's move away from the rural deep South to the more cosmopolitan urban river city resonates with other instances of Memphis as a stepping stone to the North and to freedom. Finally, Celie's return to the South—marked as it is by her successful though revolutionary business and by her attainment of a home and a nurturing community—represents Walker's argument for black reclamation of a southern homeland. Thus, Walker liberates her great-grandmother from history. Though she begins her life as a brutalized victim of oppression, at the end of the novel's mythohistorical cycle she, like other slave women, is reunited with her children and redefines the terms of her existence in the South.

The beginning of *The Color Purple* reads like an account of slavery and of the sexual brutality slave women experienced at the hands of their owners. "Pa"'s "theft" of Celie's children directly parallels slaveholders' sale of children away from their mothers, with no regard for familial or maternal ties. As Michael Awkward argues, this theft "suggest[s] that the conditions of [Celie's] life are not substantively different than those of female slaves whose children—including those produced through male slaveowners' coercion and rape—were frequently sold for financial gain" (140). Similarly, the scene in which Mr. _____ comes to "look over" Celie with thoughts of marrying her parallels the auction block of slavery, and her position as chattel is underscored when "Pa" reminds Albert that the cow is coming (20). Finally, Celie and Nettie's attempts at literacy, knowing, as Celie says, that "we got to be smart to git away" (19), parallel the connection between literacy and freedom in slave narratives.

If early portions of the novel parallel black life in the antebellum South, the novel's long middle section focuses on the tension between southern blacks and whites during Reconstruction and most of the twentieth century. Walker shows that racism informs all aspects of black life in the white South. The novel bristles with racial tension on every page; by illustrating how isolated incidents can set off long strings of racist interactions, Walker makes clear that she is barely scratching the surface of southern racism. One such incident is the lynching of Celie and Nettie's father, an act that defines most of Celie's early life, making way as it does for her rape by "Pa," the giving away of her children, her marriage to Mr. _____, and her unknowing dispossession of her homeland and inheritance. By the end of the novel, however, these actions have come full circle, and what began as the ultimate act of racism becomes the foundation on which Celie can build her alternative business.

The insidious effects of a culture dominated by a white racist patriarchy, however, makes itself most felt in damaged relationships between blacks, as can be seen in the ways in which the lynching leads to "Pa"'s abuse of Celie and his oppression of other blacks. "Inheriting" his business and farm from Celie and Nettie's real father, he determines to avoid his predecessor's mistake of not catering to white expectations. He tells Celie late in the novel: "[T]he fact is, you got to give 'em something.

Either your money, your land, your woman or your ass" (167). To satisfy whites and to succeed financially, "Pa" oppresses other blacks, by virtually robbing the store, the farm, and the home from Celie, Nettie, and their mother, essentially killing their mother, raping and breaking the spirit of Celie, exiling both Celie and Nettie from their home, and eventually perpetrating similar crimes upon other black women. "Pa" extracts sexual favors and free labor from blacks whom he subjugates socially and economically and, in so doing, replicates the traditional southern white "boss," who keeps sharecroppers forever indebted to him or the company store.

Although Walker depicts all blacks as being capable of oppressing other members of their community, she focuses much attention on the ways in which black men constantly brutalize black women. Young women are sexual objects: the young Celie's body is raped by "Pa" and her spirit by Mr. _____ ; the young Nettie must be clever and work hard to slip out of the clutches of both "Pa" and Mr. _____ ; and Sofia notes that "[a] girl child ain't safe in a family of men" (46). Perhaps an even greater oppression black men wage against black women, however, is economic, often marrying their wives for the labor they can provide. For example, "Pa" values Daisy not simply as an outlet for his sexual aggression but also for her ability to work. Likewise, when Mr. _____ considers marrying the young Celie, he notes one of his primary objectives in finding a wife: "[M]y poor little ones sure could use a mother" (17). Moreover, Mr. _____ is not interested in Celie simply for her ability to serve as a stepmother but also for her ability to work hard on the farm. Indeed, one of "Pa"'s selling points is that Celie "can work like a man" (18), and later in the novel Celie is seen to be the only one working hard on the farm. Walker argues, then, that the sexual and economic oppression of black women by black men are tightly linked.

Celie is the nexus of all these oppressions—sexual, physical, social, economic. Beaten down so long she cannot fight back, Celie at first internalizes black men's readings of her. "Pa" provides an early reading: "She ugly. Don't even look like she kin to Nettie. But she'll make the better wife. She ain't smart either, and I'll just be fair, you have to watch her or she'll give away everything you own. But she can work like a man" (18).

Mr. _____ succeeds "Pa" in his repeated attempts to define—and thus control—Celie. When she announces her decision to leave the farm and go to Memphis with Shug, he says, "Who you think you is? . . . You black, you pore, you ugly, you a woman. Goddam, he say, you nothing at all" (187). Here both "Pa" and Mr. _____ function as the community's enforcers of the dominant ideology, keeping Celie and other women in their place by imposing definitions and readings of these women upon them. Rather than allowing them to assert their own interpretations of their existence, "Pa" and Mr. _____ contain possible threats to their position of power by controlling the keys to self-interpretation.

In one of the novel's most memorable passages, Celie refutes not only Mr. _____'s reading of her but also those that other characters impose upon her and that she has internalized. On a larger level, she also refutes the readings and controls imposed upon all blacks, especially black southern women. She says, "I'm pore, I'm black, I may be ugly and can't cook. . . . But I'm here" (187). Just as she worked to create her own system of bringing an ordered understanding to her experience (in her decision to write letters to God), so here she begins to seize the tools of interpretation, to assert control over the readings (and writings) of her existence. Moreover, this passage signals not only the turning point in Celie's life but also the moment at which Walker explicitly begins to explode the racist, sexist, and regional oppression that informs the novel up to this point.

It is in this moment of self-definition that Celie asserts her decision to go "North," that is, to move to the symbolic urban land of liberation. Like the slaves who equated the North with freedom and like Richard Wright who saw Memphis as the stepping stone to the North, Celie sees her chance to go to Memphis with Shug as an act of liberation. Here Walker makes a major shift in her South-North-South pattern. Though the first three-quarters of the novel are set in the racist, patriarchal South, its focus now moves to the urban Memphis. Throughout *The Color Purple,* Memphis and the symbolic North are presented as entirely different places, far removed from the restrictions of the South. Memphis, like the North for the black community in general, symbolizes the point of supposed liberation for Shug as well. When she can no longer mold herself to the rigid values of the South, she is forced to search for a freer life. She tells Celie, "[T]he last baby did it. They turned me out. I went to stay with my mama wild sister in Memphis. She just like me, Mama say. She drink, she fight, she love mens to death. She work in a roadhouse. Cook. Feed fifty men, screw fifty-five" (116). For Celie as well, the move to Memphis and symbolically to the North becomes a crucial moment in her struggle for independence. Shug refuses to take advantage of Celie economically as "Pa" and Mr. _____ had; rather, she wants her to use her time in the North as a time of healing. She tells Celie: "You not my maid. I didn't bring you up to Memphis to be that. I brought you here to love you and help you get on your feet" (190). Getting symbolically out of the South and literally out of the country opens up a new world for Celie: she meets new people, gets her first taste of designing her home and space, starts a wildly successful business, and in general has increased access to the larger world. In fact, not until Celie's move to Memphis does Walker include references to world events (189–90), suggesting that the move out of the South and into the symbolic North represents greater awareness of the entire world.

But just as for Douglass and Jacobs as well as thousands of other migrating slaves, the "North" represents for Celie not only liberation but potential loss of identity as well. Not surprisingly, in a novel about language and interpretation, the tangible marker of this potential loss is Celie's struggle over her country dialect. Her rural (southern) dialect clearly marks her; in fact, her employee Darlene tells her that her mode of speaking is simply not acceptable in the city (the North). Celie writes: "Darlene trying to teach me how to talk. She say US not so hot. A dead country give-away. You say US where most folks say WE, she say, and peoples think you dumb. Colored peoples think you a hick and white folks be amused" (193). But Celie, who has reached a new level of self-awareness and who is beginning to achieve cultural pride and self-acceptance, balks at this advice. When Celie and Darlene ask Shug what she thinks about Celie's dialect, Shug explodes regional and class distinctions: "She can talk in sign language for all I care" (194). Hence, to Shug, saying "us" instead of "we" may mark Celie's place of origin but in no way marks her intelligence or worth as a human being. Celie concludes: "Look like to me only a fool would want you to talk in a way that feel peculiar to your mind" (194). Though the North may represent economic freedom, it also symbolizes cultural conscription. To make it in the North, Celie—and the black community in general—will have to give up cultural identity and will instead have to talk and (re)present themselves in "way[s] that feel peculiar to [their] mind[s]."

This tension between potential liberation and the equally potential loss of identity makes itself felt tangibly in Celie and Shug's discussion of their ideal home. Celie's initial description of Shug's house indicates Shug's wealth and high standard of living. Her house is "big and pink and look sort of like a barn" and, in addition to plenty of bedrooms and bathrooms, has "a big ballroom where she and her band sometime work." There are "plenty grounds round the house and a bunch of monuments and a fountain out front" (188). Despite this grandeur and the economic liberation it suggests, the house still falls short of Shug's ideal conception of a home: she wants to build a "round house" but "everybody act like that's backward" (188). Thus, her attempts at self-definition are not yet fully realized, and she still encounters those who resist the woman she wants to become.

Most important, however, in this passage Celie takes yet another crucial step in developing her concept of self. She and Shug imagine building a home, thereby achieving wholeness together:

> Us talk bout houses a lot. How they built, what kind of wood people use. Talk about how to make the outside around your house something you can use. I sit down on the bed and start to draw a kind of wood skirt around her concrete house. You can sit on this, I say, when you get tired of being in the house.
>
> Yeah, she say, and let's put awning over it. She took the pencil and put the wood skirt in the shade.
>
> Flower boxes go here, she say, drawing some.
>
> And geraniums in them, I say, drawing some. (189)

Shug and especially Celie take a significant step in visualizing new spaces—physical and spiritual—for themselves. As Celie says, "By the time us finish our house look like it can swim or fly" (189).

It is not until Celie returns to the South, however, that she actualizes her dreams of a home or, as Houston Baker puts it, realizes the imagined "prior unity," the Eden implied before page 1 of the novel. Celie is correct in implicitly connecting her dream house to her spiritual and emotional well-being, for it is in her repossession of her family home in Georgia that she finally comes totally and fully into her own. On her first visit with Shug back to her home place, long before she knows it is her rightful inheritance, its beauty startles her. Once the site of brutal physical, sexual, and emotional abuse, it has always remained a dark and threatening part of her past. Her description of seeing the house and land again suggests the deep ambivalence she feels:

> Well, say Shug, all this is pretty enough. You never said how pretty it was.
>
> It wasn't this pretty, I say. Every Easter time it used to flood, and all us children had colds. Anyhow, I say, us stuck close to the house, and it sure ain't so hot.
>
> That ain't so hot? she ast, as we swung up a long curving hill I didn't remember, right up to a big yellow two story house with green shutters and a steep green shingle roof.
>
> I laughed. Us must have took the wrong turn, I say. This some white person's house. (165)

This passage is interesting for two reasons. First, it articulates the separation from the place of origin Celie feels as well as the memory of the pain she experienced there, paralleling the entire black community's separation from and painful memories of the South. Second, in the last line of the passage the reader gets a glimmer of Walker's subversive message: that which is southern and white—either by definition or through ownership—can now be reclaimed as black. When blacks return to the South, they may encounter plantations (or remains of them) and homes and farms that thrive because slaves and sharecroppers built them, maintained them, and worked them. Though these things may appear to be "some white person's house," in actuality they are the rightful inheritance of the black community. They are only waiting to be reclaimed.

Celie's description of the idyllic conditions on the day she and Shug visit the home place indicates the fertile economic and social conditions blacks may increasingly find as they return South. Celie describes the day:

> Well, it was a bright Spring day, sort of chill at first, like it be round Easter, and the first thing us notice soon as we turn into the lane is how green everything is, like even though the ground everywhere else not warmed up good, Pa's land is warm and ready to go. Then all along the road there's Easter lilies and jonquils and daffodils and all kinds of little early wildflowers. Then us notice all the birds singing they little cans off, all up and down the hedge, that itself is putting out little yellow flowers smell like Virginia creeper. It all so different from the rest of the country us drive through, it make us real quiet. I know this sound funny, Nettie, but even the sun seemed to stand a little longer over our heads. (164–65)

Not coincidentally, Celie makes this pilgrimage back to her home place at a time "like it be round Easter." Renewal, redemption, and rebirth are imminent—both for Celie and for the entire black community.

Significantly, this passage also echoes Walker's 1975 essay, "Beyond the Peacock: The Reconstruction of Flannery O'Connor," in which Walker contrasts the stately O'Connor home with the nearby "share-farmer shack" her own family occupied. As she considers the fact that O'Connor's house was probably built "brick by brick" by slaves—possibly even Walker's own ancestors—and as she realizes that there is a caretaker still tending O'Connor's house while Walker's own home has fallen into disrepair, she states, "Her house becomes . . . the symbol of my own disinheritance" (57). Here, as well as in the passage from *The Color Purple*, Walker makes clear that blacks are the rightful owners of these houses, this land, this region. Despite the sense of disinheritance, however, she is still able, like Celie and Shug, to see the beauty of the land: in both passages daffodils abound, Walker and the characters are "amaz[ed] how beautiful [the] setting is" (44), and Walker remembers that her most profound feeling about this home as a child was that "it represented beauty and unchanging peace" (45). The lengthy passage in

The Color Purple becomes, in a sense, the novel's centerpiece, the point around which everything else revolves. Linking Celie's experience so carefully and explicitly with her own experience, Walker underscores the deep connection southern blacks and women feel to their homes, the "disinheritance" they feel from these homes, and the powerful role the reclaiming of the home plays in allowing blacks and women to redefine the terms of their existence in the South.

When Celie discovers that the house, the farm, and the store are her and Nettie's rightful inheritance, she proudly reclaims them, again suggesting the way blacks might reclaim the region where their ancestors were born and raised, worked and died. But like the black community, Celie and Shug realize it is not enough simply to move back and reclaim the land. They must also exorcise the demons of oppression and abuse that have dominated the land for so long. Celie says Shug "took some cedar sticks out of her bag and lit them and gave one of them to me. Us started at the very top of the house in the attic, and us smoked it all the way down to the basement, chasing out all the evil and making a place for good" (217). That done, she can truly enjoy her home. She writes to Nettie:

> I can't get over having a house. Soon as Daisy leave me with the keys I run from one room to another like I'm crazy. Look at this, I say to Shug. Look at that! She look, she grin. She hug me whenever she git the chance and I stand still. You doin' all right, Miss Celie, she say. God know where you live. (216–17)

In addition to bringing Celie physically home to the South, the final quarter of Walker's novel also stresses the need to come home spiritually and emotionally. Thus, Walker argues, to heal itself and to make peace with the South, the black community needs to work toward new definitions of the relations between the races and the sexes and ultimately toward new ideas of self-definition. In examining these ideas, Walker explicitly challenges racial boundaries, portraying new ways blacks and whites can create a shared sense of community. Eleanor Jane, for example, begins to understand her complicity in the division between whites and blacks and takes a step in correcting the imbalance by going to work for Sofia. Shug and Celie revision a non–racially centered alternative theory of spirituality, and Celie blurs racial lines in her store by hiring Sofia as a clerk.

Walker challenges gender boundaries throughout the novel as well. Three women in the novel—Nettie, Sofia, and Shug—particularly exemplify the decision to go beyond strict southern definitions of black womanhood. Nettie's education, for example, proves to be her ticket out of the South and into the larger world; it allows her to overcome gender boundaries. Early in the novel, education, particularly the ability to read, is linked to liberation (19), and later it becomes clear that Nettie's opportunity to work in Africa with Corrine and Samuel comes as a result of her ability to help them "build a school" (124). An even greater blurring of gender roles can be seen in the "stout and bouncy" Sofia (81), especially in her relationship with Harpo. For a while their relationship, with Sofia working out in the fields and Harpo taking care of the domestic chores, makes them quite happy. But Harpo's socially conditioned desire to dominate Sofia first causes them to fight "like two mens" (44) and then leads to their long separation. By the end of the novel, however, Harpo and Sofia make their peace, fully accepting each other, regardless of whether either of them falls within acceptable gender boundaries. Even more than Sofia, Shug represents a total flaunting of society's prescribed roles for women. An early photograph of Shug, reminiscent of Walker's description of a photo of Zora Neale Hurston,[3] captures her essence: a daring but unhappy woman who goes against strict southern mores. Celie eventually discovers Shug's price for her unconventional freedom: separated from her children and her family, she fails to find answers for herself in the pages of white fashion magazines. Ultimately, both Shug and Celie work toward a more wholly satisfying alternative vision of sexuality, religion, and social relations.

By the end of the novel, significantly in the portion of the novel in which Walker creates a utopic vision of new southern community, Mr. _____ begins to revise his attitudes toward women, gender roles, and other human beings in general. Although he brutalizes Celie throughout most of the early parts of the novel, he is not the static "sexually driven beast" some critics claim. Though Walker criticizes him and the type of men he represents for his abuse of Celie and his attempted abuse of Nettie, she shows that even Mr. _____ is not beyond salvation. His portrayal as an abusive patriarch throughout most of the early novel, in fact, is not absolute. His love for Shug indicates that he can love and care for someone else. After Shug leaves both of them and Celie has returned to Georgia, Mr. _____ talks to Celie about loving Shug and, in doing so, reaches a better understanding of Celie. Their shared love for Shug and Celie's decision to take control over her life and leave Mr. _____ are ultimately the keys to his transformation into "Albert" and to a renewed and healthy, if nonsexual, relationship with Celie. Celie writes of the new Albert, "I mean when you talk to him now he really listen, and one time, out of nowhere in the conversation us was having, he said Celie, I'm satisfied this the first time I ever lived on Earth as a natural man. It feel like a new experience" (230). This is not the biased depiction of a hopelessly sexist and brutalizing black man; rather, it is an honest sketch of the way racial and economic forces oppress black men. Most important, however, Walker demonstrates here, as in other parts of her novel, the possibility of salvation for all human beings, even those who brutalize and dehumanize others. Just as the change of spirit in Eleanor Jane represents the chance for breaking free of racial boundaries, so too Mr. _____'s redemption argues for the possibility that all gender lines might be blurred beyond recognition.

Ultimately, then, Celie, emblematic of all African Americans, works out a new relationship with the South. Not only does she reclaim her family's home, farm, and business; more important, she also exorcises the pain of the past and challenges racial and gender divisions. Here, finally, Walker liberates her great-grandmother from history. Though Celie, like innumerable slave women before her, had her children taken away from her, at the end of *The Color Purple* they are restored to her, suggesting a symbolic reconciliation with the South and an end to the patriarchal and racial oppression that constituted slavery and informed Reconstruction and life in the twentieth-century South.

But as Susan B. Willis points out, reclaiming the land, the home, and the store does not mean that Celie succeeds in life (or that blacks will achieve parity) because she has become a good capitalist (119).

Rather, her ability to create new definitions and to make them tangible reality signal her triumph. Her home is a place for her new idea of family or her "people": not only does she welcome Shug and eventually Nettie, Samuel, and "their" children, but she also ultimately welcomes the changed Albert into her home as one of her "peoples" as well. When she writes to Nettie of their inheritance, she says, "Oh, Nettie, us have a home! A house big enough for us and our children, for your husband and Shug. Now you can come home cause you have a home to come to!" (217). Celie's home represents, as Willis argues, "the basis for a wholly new community" (119). Her business too represents changed attitudes. No longer a place where whites can humiliate blacks, it is now a space where women's traditional arts are valued and used to revolutionary ends (in Celie's creation of "folkspants"), where black women can exercise their talents as merchants, and where blacks can be served by members of their own community. As Lauren Berlant argues, "Celie's business is as perfectly biracial as it is unisexual, employing both Sofia and a white worker to sell her goods so that *everyone* will be well served" (853). Willis describes the new South Celie creates for herself: "*The Color Purple* defines return in . . . auspicious terms and offers not a prescription for but a suggestion of what a nonsexist, nonracist community might be" (119).

Celie's inheritance and acceptance of her home place is clearly a parable of the way blacks might reclaim the South as their home. The idea of the "South-as-black-homeland" is not unique to Walker, however. Walker's closest predecessor in this and other regards is Zora Neale Hurston, who also dealt in her work with the issue of identity and place. As Melvin Dixon notes, Hurston's argument about the return to the South is closer to Walker's than are the treatments black male writers give the South:

> Hurston's South presents neither a Toomeresque swan song, nor a Wrightian sense of doom. . . . [S]he was acutely aware of the importance of land and ancestry. . . . Most writers of her time wanted to reject the South because of its racism; few wanted to celebrate its flourishing black culture. (85)

Walker, then, searches for many of the same things as Hurston and dreams the same dream of a black southern homecoming. Dianne F. Sadoff notes that, like Hurston, Walker

> has gone north, has become semi-assimilated to a white male literary world; she seeks her rural, southern heritage with an idealism that tempers and compensates for her own lost past. Walker takes her trips back south to look for wholeness because, she believes, experience has fragmented and split apart herself and her people. (14)

Indeed, in her essay on Flannery O'Connor, Walker refers to the "wholeness" one can achieve when making peace with one's past and with one's region. It is not surprising, then, that she advocates this return to roots for other blacks as well. As Thadious Davis points out, the South is a place "that is not without a history of pain, but it nonetheless connects generations of blacks to one another, to a 'wholeness' of self, and to 'the old unalterable' roots" ("Alice Walker's Celebration" 46).

As in her other works, Walker patterns *The Color Purple* on the South-North-South model, but even more than in *The Third Life of Grange Copeland,* she holds out the promise that the return to the South can be a time of redemption and healing. Shug, who abuses herself in her fast life-style, finds her ultimate healing in the arms of Celie, who nourishes her on "home cured ham" (56). Mary Agnes discovers that leaving the South only means being on an extended, and extremely nonproductive, high. Celie similarly learns that though she can make it in Memphis, her real home remains in Georgia. And as Frank W. Shelton points out, even "Nettie, her family, and Celie's children must return to the American South to find integration into a true community" (389). In short, the return of these characters—and on a larger scale, that of the entire black community—represents a mythical return to their "mothers' gardens."

I strongly believe Walker intended *The Color Purple* to be read as "A Moral Tale" about envisioning a better future for African Americans. The image of Celie's home as rightful inheritance and transformation of community makes tangible Walker's dream. The novel's final letter finds Celie presiding over her home, a home into which she welcomes her "peoples," Shug and Albert. It finds Nettie also finally making a return "home" to America, to the South, to the original home place. It finds a transformed world, in which women and men genuinely and sincerely work toward active self-definition and in which they renegotiate the terms of their existence within their own world and within the dominant white southern society. The events of this last letter appropriately take place on Independence Day. Traditionally a day for white Americans to celebrate their independence from England, blacks have in the past "spen[t] the day celebrating each other" (250). In a clever twist, Walker uses this traditionally white holiday to mark the emotional, social, economic, and spiritual independence of Celie, her family, and homeward-bound blacks in general. Indeed, this day marks the birth of a new black nation. Hence, when Celie says at the end of the novel, "Matter of fact, I think this the youngest us ever felt" (251), she signals her triumph, her ultimate ability to transcend the pain of the past and to reach beyond it to the Edenic days before oppression.

What finally makes Celie's transformation successful is not her return to the South, nor merely her creation of an alternative community. Rather, as the novel suggests all along, the key to self-transformation lies in the ability to take control over defining oneself, naming oneself, and, in the tangible realm, gaining access to the dominant culture's tools of definition, specifically to such social weapons as reading and writing. *The Color Purple* is precisely about the nature of reading, writing, and constructing meaning out of experience. Celie, heretofore defined and controlled linguistically by others, must move toward wholeness by asserting herself as a person or, in other words, by proclaiming her self-definition. This begins on the day she announces that she will leave Mr. _____ to live with Shug in Memphis; she states, "I'm pore, I'm black, I may be ugly and can't cook. . . . But I'm here" (187). In this passage, however, Celie can only define herself in opposition to Mr. _____'s terms. Later, in a letter to Nettie, she articulates a new and more positive vision of herself and in so doing creates her own vocabulary of self-interpretation: "I am so happy. I got love, I got work, I got money, friends and time. And you alive and be home soon. With our children" (193). And although Celie has never signed her letters before, she does so now emphatically:

Your Sister, Celie
Folkspants, Unlimited
Sugar Avery Drive
Memphis, Tennessee

This inscription of her identity confirms her new place in the world: she defines herself through her family relationships ("Your Sister"), her business and creative endeavors ("Folkspants, Unlimited"), her love relationship and participation in creating a home ("Sugar Avery Drive"), and her movement into the outside world ("Memphis, Tennessee"). Surely this self-inscription represents a profound transformation from the young girl who could not even claim control over the words "I am" (11). Finally, her ultimate act of self-definition occurs after her return South. As she walks past Mr. _____'s house, he does not even recognize her, confirming that she has truly internalized this new vision of herself:

> I feels different. Look different. Got on some dark blue pants and a white silk shirt that look righteous. Little red flat-heel slippers, and a flower in my hair. I pass Mr. _____ house and him sitting up on the porch and he didn't even know who I was. (195)

In her radical and enthusiastic process of self-definition, Celie seizes control over her own being so well that she places herself outside of the reaches of those who had power over her before. In creating her own vocabulary of self-interpretation and in actively redefining her place in the world, Celie resists containment by the dominant culture and counters the master narratives that would consign her to a position of powerlessness.

Midway through *In Country*, protagonist Samantha Hughes is rooting around the basement of her family home, looking for her uncle Emmett, whom she irrationally fears may be dead. As she pokes around, she discovers remnants of her family's past—the dried-up remains of her great-aunt Bessie's flower tubs. "Sam remembered," writes Mason, "when the plants would stubbornly send up green shoots in the spring, in the dark basement, but finally all the plants had given up seeking the light. . . . The dead stalks in the tubs made her cringe. They were oppressive, something useless and ridiculous that she had had to look at all her life" (217). This passage signals longtime female identity with this family home, the thwarted potential of women's creativity, and the apparently dead roots with which Sam must reconnect if she is to have any hope for a sustaining life in the South. Here, in this almost invisible link back through Sam's female ancestry, Mason reminds us that this novel is fundamentally concerned with a family in flux in the changing South and especially with young Sam as she attempts to bring dead stalks back to life, to seek her own light. This scene—buried as it is under constant references to popular culture and the pervasive surface story about the legacy of Vietnam—could be all too easily overlooked by the casual reader. But like the many other passages in the novel that deal with the physical disintegration of Sam's family home, this scene reminds us that home and family are as important as the more obvious focus on Vietnam and that Sam must travel the roads to both places— home and Vietnam—in order to gain a deeper sense of herself and to re-create a more satisfying sense of family.

Although most critics read *In Country* as a Vietnam novel,[4] a closer look reveals that it is equally concerned with a young woman's coming of age in a changing region. Indeed, Mason's original plans for the novel did not involve Vietnam at all; rather, she intended to focus on the adolescent love affair between Sam and Lonnie (Wilhelm, "Interview" 30). Therefore, the Vietnam story, though a major focus of the novel, may be only a mirror for the larger story at work. As Mason tells Sam's story, she is fundamentally concerned with the South as a changing region and Sam's own changing position within that region. Her mother's departure causes Sam to doubt her family's security and stability, and in an unconscious attempt to reclaim a sense of family and home, Sam looks back through her mother and uncle to her father, who died in the Vietnam War before Sam was born. Viewed in this light, Sam's preoccupation with the Vietnam War parallels not only the traditionally southern preoccupation with history and defeat (as Owen W. Gilman, Jr., suggests)

but also speaks to her deep-seated and equally southern need for a sense
of family, home, and belonging. As Sam tries to make sense of the relationship between landscape and identity, of the options available to
her as a young southern woman, and, like Walker's Celie and McCorkle's
Virginia, of her home as a physical manifestation of these issues, she,
like the reader, must reach beyond the surface layer of popular culture that threatens to engulf the South and must look instead for the
deeper elements that root her to her region and her home. Only then
can she, like Celie, hope to reclaim a sense of "prior unity," to recapture
an empowering and sustaining sense of family and womanhood.

Kentucky has traditionally been considered a border state, poised in
a regional and cultural limbo between South and North, and, as such,
may be even more susceptible than the rest of the South to the encroachment of homogenized American culture. In focusing on her native
state, Mason highlights the changes it faces. As she said in an interview
with Albert E. Wilhelm, "I'm not nostalgic for the past. Times change
and I'm interested in writing about what's now. To me, the way the
South is changing is very dynamic and full of complexity" ("Interview"
37). Although a number of critics have claimed that Mason's Kentucky
can no longer be identified distinctively as southern,[5] and though many
see her landscape as an empty morass of mass culture,[6] Mason, like
McCorkle and Smith, argues that just because the South is confront-
ing change does not mean it has completely lost its cultural identity.
Though her frequent references to popular culture (e.g., Bruce Springsteen, "M*A*S*H," Boy George, Exxon, McDonald's, HBO, and Howard
Johnson's) threaten to obliterate the repeated references to southern
culture and values (e.g., pit barbecue, swamp rabbit, Confederate flag
tee-shirts, "[a]ntiques and Civil War stuff" [113], church, family, home,
marriage, and motherhood), they have not yet completely taken over.
The "nonminimalist reader," to borrow Fred Hobson's phrase (19), goes
beyond the surface details of this minimalist novel to discover a text fundamentally concerned with traditional southern questions—questions
about past, region, home, and family.

What may throw many readers off is Mason's deliberate redefinition of
the term "southern." Traditionally, southern literature has been said to

focus on upper-middle-class southerners, the descendants of the plantation aristocracy. Yet Mason and many of her contemporaries focus on
decidedly lower-class characters; as Hobson puts it, Mason writes about
"working-class people unselfconsciously and . . . approvingly" (21). The
temptation here is to conclude that, because contemporary southern
literature is written by southerners from different backgrounds, the concerns in this fiction have shifted. On a surface level, this may indeed be
the case. As the region experiences "economic growth and . . . consequent cultural changes" (Mason qtd. in Shomer 87), there is a great shift
in class as well. "I'm constantly preoccupied with the class struggle,"
Mason says, "and I'm exploring various kinds of culture shock—people
moving from one class to another . . . people being threatened by other
people's ways and values" (qtd. in Havens 95). But though these characters are from less privileged backgrounds, and though the day-to-day
material concerns are markedly different from those of their upper-crust
counterparts, the deeper fundamental issues remain. For Mason's characters, as for many characters of "traditional" southern literature, ties to
the past, to the region, to home, and to family are the inextricable bonds
between southerners and their homeland. It is undeniable that Mason is
concerned with a changing region and with a working class facing up-
ward mobility and encroaching mass culture; but it is also true that her
more emotionally whole characters—especially those in *In Country*—
continue to understand themselves in terms of region, home, and family
and struggle to maintain these values even as they face personal and
cultural change.

Sam, like other southerners, is trying to find her direction in the
changing region and to discover a way to retain the valuable parts of
her southern heritage while moving ahead. Her passion for running, her
yearning for a car, her longing to travel and see the world, and her reading of Jack Kerouac's *On the Road* indicate that she longs to break free
from the old South that holds her back. But her equally strong desire
to learn about the past, particularly her parents' past, her devotion to
her Uncle Emmett and to maintaining their sense of home, and even
her visits to her grandparents' homes suggest also that she feels a bond
with the South and that she will lose, as well as gain, if she moves to

Lexington to attend college. As Gilman puts it, "Sam embodies the spirit of rebellion against the ways of the past," but at the same time "her character is balanced by the southern need for history" (49). The trick, as for McCorkle's Virginia, is to be like her foremothers while simultaneously becoming more than them.

Although the novel's opening and closing sections depict Sam, Emmett, and Mamaw's trip to the Vietnam Veterans Memorial in Washington, D.C., and Sam's exposure to the greater world, Mason spends the much lengthier "inside" of the novel underscoring Sam's need to discover the roads closer to home. Sam's exploration of the roads surrounding Hopewell, of her grandparents' homes, of the imaginative merging of Kentucky and Vietnam, and of the wildness that is the South both is prompted by and is a tangible outcome of her search for home and family. In her constant layering of images and meanings, Mason suggests that there is an essential connection between Sam's quest to come to terms with the links between the past, the legacy of Vietnam, and her wild roots in western Kentucky and her attempts to re-create a meaningful sense of home and family, to recapture a sense of "prior unity." Sam's quests may seem on the surface to be disconnected; if we squeeze to a deeper level, however, we discover that these parallel quests are inextricably fused into one whole and entire process of coming to know herself, her home, and her region.

Sam's mother sets the tone for Sam's explorations, taking Emmett and Sam on an unexpected detour:

> "Here it is," Irene said . . . , as she rounded a curve on a small hill. She pulled into a dirt lane and stopped. "Look," she said. . . .
>
> Irene had to explain that what she wanted them to see was the landscape, some fields and trees along a hillside. . . .
>
> "I always thought this place was so pretty," Irene said. . . .
>
> "The reason I like this so much," Irene went on, "is that it's just like England. I've seen pictures of England that look like this. . . . That's a place I always wanted to go, but I don't guess I'll ever get the chance." (232–33)

This scene is interesting for two reasons. First, it indicates the characters' physical separation from their homeland. Irene and Emmett were raised in a rural area nearby, and Sam's father grew up on a farm not far from this vista. But Irene's decision to drive home through the country is no longer part of the characters' daily routine. Second, this scene suggests all three characters' emotional and spiritual alienation from the rural South. Emmett and Sam literally cannot see it: Irene has to point out to them what she wants them to see ("the landscape, some fields and trees along a hillside"). Irene, though she appreciates the view, can only see it through her yearning to break free from the South, can only embrace it if she sees it as other than southern.

Like her mother, Sam is curious about place and landscape, but during the first half of the novel, her lack of a car compels her to spend most of her time in Hopewell, her frequent runs indicating an intimate knowledge of her town's physical and social geography. Once Sam gets a car, however, she begins to explore the surrounding countryside, in particular spending time on the roads that lead to her father's family farm. Mason writes: "She passed the place her mother said looked like England. She was far out in the country, and soon she turned off on a smaller road. She passed old farms that looked unchanged since the time her father had lived out here" (273–74). Mason implies that an essential quality of the countryside remains "unchanged," that national homogenization has not yet touched these rural outbacks off of "smaller road[s]." Yet a bit later, Sam notices details that indicate even rural Kentucky is not exempt from mass culture:

> The road meandered past an overgrown graveyard. Some new house trailers perched on blocks in bare fields. She passed through an abandoned settlement, with an old feed mill and a boarded-up store with a rusted Orange Crush sign. The Methodist church was whitewashed and had a newly graveled parking lot and a marquee on wheels that said KEEP THE CHRIST IN CHRISTMAS. (275)

Here, Mason refers to particulars of the landscape that suggest the encroachment of the outside world: "new house trailers" indicate an element of impermanence; an "abandoned settlement" and an "overgrown graveyard" mark the loss of the area's previous population; the "bare fields" and the "old feed mill" signify the decreasing importance of farming; a "boarded-up store" symbolizes the decline of commerce; and a "rusted Orange Crush sign" bears witness to the effects of mass advertising and the ability of national products and fads to reach even the most rural of areas. However, this passage also suggests the continued, if changing, vitality of the area. The house trailers are "new," suggesting new residents in the area, and the Methodist Church has enough business to be "whitewashed" and to have a "newly graveled parking lot." The role of the church is still paramount in this community: it has so much business it can afford a "marquee" and thus can promote its traditional message to "KEEP THE CHRIST IN CHRISTMAS."

But though Mason focuses on rural Kentucky, she does not present it as a monolithic harbinger of conservative values. Rather, the tension she establishes between the traditional country and the suburban country (which I will call hereafter, for convenience, "rural" and "suburban") allows her to explore the shifting southern landscape and culture. The rural country Sam's paternal grandparents inhabit is a region—culturally and physically—to which Sam has had little exposure but which she needs to experience in order to make satisfying connections to past, region, family, and personal identity. Visiting Mamaw and Pap's farm represents not only a link to her father (and, by extension, family) but also an essential step in defining herself: "She was seeing the place her dad knew. . . . Her roots were here, and she had been here often enough for the place to be familiar, but not enough to really know it. She felt she was seeing it for the first time" (284–85). But Sam has difficulty facing the Hugheses, their home, life-style, class status, and especially what they represent in terms of Sam's definition of herself. She struggles to come to terms with what she perceives as backward poverty:

Maybe she should just forget about her father and dismiss the whole Hughes clan along with him. They were ignorant and country anyway. They lived in that old farmhouse with the decayed smell she always remembered it having—the smell of dirty farm clothes, soiled with cow manure. In their bathroom earlier, she had almost slipped on the sodden rug that lay rotting around the sweating commode. In the living room, the television was missing a leg, and a complicated old antenna—all claws and a fan of rods—sat in a

corner, looking like a monster from outer space. The contraption
was an effort to pick up cable so that Pap could catch the Wildcats'
basketball games. Mamaw picked peas in a rusty bucket with a rag
plug stopping up a hole. (295–96)

Sam is embarrassed by this lower-class home and compares it with
her other grandparents' home in the suburban country, a region showing
the effects of change, transition, homogenization, and, importantly, class
mobility. As Irene and Emmett grew up, the house and the country were
isolated. Sam thinks about the way her mother's personality was shaped
by her upbringing in the country: "Grandma Smith always said Irene
had felt inferior in the city school because she was self-conscious about
being from the country and so she did rebellious things to get attention"
(274). Now, however, the Smiths' home is not so isolated, its distance
of five miles from Hopewell making it seem fairly close in. Five miles,
Mason argues, has become a much shorter distance. In its proximity to
town, the Smiths' house has become modern and suburban: it has "fake
brick siding and a new kitchen and a den and a brick fireplace" (208).
The Smiths may still live in the country, but their version of country is
decidedly more up-to-date and middle-class.

It is not enough, however, for Sam to examine the surrounding
countryside; in order for her to reconnect with her region, home, and a
more fundamental sense of place, with her father and a deeper sense of
family, Sam must also explore the connections between Kentucky and
Vietnam. "In country" was, as Mason notes several times throughout the
novel, the soldiers' term for serving in Vietnam, and in many ways, it
becomes a metaphor for understanding the changes in a region traditionally held to be separate from the rest of America. Southerners, Mason
suggests, are also "in country." This connection is one all of the Vietnam vets make—either during their tour of duty or once they return
home. In his letters and diary, Sam's father, Dwayne, consistently collapses the distinction between Vietnam and Kentucky, so much so that
Sam gets frustrated at Dwayne's insistence on reading Vietnam through
a filter comprised only of that which is familiar to him: "She was disappointed that her father didn't say what Vietnam was like. His mind was

on the fish in Kentucky Lake, not on the birds and fish over there" (258–59). And one of Emmett's friends, Pete, while in Vietnam, has a map of "the Jackson Purchase region of western Kentucky tattooed on his chest" (65), transforming Kentucky into a literal, physical part of himself that he can carry with him while "in country." Although the symbolic representation of Kentucky is completely fused with Pete's own body, his strategy to strengthen his bond with his native region backfires: "I look at it upside down and in the mirror it's backwards" (69).[7]

But the Vietnam vets are not the only ones who can no longer see or experience their home region "right side up" and who, by implication, have lost their emotional or spiritual connection to it. In this novel, as in countless short stories, Mason suggests the pervasive degree to which southerners have been cut adrift from cultural traditions and from the region itself. If this generation is to reconnect, Mason suggests, it must remember the past and confront the secrets of the region just as previous generations did. For Sam, this means not only coming to terms with the legacy of Vietnam in her own life but also making a larger connection, as the vets did, between the marginalized status of both Vietnam and Kentucky. She first understands the connection between the two "countries" when she is only eight or nine. She remembers watching television:

> The landscape was believable—a hill in the distance, a paved road with narrow dirt shoulders, a field with something green planted in rows. The road resembled the old Hopewell road that twisted through the bottomland toward Paducah. For the first time, Vietnam was an actual place. (72)

Sam instinctively comprehends the enigmatic relationship between Vietnam and the South and at this early age sets in motion her deep desire to understand the implications of her father's past in Vietnam for her present in the South.

In her need to connect with her father and, more largely, to foster a sense of home and family, Sam spends the entire novel trying to find out more about Vietnam: she reads history books, talks to vets, goes to a dance in honor of the vets, reads her father's diary and letters, asks family members what they remember of her father, and even goes to bed with one of the vets. Ultimately such methods are not enough; Sam wants to know what it was really like and she finally concludes she must spend the night in Cawood's Pond, "the last place in western Kentucky where a person could really face the wild" (299). She goes out to "hump the boonies," to replicate the experience of being "in country." She takes "rations," a sleeping bag and canteen, a flashlight and her father's diary, and—in an evening reminiscent of Quentin and Shreve's imaginative reconstruction of events during the Civil War in Faulkner's *Absalom, Absalom!*—attempts to re-create the feeling of being in Vietnam. She goes out to "face facts," even if Cawood's Pond is "as close to the jungle as she [can] get, with only a VW" (303). Mason writes:

> She knew that whenever she had tried to imagine Vietnam she had had her facts all wrong. She couldn't get hickory trees and maples and oaks and other familiar trees, like these cypresses at Cawood's Pond, out of her head. . . . Humping the boonies. Here I am, she thought. In country. (302)

All of these scenes—Sam's exploration of the rural landscape surrounding Hopewell, the vets' insistence on collapsing the geographical distinction between Kentucky and Vietnam, and Sam's attempt to make contact with the wilderness of her region—underscores Mason's argument that understanding one's ties to a region is fundamental to understanding one's self. Until Sam explores her region with depth and awareness, until she "humps the boonies" of the South, she will not be able to make the larger leap to discovering the wild places within herself, to look for ways of becoming her fullest self while remaining "in country" in the South. Although the novel is, on one level, about Vietnam and Sam's search to understand what happened there, on a deeper level it is about her search to understand herself as a southern woman. At eighteen, she is on the brink of adulthood and, more important, on the verge of making a choice about the kind of southern woman she will be. On her runs around Hopewell, in her conversations with Emmett's friends, in her relationship with Lonnie and later her affair with Tom, in her friendship with Dawn and her talks with Anita, in her frustration with her mother and her need to see both of her grandmothers, in all of these events and experiences Sam is trying to come to an understanding of herself and of how the patriarchal South constructs her identity and constricts her options.

Here, Sam's ability to read and consider all possibilities comes through most clearly as she struggles to understand the options available to her: to acquiesce to the narrow definitions of southern womanhood that small-town Kentucky allows or to break free from these roles and create a new space for herself. In making these choices and considering these possibilities, however, Sam seeks a point of equilibrium at which she might be able to retain her connection to the past and to her cultural heritage, while at the same time creating a new vision for herself as a woman in the South. As she searches for possible role models, Sam discovers that no woman she knows is successful in balancing a sense of cultural heritage with forward-thinking behavior. Yet she also makes the important realization that almost every important woman in her life embodies some positive aspect of southern womanhood. It is tempting to label Sam's choices as either bad or good, with Mamaw and Dawn representing limiting choices and Sue Ann, Anita, Grandma Smith, and Irene representing more positive options. Yet Sam, in her astuteness as a careful reader, refuses to place these women in superficial categories.

Of the women she knows in town, Dawn, Sue Ann, and Anita are those she knows best or whom Mason considers to some degree. Sam's best friend, Dawn, is presented as a young woman bound to the rigid category of "southern woman." Although Dawn joins Sam in asserting that they are "the baddest girls in Hopewell," Mason portrays Dawn's rebelliousness as a brief prelude to a lifetime of playing southern wife and mother. Unlike Sam, Dawn cannot imagine herself in other places, leading other lives. When she becomes pregnant, she willingly succumbs to traditional expectations to get married and have the baby. Although Sam tries to suggest on several occasions that Dawn has other options, Dawn resists, instead insisting on following the most traditional path. In a key scene, Mason depicts both Dawn's narrow vision of her future and Sam's desire to break free of sexist roles for women:

> Sam said, "Look, Dawn, you're always wanting to do something wild. Get an abortion—for your own good."

"But having a baby would be as wild as anything I can think of. And besides, I think Ken will have some say-so in it."

"No!" cried Sam, banging the steering wheel. "Having kids is what everybody does. It doesn't take any special talent." (253)

The impending changes in Dawn's life worry Sam because they indicate a lack of control over choices. Where Sam searches frantically for other options, Dawn sees only one possible outcome. Unlike Sam, she does not read all the alternatives.

Sue Ann and Anita, however, are more successful at imagining other lives for themselves, but for both the price for such lives may be too high. Sue Ann's decision to accept a job in Lexington not only threatens her marriage but also threatens Jim's security in her role as a traditional southern woman. Emmett explains it this way: "I guess Jim's afraid Sue Ann might decided [sic] to run for President or something" (316). Anita, too, finds that traditional expectations for women do not offer enough choice. Though she has decided to stay in the small-town South, she resists the restrictive definition the community tries to impose upon her. Married as a young woman and subsequently divorced, she remembers having no awareness of other options available to her: "I was eighteen, and it was just what you did back then. I didn't know what else there was to do" (88). Her husband, like many men of his era, "didn't know what to make of me. He wanted me to be a picture. That's all I was supposed to do, just be beautiful" (89). Instead of choosing to stay in a dead-end marriage, she decides to "improve" herself. She gets a divorce, becomes a dental hygienist, finds time to read in the evenings, and dresses unconventionally, looking, as Sam puts it, "like a flamingo in a flock of chickens" (144). To Sam, Anita becomes a positive image of a woman making her own choices in the inhibiting South but who, at the same time, cannot find a man who is comfortable with her progressive thinking.

It is the women in Sam's family, however, whom Sam most thoroughly reads as she considers her options as a young woman in the South—and, again, each woman embodies both strengths and limitations. Mamaw, for example, has internalized the South's views of women but at the same time provides Sam's most important links to the past. Although both of Sam's grandmothers are tied to a strong sense of southern cultural heritage, Mamaw is, if possible, even more old-fashioned in her beliefs than is Grandma Smith. Although her lower class status would never place her in the role of southern lady, Mamaw's ideas of proper behavior for a southern woman are nevertheless very much defined by this prescription and are rooted in an earlier era and in a more isolated place. Yet the fact that she has saved Dwayne's diary and that she now gives it to Sam suggests her awareness of the need to preserve and pass on a sense of the past, of cultural heritage. While she may be an anachronism, she also allows Sam access to her past. Grandma Smith, on the other hand, retains her belief in certain traditional southern values, particularly religion and family, yet is beginning to perceive herself as a southern woman ready to move ahead. Having updated her look, she considers breaking free of other prescribed behaviors by breaking free of the region itself. Florida becomes for Grandma Smith a symbol of what could be, a symbol of liberation from her life in Hopewell, and may also suggest the higher class status she has achieved.

Although Mamaw and Grandma Smith provide important contrasting examples of options available to women in the South, it is Irene whom Sam reads most carefully and most fully. Not surprisingly, Mason chooses Sam's mother as the richest but most conflicted example of a woman striving to reach new visions of what it means to be a southern woman. While Irene is successful at moving out of Hopewell and away from conventional roles for southern women, she does so at what Sam sees as the unacceptable price of her cultural heritage and her sense of the past. Like Anita, Irene begins her adult life as a traditional southern woman. She marries Dwayne at an early age, and it appears from his letters to her that theirs was a conventional relationship. Later, as a widow, she moves to Lexington with her new lover, Bob, but eventually returns to Hopewell to take care of Emmett and to be near her family. She tells Sam, "I got stuck. I had to take care of things at home" (336). Despite her beginnings as a traditional southern woman, Irene always had a different spark, an urge to defy the patterns imposed upon women. She always dreamed of going other places, whether England or California. She was bold and rebellious; Mamaw says, "She'd do anything" (280), and Granddad remarks, "Irene never would do things the normal way" (212). Eventually Irene's different spark drives her to break free from Hopewell's conservatism. She marries Larry and moves to Lexington to create a new life for herself. Despite the distress to herself and to others, Irene is somewhat successful this time at moving ahead. But though she leaves behind the painful parts of the past, she also apparently forsakes happier memories; and while she retains affection for her family, her relationship with them suffers to some degree.

With Irene's second move to Lexington comes not only a marked step up in class status but also a growing awareness of choices for southern women. Now that she has moved to Lexington, Irene has created a new life for herself that suits her and that will last. It is certainly a different life: instead of listening to the Beatles and Bruce Springsteen, she now tunes in "the easy-listening station" (147); she suggests using "brewer's yeast" as a natural remedy for Emmett's skin problems (248); she feeds her baby "natural foods that I fix in the food processor" (223); and though she has an ivory necklace it was not made at the expense of "kill[ing] an elephant" but rather from "recycled piano keys" (225). She has raised her awareness of feminist issues, correcting herself when she refers to an adult friend as a "girl." Most important, Irene realizes college is an essential part of being able to make new choices. She repeatedly tells her daughter, "You *have* to go to college, Sam. Women can do anything they want to now, just about" (239–40). Yet such passages suggest Irene's overemphasis on materialism and class status as well as her limited and superficial understanding of political and social issues. While she wants to enable Sam to make new choices in her life (particularly in terms of going to college and moving to an urban area), she only understands Sam's material and economic needs. Having jettisoned her ties to the past so readily herself, she cannot read clearly Sam's more spiritual needs, particularly her need to maintain a strong tie to her southern past.

Though Sam may ultimately construct a different identity as a southern woman, she nevertheless shares many of her mother's strongest qualities and hence may face many of the same challenges as she seeks to find a place for herself in the South. Most important, Sam shares a wild and rebellious spirit with her mother. As Mamaw puts it, "She always *was* touchous" (278). In the novel's opening section, Mason tells us that "Sam never really cussed much before this summer. But now she feels like letting loose. She has so much evil and bad stuff in her now. It feels good to say shit, even if it's only under her breath" (10). And Sam takes seriously her assertion that she and Dawn are "the baddest girls in Hopewell" (56): she wants to wear "black leather pants" and "a lot of metal" (269), longs to "take off in it [her car] for parts unknown" (270), and warns that she is "liable to kick a door down" (271). And when she spends the night at Cawood's Pond, she not only connects herself imaginatively to the Vietnam vets but also asserts her independent vision of being a woman in the South: "Lonnie would be totally disgusted with her. His mother would think Sam had lost her brains. Grandma would have a heart attack just at the idea of the snakes. Sam enjoyed thinking of their reactions. Maybe her mother would think the idea wasn't so ridiculous. Her mother had done braver things" (307).

But a rebellious spirit, Sam realizes, is not enough. She also needs to consider carefully what she is doing and why. As she says, "There was so much she had to find out before she took off the way her mother had. Her mother had gotten rid of her memories" (272). If she moves away from Hopewell, she wants to do so while still maintaining meaningful relationships with the important people in her life. Though she is concerned about their problems, however, she realizes the main thing on her mind is not the other people in her life or even Vietnam. Rather, the primary issue she is struggling with is determining if there is a place for her in this society:

> Maybe she was going nuts. It wasn't just Tom. Or just Emmett. Or Lonnie. Or Dawn's predicament. It was her. She was the center of all these impossible dramas, and somehow she was feeling that it was all up to her. But she didn't really know where she was, or who she would be if all those people left town and walked into the sunset to live happily ever after. If she got all of them straightened out, what would she do? (254–55)

Mason makes explicit here that *In Country*'s primary focus is not Vietnam nor an adolescent love affair. Rather, her main goal is to look at the changing South and at a young woman's role within that South.

In this novel, then, Sam inhabits an unsettling limbo between the local and the global, between the personal and the regional, between the old and the new, between stability and change. As she searches to find a point of empowering equilibrium, she instinctively reaches back to the past—to her father and to the legacy of Vietnam—in an attempt to find meaning in the present, and she just as instinctively connects with the women around her, looking to them for models of southern womanhood. Nowhere are her concerns with change and flux, place and identity, made clearer, however, than in her concern over the home she shares with Emmett. Throughout the novel, Sam—like McCorkle's Virginia and Walker's Celie—struggles to come to terms with the changing conception of what constitutes home. Having lived all her life in the Hopewell house with her mother Irene and her uncle Emmett, she now faces her mother's decision to remarry and move to Lexington and her uncle's refusal to take positive steps toward becoming an active part of the outside world again.

As Sam grapples with the issue of whether to remain in Hopewell—taking care of Emmett, dating Lonnie, working at the Burger Boy and going to the nearby state college—or to move to Lexington—living with Irene and her new husband and baby and going to the University of Kentucky—she contemplates the idea of home. Attached as she is to the familiar life of Hopewell, she leans throughout most of the novel toward staying there. Such a decision would make a lot of her friends and family happy. As Mamaw says, "If she went up there [Lexington], look how she might turn out. I think it's fine when children want to stay where they was brought up" (277). Regardless of the decision Sam will make (and by the end of the novel, though she has not articulated a decision, she seems to be leaning more heavily toward moving to Lexington), a secure sense of home and family will be essential to Sam's emotional well-being. When Emmett disappears and his cat Moon Pie escapes, for example, Sam is nearly beside herself. She feels threatened with the loss of the remaining fragments of home. However, when Irene shows up with her infant daughter and a hungover Emmett in her car, Sam feels better. When Moon Pie returns that night, everything feels complete once again: "Sam saw Moon Pie streaking through the rain across the yard toward the porch. Everyone was home now" (227).

Sam's terror at the potential loss of her family and sense of home comes up repeatedly in the novel, but as is usual with Mason the suggestion of this fear is subtle. In other words, the reader must read between the lines to discern Sam's fear. She complains constantly about the state of the house. She grumbles, for example, about Emmett's characteristic stop-gap attempt at insulating the house. She tells him, "Taping plastic on the windows is what poor people do. . . . I'm tired of everything being so tacky" (154). Here, Mason points to Sam's growing dissatisfaction with the house's physical decline as well as her increasing sense that it represents a decline in her family relationships as well. Irene, too, in her criticisms of the house, suggests its physical deterioration as well as the threatened disappearance of the family bond holding it together. While Emmett may respond to this problem in his frenzied and intense efforts to fix the house's foundation (indicating an attempt to fix both the house's physical and the family's symbolic disintegration), Irene responds by wanting to throw out the old "junk" and by wanting to move ahead to a new house. She says, for example, to Sam: "I wish y'all would clear that room out—the whole house out—and have a yard sale. This house is going to fall apart from the weight of all the junk in it" (242). Yet Irene's desire to start over by throwing everything away disturbs Sam. Irene believes the best way to strengthen shifting familial bonds, especially between her and Sam, is to move to a new home and to create a totally new sense of what family might mean; but Sam finds such a proposition quite frightening. Instead, Sam's vision of home, of family, and of southern womanhood will be, like Celie's, one in which she maintains a rich sense of her familial, cultural, and regional heritage while simultaneously creating new spaces—social, economic, and spiritual—for herself as a woman in the South. In this way, she will bring new life to Aunt Bessie's dead stalks and reclaim her link to her region, her home, her family, and her female ancestors.

FIVE

ERASING THE SOUTH:
THE CREATION OF "UNIVERSAL" FILMS

There was *truth* in Georgia; it resonated from the book and Alice
Walker's experiences in writing about these people, but it just wasn't as
pretty as the farm we found in North Carolina, so we shot North
Carolina and called it Georgia.

STEVEN SPIELBERG

While Samantha Hughes's major concerns are reading her position
as a young woman in the South and in her family, her vehicle into these
issues is her study of the Vietnam War. Throughout *In Country,* Sam
tries to recapture a sense of family and belonging through reconnecting
imaginatively with her father and his experiences in Vietnam. Her early
attempts involve talking to other vets, reading books on Vietnam, and
so on—the basic research we expect of a reasonably curious person. But
Sam discovers that this basic research is not enough and increasingly
finds that she needs to bring more of herself to her research. Thus, she
drives out to her father's family farm, spends time with her paternal
grandparents, and gains access to the diary her father kept while "in
country." It is this diary—the tangible text of her father's experiences—
that spurs Sam's pivotal realizations about his experiences in Vietnam
and about her ultimate limitations as a reader of these experiences.

Sam is shocked when she reads her father's diary, not only because she
learns surprising truths about him but also because she realizes that the
father she thinks she knows is just a myth: "Mamaw and Pap must not
have even read the diary. If they had read it, they would have realized
that he smoked and drank and murdered. Maybe they read it but didn't
want to remember their son that way. Or they pretended they couldn't
read his handwriting" (295). Read on a larger, cultural level, this passage speaks to the tendency humans have to misread those around them.

The diary is the most direct and uncensored account of Dwayne's experiences in Vietnam, but because his parents cannot accept this text,
they have only three alternatives. They can refuse to read it, rendering
the text invisible. They can read it and deliberately misunderstand and
distort it. Or they can read it and pretend to be unable to interpret its
meaning.

   This passage—coupled with the much earlier passage about
"squeez[ing] one layer deeper" (9)—challenges us to consider our own
positions as readers, to consider the lenses through which we examine
texts, and to consider the ways in which we seek to impose prescribed,
comfortable, even stereotypical patterns on texts we do not understand
or find threatening or subversive. Stanley Fish argues that these positions, lenses, and patterns, these "interpretive strategies," "exist prior to
the act of reading and therefore determine the shape of what is read
rather than, as is usually assumed, the other way around" (14). Or as
Martin Nystrand puts it, "'[W]hat you see' . . . depends on 'how you
look'" (79). While Dwayne's parents have approached his diary with
inadequate reading strategies and have consequently found an upright
young man where they should instead have found someone who "smoked
and drank and murdered," the human tendency to misread the "Other"
is even more damaging for women and especially for southern women.
Traditionally expected to refrain from challenging the white southern
patriarchy (as white women they were to be subservient ladies on pedestals, as black women they were to be sexual chattel with no agency or
voice), southern women may now construct texts that—if read carefully—show them to be much more assertive, subversive, and radical in
their intent. They may be, like Sam, "liable to kick a door down." Many
readers come to southern women's texts ill-equipped to hear what they
have to say and fail to discover the maps of reading they embed in their
texts. Consequently, southern women's texts are obscured or misrep-
resented, and the truly subversive and radical dimension of their lives
goes unheard.

   Sam herself attempts to correct this tendency toward misreading by
mimicking her father's experiences in Vietnam; she goes to Cawood's

Pond to "hump the boonies," to face the wilds of the South in a vicarious attempt to understand the wilds of Vietnam. She has expanded her interpretive strategies, tried to find other ways to look, but ultimately discovers that even these creative and imaginative leaps fail to close the gap between her father's experience and her own. She finds that spending the night in Cawood's Pond is not enough: "It hit her that this nature preserve in a protected corner of Kentucky wasn't like Vietnam at all" (308). Still, her night spent "in country" changes her and makes her at least more sympathetic to the way the veterans felt as they returned home:

> It is a good country. But she [Sam] keeps getting flashes of it through the eyes of a just-returned Vietnam soldier. The day they came back from Cawood's Pond, she felt she was seeing that way as they drove into town. . . . She didn't fit in that landscape. None of it pertained to her. . . . The soldiers must have felt like that, as though they belonged nowhere. (332)

Here Sam realizes the limitations of her ability to imagine the vet experience fully and sympathetically. But though she has developed an awareness of her limits as an interpreter of others' experiences, she also importantly comes to a fuller understanding of more responsible reading. Unlike her grandparents, she refuses to ignore her father's text, to distort it, or to pretend she does not understand it. Unsettling though it may be, Sam faces the text head on and attempts to respond to it by bringing as much of herself to it as she possibly can.

It is this type of responsible reading that both Mason and Walker call for from their audiences, and both make clear the disastrous consequences for women if their texts are not read with care or sensitivity. And like Fredric Jameson and Teresa de Laurctis, both Walker and Mason are concerned with the ways in which those in positions of textual and narrative power use their texts and stories to reinforce dominant ideology and to contain subversive texts. Those in positions of interpretive power—in this instance, Steven Spielberg and Norman Jewison as the film adaptors of Walker's and Mason's novels—read "Other-ed" texts through filters informed on every level by master narratives; that is, instead of reading a writer's text from within that text's own internal interpretive map, instead of reading deeply and sympathetically as Sam does, the reinforcer instead interprets the text by superimposing the master narrative and its dominant interpretive ideology onto the subversive text. The marginalized text is contained and disempowered when read according to the dictates of the master narrative.

Not surprisingly, those in positions of dominance may perceive the assertion of cultural and gender difference as potential fragmentation and may scramble to assert instead the oneness of the social fabric; consequently, they may seek to erase difference in favor of claiming the universality of all experience. Spielberg and Jewison do just this. Their interpretations of Walker's and Mason's novels indicate their profound discomfort with cultural, racial, regional, class, and gender difference and their consequent attempt to assert hegemonic dominance. To counter this process of universalization, that is, the process of containing the assertion of difference that threatens to fragment or split the dominant societal view, Jameson argues that readers need to approach texts by marginalized writers not simply as "the pluralistic rediscovery of other isolated social groups" but rather must create "an ultimate rewriting of these utterances in terms of their essentially polemic and subversive strategies [that] restores them to their proper place in the dialogical system of the social classes" (86). In other words, readers must counter the reinforcer's trend to universalize and contain texts by Others by reading the texts on their own terms, according to their own internal maps of reading, and must allow them to remain dynamically and threateningly on the (cutting) edge of dominant ideological discourse.

Though Walker's and Mason's inscribed maps of reading assert the need for particularity and an understanding of the local, Spielberg and Jewison substitute their own methods of reading according to master narratives and thus not only miss the points of the novels but also substitute the universal for the particular. Hence, as de Lauretis might put it, by (re)producing dominant ideologies, they "technologize" not only gender but race and region as well. A comparison of Walker's and

Mason's inscriptions of southern women's experience with Spielberg's and Jewison's readings of these experiences can illustrate the ways southern women's texts can be appropriated, commodified, and ultimately contained by white middle-class America.

As the preceding chapters make clear, the twentieth century has seen a substantial number of important southern writers—not only the many women writers I have mentioned but also rich and provocative male writers. With few exceptions, these writers can be termed serious writers; that is, they treat the South and the people of the South with seriousness and respect. There are virtually an equal number of film treatments of the South as there are novels. A brief listing might include such landmark films as *Birth of a Nation* (1915), *Gone with the Wind* (1939), *Cabin in the Sky* (1943), *Song of the South* (1946), *A Streetcar Named Desire* (1951), *Bonnie and Clyde* (1967), *Easy Rider* (1970), *Deliverance* (1972), *Sounder* (1972), *Nashville* (1975), *Roots* (1976), *Smokey and the Bandit* (1977), *Norma Rae* (1979), and more recently, *Crimes of the Heart* (1987), *Mississippi Burning* (1988), *Steel Magnolias* (1989), *Driving Miss Daisy* (1989), *Wild at Heart* (1990), and, of course, *The Color Purple* (1985) and *In Country* (1989). Indeed, Wade Austin notes that "the South as a setting and the Southerner as a character type have been fixtures in American motion pictures" (83).[1]

But except for a few truly well done films, many of these movies depend on misreadings of texts and on stereotypes of southerners. As Warren French points out, the "Southern" before World War II tended to glorify the Old South while films since then have presented the South as a kind of "decadent backwoods and backwaters" "hell" (4–5). Despite a handful of excellent independent southern filmmakers,[2] most of the films about the South continue to be made by nonsoutherners. This geographical distance between the region being filmed and the region funding the film plays a large part in creating the gap between the serious literature of the South and its filmic debasement. Southerners have not been regarded as legitimate filmmakers—as Linda Dubler argues, those in power assume that southerners would not be up to the "technical standards" of "their peers in Manhattan or Los Angeles" (39)—and their nonsouthern counterparts are instead chosen to make films about the South that further reinforce the idea that the South is culturally, morally, intellectually, and technologically backward.

But the greatest difference between novels about the South by southerners and films about the South by nonsoutherners is not just a matter of those who are inside or outside that culture. Rather, the greatest difference—though connected to this concept of experiential authority in reading and rendering the South—lies in the novelists' insistence on particularity and locality, that is, on the characteristically southern sense of place, and the filmmakers' equally strong desire to focus either on stereotypes about the South or on the universal aspects of southern experience. Given the wide gap in perceptions of the South that exist between southern novelists and Hollywood[3] filmmakers who seek to capitalize on mainstream misperceptions of the South, it should not be surprising to discover that Steven Spielberg and Norman Jewison in their adaptations of Walker's and Mason's novels create misreadings that fall short of the mark for precisely the same reasons most other filmic treatments of the South go awry.

Both the Hollywood-based Spielberg and the Canadian Jewison are closely aligned with the establishment film industry. Spielberg has dominated the money-making end of film for the last fifteen years. Never noted for his treatment of serious subjects, he is heralded instead for his blockbuster adventure and fantasy movies, including *Jaws, Close Encounters of the Third Kind, E.T.,* and the Indiana Jones movies. Jewison, on the other hand, is better known for his treatment of controversial issues in movies such as *A Soldier's Story,* but he is also noted at times for his "distressingly conventional approach" (A. White 12). In other words, neither Spielberg nor Jewison is ever accused of taking dangerous stances in films. Moreover, in their positions of economic power in Hollywood, both Spielberg and Jewison function as reinforcers and reproducers of dominant ideologies who perpetuate restrictive notions of gender, race, and region. Or as Jameson puts it, they engage in "the process of cultural 'universalization,'" which "repress[es] . . . the oppositional voice" and creates "the illusion that there is only one genuine 'culture'" (87).

Not surprisingly, the film versions of *The Color Purple* and *In Country* are informed by the phallocentrism, racism, and regionalism inherent in most Hollywood productions. As de Lauretis argues, Hollywood functions as a technology system that reproduces the dominant ideology: Hollywood technologizes gender and, by extension, race and region as well. The emphasis on masculinist readings did not escape the making of *The Color Purple,* in which three out of the four producers were men, two of them white. Virtually all important aspects of making the film were assigned to men. And in a film based on a black womanist's novel about black women's community,[4] even the opening credits indicate the dominating role of men: Danny Glover, who plays "Mister," and Adolph Caesar, who plays his father (indisputably a minor character), are listed before any of the female leads. Besides the credit to her as the original novelist, Walker gets one other mention as project consultant during the closing credits, where her name shares the screen with the makeup director. Such deemphasis of the text's original author may be a film convention, but it nevertheless underscores the degree to which Walker was erased from the making of this film. In addition, the predominance of men involved in making the film—especially the predominance of white, nonsouthern men—makes it clear that the readers in this case are far removed from the womanist vision that shaped the original writing.

Likewise, Jewison's *In Country* was shaped predominantly by men and by a number of nonsoutherners as well. Frank Pierson and Cynthia Cidre wrote the screenplay, both of the film's producers were men, and most of the other leading participants in the film were men as well. In addition, the Canadian Jewison may have set the tone for nonsouthern control over the production. As in *The Color Purple,* the opening credits of this film are instructive. Bruce Willis, as Sam's Uncle Emmett, gets top billing, suggesting not only that Willis is the biggest name attached to the film but also that Jewison sees this movie as the Vietnam veteran's story. To Jewison's credit, *In Country* was shot mostly in Kentucky: the film's closing credits thank the Kentucky Film Commission, the city of Paducah, the town of Mayfield (Mason's hometown and the model for Hopewell), the Kentucky National Guard, and the Vietnam Veterans of Paducah. Moreover, Jewison consulted with a number of veterans from Kentucky; such input may be largely male, but at least there is a modicum of southern influence on this film.

Spielberg's and Jewison's distance from Walker's and Mason's texts in terms of region, culture, race, and gender, i.e., their position as non-southern white men, does not in itself make them reinforcers of dominant ideology. Rather, their insistence on universalizing the particular and on containing Walker's and Mason's more difficult messages defines them as such. Although Spielberg, for example, insists his Jewishness allowed him to empathize with his characters,[5] and although he took some comfort from Quincy Jones, who made "me feel that I wasn't too white" (qtd. in Turner, "Spielberg" 63), his belief in the novel's universality and his ability to see the South through a filter of stereotypes shapes his particular reading. Spielberg has repeatedly asserted that Celie's story is universal: "I determined early on that this wasn't just a story about race or color or intellect or station in society, it is really a story about humanity" (qtd. in Turner, "Spielberg" 59). Whoopi Goldberg, who played the role of Celie, joined him in stressing the story's universal significance: "*This is not a black story. The Color Purple* is a story about human beings in odd situations, and it could have been done with Chinese people, or white people, or Spanish people" (qtd. in Kearney 26; my emphasis). In addition to reading Celie's story as universal, Spielberg also reads it through a haze of stereotypes. Thus, Spielberg reads the story of poor black southern women through the same filter he uses to understand and render the story of E.T. In treating Walker's novel as a cartoon or fantasy, Spielberg not only rips the story from its gritty sociocultural context; he also deprives it of its real significance, robbing it of its power to challenge white male authority. Where Walker's serious novel is very much about race and region, Spielberg's "coloring book version" (Bush 66) puts Celie in a context even Spielberg and his associates agree has little to do with race.

Like many directors before him, Spielberg asserts his authority as a reader of this novel; at the same time, he erases (and, thereby, contains) difference by relegating negative stereotypes as peculiar to the South or to blacks and simultaneously recategorizes positive aspects of southern blacks as part of universal experience. Similarly, Norman Jewison ignores the impact of his perspective as a Jewish Canadian man on the creation of a film about a young Protestant southern white woman coming to terms not only with Vietnam but also with her role as a woman in the South. Like Spielberg, he attempts to get off the hook by arguing that the film is not about the South but, rather, America. Jewison unself-consciously uses the term "America" (read: "universal") as if it were a monolith we all recognize. While Spielberg at least expresses some initial discomfort in appropriating a black text, Jewison never blinks an eye about distorting a white southern woman's text. He does not defend—nor does he ever address—his decisions to erase some aspects of southernness, to distort others. The promotional materials for *In Country,* in fact, label the film as "The Story of an American Family." Jewison claims, "I want to make sure that people understand the momentous effect this war had on the American family, which Bobbie Ann Mason wrote about" (qtd. in J. Scott 12). Nowhere does Jewison mention the South or his concern to depict the South accurately.

One can learn a great deal about both films—and about the practice of (mis)reading southern texts—by considering Spielberg's and Jewison's supposed motives in making their films. Indeed, I find it most compelling to look at the films as very specific readings of the novels. In other words, looking at the films allows us to gauge how those in dominant positions read (black) southern women's texts. To examine a film as a reading of a novel is not stretching matters; as Adam Mars-Jones notes, "[E]very film of a book is an involuntary act of literary criticism" (27). It is entirely possible that Spielberg and Jewison brought a true empathy to their making of *The Color Purple* and *In Country.* And it is, of course, possible to make a good film about the South if one is an outsider, just as it is possible to read and interpret southern or African-American fiction if one is not southern or black. Yet as many literary scholars realize, the ability to do the latter depends upon a real willingness to recognize and confront one's own sociocultural background and the distance it creates between the text and the reader. In other words, one might wish Spielberg and Jewison would acknowledge less dismissively their roles as Jewish male directors from Hollywood and Canada. An examination, then, of Spielberg's *The Color Purple* and Jewison's *In Country* can illustrate the way southern women's texts are misinterpreted, appropriated, commodified—in short, the ways they are put to use by white middle-class America.

Spielberg's skill at sugarcoating comes through most boldly in his depiction of the South as place, of the economic realities of black life in the South, of black southern women, and of the alternative spirituality at the heart of Walker's novel. Moreover, Spielberg's film spends the bulk of its 152 minutes on the story's first southern phase, with very little attention to the North's role in Celie's transformation or to the new vision of community in the story's second southern phase. As he ignores the importance of place, as he creates a homogenized treatment of black socioeconomic status in the South, as he recodifies gender lines, and as he reinserts a depiction of organized religion, Spielberg works to create a universalized portrait of black southern life and, by doing so, contains Walker's radical message. Or as *Nation* reviewer Andrew Kopkind puts it, Spielberg's "secret technique" is to move the film into "a safe and familiar form to compensate for its difficult and threatening content" (124).

Though Walker claims Spielberg had an instinctive sense of the novel's essence, he clearly did not see evocation of place as central to the book's theme. First, he did not recognize the sense of place that marks Walker's novel as a decidedly southern text. Second, Walker's interest in the South as place goes beyond pure evocation to a striking emphasis on the South as an African-American homeland. Yet Spielberg's film has nothing at all to do with Walker's revolutionary idea of black reclamation of the South; there is nothing, as there is in Walker's novel, that makes the leap to a higher plane of utopian possibility.

Instead, Spielberg sees place as mere backdrop. He and his associates proudly talk about the way they shot the South to look "pretty" and had no qualms about polishing the rough edges of southern experience. In addition, they pat themselves on the back for their diligent efforts at creating realistic environment. As cinematographer Allen Daviau states, "Steven Spielberg is always concerned about the audience understanding

the geography—whether it be this entire farm or what's happening inside a single room. He never wants anybody to be confused as to where
they are" (qtd. in Harrell 56).

The film's skewed presentation of the South-as-place results, then,
because Spielberg himself is confused as to where he is. Shot on location on a farm outside Wadesboro, North Carolina, *The Color Purple*'s
scenery is far removed from the red clay region of Walker's Georgia.
Though Spielberg himself did not select the shooting location, he was
nevertheless impressed with production designer Michael Riva's choice.
"When I got there," Spielberg recalls, "I was flabbergasted at how beautiful everything was" (qtd. in Turner, "Spielberg" 60). What is problematic
here is not that Spielberg found the South beautiful but that he felt no
qualms in exchanging the North Carolina countryside for Walker's flat,
earthy Georgia. To make North Carolina look more like Georgia, they
imported "tons of red clay-like earth" to create a sense of "the Georgia
red clay," and for their surprisingly numerous snow scenes they brought
in biodegradable material that gave a snowlike effect (Harrell 56). To
enhance the natural beauty of the location, the cinematographer deliberately shot most of the film's scenes in the early morning, during what
he and Spielberg called the "magic hour" (Turner, "Daviau" 81). As John
Simon notes, the cinematographer was "made to shoot the film as a series
of picture postcards" (56).

Many critics also complain not simply because the movie's landscape
does not closely resemble Georgia but also because Spielberg's depiction of black rural life in the South seems skewed. Of course, both
Walker and Spielberg claim they were depicting middle-class blacks in
the South. Spielberg states, in fact, that the company "based Celie and
Mister's house on pictures Alice showed us," pictures of her "well-off"
and "successful" grandparents' house (qtd. in "Dialogue" 14). In Walker's
novel, however, "Pa" seems to be wealthier than Mr. _____: he owns not
only the house Celie and Shug later declare to look just like "some white
person's house" (165) but also a large farm and, more important, a store.
But in the film, Mr. _____ lives in a much more spectacular home than
does "Pa," and it appears that marriage to Mr. _____ is at least an economic step up for Celie. What Walker and Spielberg both distressingly

fail to clarify is how anyone in the South, especially rural blacks, sur-
vived the Depression with such economic prosperity. Similarly, where
Walker makes clear that Celie spends a lot of time out in the fields,
Spielberg rarely, if ever, shows her or anyone else at work on the farm.
Critics complain about the film's "too perfect and homogenized" view of
southern black life (Greenberg 16), criticize its depiction of people who
"seem to be doing a lot better than simply eking out a living" (Greenberg 16), take Spielberg to task for creating a farm that "prospers for
decades, even during the depths of the Depression," a "healthy looking"
and "large" farm that apparently tends itself (Maslin 181), and even note
that "Mr.'s house inexplicably oscillates between a cabin and an antebellum mansion, depending on whether you're looking out front or back"
(Hoberman 76). Thus, the production is overwrought and far removed
from the brutal economic reality of rural Georgia.

In addition to erasing a true sense of southernness from his film,
Spielberg also distorts images of black women in the South and recodifies the gender lines Walker worked so hard to blur. At the center of
Walker's novel, of course, is the women's community, which Spielberg
gestures at in the brief allusion to the lesbian relationship between Celie
and Shug, in the helping and caring relationship between Celie and
Sofia, and especially in the close and lifelong bond between Celie and
Nettie. But even here much of the woman-to-woman bond is erased: the
cooperative mothering between Sofia and Squeak, the intense passion
between Shug and Celie, even Celie's problematic relationship with her
mother. Instead of focusing his energies on the womanist implications
of Walker's text, Spielberg alters and adds, investing his reading with
an even deeper division between men and women. Sadly, though not
surprisingly, he fails to take on the issue of Celie and Albert's eventual emotional—though nonsexual—reconciliation. It is much harder
to categorize as black and white, to divide as men and women, if Celie
and Albert find some new ground to stand on, some new way to coexist
and be together. Thus, where the novel ends with Celie at home with
Shug *and* Albert, where it ends with her introducing them to Nettie as
"my peoples," the film shows Albert passing by on the road unnoticed
and unrecognized. Indeed, the closing shot of the old Celie and Nettie

playing together once again is interrupted by the sight of "Mister" passing through them, suggesting that he still holds power, that he can still
intrude and divide.[6]

Such a division refuses to acknowledge and bring to life the grays
of the world Walker works toward in her novel. She might begin her
novel with references to stereotyped views of women and of blacks (e.g.,
"smart women will never attract men," "wives need to mind and thus you
should beat them"), but she quickly blurs these distinctions. Spielberg
all but erases these blurred gender boundaries and instead lines things
up neatly as male and female, black and white, good and evil. Hence, the
complexity of the relationships, especially the ambiguity at the center
of male-female relationships, is not present in Spielberg's film. In fact,
when it becomes impossible to fit a particular relationship within appropriate male-female categories, as in the relationship between the "weak"
Harpo and the "dominating" Sofia, Spielberg has no choice but to treat
these characters comically.

Most frustrating in Spielberg's film is his insistence on taking the
novel's two main examples of strong southern womanhood—Sofia and
Shug—and explaining their power away. He paints Sofia as a clown,
robbing her of the dignity and respect that would cause an audience to
take her character as a serious alternative vision of southern womanhood. Similarly, he waves his magic wand and transforms Shug, not into
the magician or honeybee figure she is in the novel, but into a classic
Freudian example of the daughter seeking approval from the estranged
Father. To Spielberg, it does not matter that the father does not even exist
in the novel, much less that Shug expresses little concern or anxiety
over a troubled relationship with her parents. Rather, what matters to
Spielberg is that he find a way to explain Shug's determination to be an
independent woman. Since it would be too threatening to conclude that
Shug is a free spirit because she defines herself as such, Spielberg makes
her waywardness palatable by attributing it to a troubled relationship
with Daddy. Spielberg is not interested in the fact that in the novel Shug
is "bound to live her life and be herself no matter what" (236). Instead, as
Molly Hite argues, Spielberg "reinscribe[s] the law of the father exactly
where Walker had effaced it, by providing Shug with a textually gra-

tuitous 'daddy,' who is also a preacher and thus the representative of the Christian white father-God explicitly repudiated in the passage that gives the book its title" (115).

Spielberg's addition of the Father allows him not only to reinforce dominant ideology's views of gender; it also allows him to overturn Celie and Shug's theory of alternative spirituality and to replace it with traditional organized religion. Here, more than anywhere else, Spielberg is determined to contain Walker's subversive portrayal of independent women who believe in decentered, nonpatriarchal, nonracist spirituality. Where Shug's spiritual wholeness in the novel comes from her rejection of organized and white-defined religion, in the film her redemption comes at the moment when she makes peace with her father by bursting into a gospel number. In the church scene, then, Shug achieves salvation as her return to church and to the Father are fused.

Moreover, the addition of the Father gives Spielberg an excuse to create what he must have felt was the obligatory black church scene. Never mind that such a scene, like Shug's father, never appears in the novel. Again, it simply does not matter because the addition of the church scene allows Spielberg to pull so many of his racist and patriarchal strands together. He might instead have shown Celie going to church a time or two; she mentions attending church a few times in the novel and, of course, addresses all of her early letters to God. Consequently, it would have made sense for Spielberg to provide early church scenes. But the addition of the church scene involving Shug and her father makes no sense at all. As Steven C. Weisenburger comments, "The preacher father is grafted onto the script not just as a way to rehabilitate the sinner, but to get the camera inside a black church because what would a black film be without a climactic scene of getting religion?" (274).

In his erasure of Walker's South, in his distortion of black southern women, and in his reinscription of organized religion, Spielberg creates a palatable commodity for consumption by his target audience—the white middle class. Spielberg claims he did not intend nor expect *The Color Purple* to be a popular film; indeed, he asserts the only problem with the movie was its popularity: "People begin to get suspicious of your intentions when the films are so wildly popular" (qtd. in "Dialogue"

16). But in another instance, Ishmael Reed claims Spielberg knew the novel to be what the book trade calls a "bodice ripper" and that as such it "attracted a mostly white feminist audience." Apparently, given the book's popularity among this crowd, Spielberg "wanted to expand the audience" for the movie (qtd. in Gates 12).

Clearly, the movie was intended primarily for middle-class whites, who can more easily afford to see first-run movies at the theater. In adapting *The Color Purple* to an even whiter audience than the book was intended for, Spielberg's goal to "make the kinds of films that I, as an audience, would want to see" (qtd. in "Dialogue" 15) seems appropriate. One reviewer argues that the film is "flagrantly meant as a racially 'crossover' film," that is, "a picture about blacks that whites will buy with a smile" and asserts that, although "readers of Alice Walker's book [should] beware," all other viewers have "nothing to worry about." In short, "*These* blacks don't mean us no harm" (Sigal 34). It is not surprising that Spielberg handily succeeded in pedalling his racist and patriarchal wares to most of the white American public. Mainstream middle-class white America—especially during the Reagan years—was eager to believe that Spielberg's film represented the truth about the South and about black women in the South.

In an interview with Holly Near before the film was completed, Alice Walker explained why she backed the Spielberg production of her novel:

> I said, if you want to get the real thing, by the end it will be a $3 paperback. Buy it, read it . . . and then you can go to the movie and point out all the things they did wrong. But for a writer like me who writes for a lot of people who don't read, I have to think of visual things, ways of reaching them. . . . I think . . . it will be progressive enough for people to see some necessary reflections of themselves. Without someone like Steven, all the people who should really see the movie wouldn't see it—it would never reach Eatonton, Georgia, my home town. (qtd. in Halprin 1)

Walker may have a point. If Spielberg, as the country's most popular reinforcer of dominant ideology, had not translated *The Color Purple* to the big screen, perhaps no one else would have ever done so, or perhaps another director would not have had the funds to distribute the film widely or the name recognition to draw large crowds. And perhaps she is right in believing that communicating part of the message about Celie and other poor black southern women was more important than communicating an accurate message about such women. But Spielberg's film is not just a watered-down version of Walker's novel. Rather, it is a flagrant misreading of a radical text. As Deborah E. McDowell said of Gloria Naylor's novel *The Women of Brewster Place* and the made-for-TV movie based upon it, "The conventions of [film], the constraints on what it constitutes as sayable, actually work . . . to reinscribe some of the very assumptions we would want to eradicate" (qtd. in Fraiman 24). Spielberg's film makes subversion nonthreatening and, in doing so, not only disempowers Walker as an author and a visionary of the black community's future in the South but also disempowers all black people— particularly poor black women—who must make a way for themselves in the contemporary South.

Spielberg's film differs so markedly from the novel that the vast majority of reader-viewers immediately discern the gap between the two. Though Jewison's *In Country* differs from its source as much as Spielberg's film, in Jewison's case such differences are not frequently pointed out by critics. One reason for this critical oversight may be that Mason's novel simply is not read nearly as widely as Walker's. Similarly, Jewison's film did not get the distribution nor the attention Spielberg's film did, substantially reducing the number of reviews actually written about the film. But the final reason for this critical oversight appears to stem from the misreadings many readers, like Jewison, were subject to.

Getting at the southernness in Bobbie Ann Mason's novel, with all its tensions and ambivalences, is even harder than in Alice Walker's novel. To get at the southernness and the deeper issues Mason addresses requires hard and careful reading. As Sam's aerobics instructor points out, you have to "squeeze one layer deeper." Given this tendency to misread Mason, it is not surprising that Jewison filmed a colossal misread as well. Erasing, or perhaps failing to see, the southernness inherent in Mason's novel, Jewison instead concentrates on *In Country* as the story of an American family. Where Mason subtly weaves parallels between the South and Vietnam, Jewison misses the point entirely. Though he casts stock southern actors and actresses as leading characters, gets his nonsouthern cast to learn the western Kentucky dialect, and shoots the film on location with the help of local Vietnam veterans, his film erases the issue of southernness on the profound level on which Mason works. In short, like many readers, Jewison sees *In Country* as just another Vietnam story. Jewison's film handles the surface story of *In Country* very well: it looks at Emmett's and Sam's attempts to come to terms with the Vietnam legacy in their lives. But Jewison's film almost never attempts to come to terms with the southern issues Mason establishes in her text. Where Mason concentrates on the changing southern cultural and material landscape, on the ways southern women are controlled by southern culture, and in particular on the choices Sam faces as a young southern woman, Jewison almost completely ignores these issues. In short, he virtually erases almost all of the southern story from his film.

That Jewison sees *In Country* as being concerned almost solely with the Vietnam issue is made clear in the film's opening. Mason begins her novel with a reference to two southern women and the connection between them; Jewison begins with the depiction of young men going off to fight in Vietnam. As the credits roll, the audience hears the sounds of marching and helicopters. The movie begins with a long shot of soldiers at attention, listening to a speech before they board the plane that will take them to Vietnam. Almost immediately, Jewison cuts to a battle shot in the jungle, with a continued voice-over about the need to fight the Vietnam War. Finally, he cuts to Sam's high school graduation and the film begins in earnest. Jewison's opening shots and voice-overs suggest he sees Vietnam as the main issue in *In Country*. Thus, asserts Stanley Kauffman, "The filmmakers . . . took a look at Mason's oblique approach and evidently said, 'The hell with *that*.' They plunk Vietnam at us right off" (30).

Of course, Jewison does set the story in western Kentucky and, in doing so, gets some of the southernness right. David Denby notes that

"*In Country* was shot in Bobbie Ann Mason territory—western Kentucky—and the sounds and tempo of a gregarious small town seemed to have soaked into the production" (130). The accents and dialects are well done and, except in the case of Mamaw and Pap, are not at all gratuitous. Nineteen-year-old British actress Emily Lloyd does a particularly fine job with her accent, rendering a very convincing portrayal as a young Kentucky woman. In addition, several of the place markers in the film add a nice touch to Mason's own emphasis on particularity; Sam's run through the cemetery marked "The United Daughters of the Confederacy Memorial," for example, indicates both the South's continued preoccupation with history and Sam's own tie to the past, particularly the military past. However, Jewison never picks up the reference again; rather than providing textual reinforcement for one of the story's major themes, he simply reinforces a stereotype about southerners still living the Civil War.

Yet despite accurate dialects and an occasional nod to southern culture, Jewison most often situates his reading of Mason's novel in a South riddled with stereotypes. Mason is noted repeatedly for her references to the particular, for her evocation of the locale and the countryside, as well as for her simultaneous references to popular culture, specifically to "M*A*S*H," the Beatles, and Bruce Springsteen. Springsteen's "Born in the U.S.A.," in fact, provides the epigraph for Mason's novel, and his lyrics are a crucial part of Mason's work. Although Jewison retains one Springsteen song (curiously enough, not "Born in the U.S.A.," Springsteen's Vietnam song), he undercuts Mason's emphasis on popular culture several times in his film. For example, each time Lonnie pulls up in his stereotypical good ol' boy El Camino, his radio is blaring country music. Jewison's Lonnie listens to Dwight Yoakam ("Honky Tonk Man") and Webb Wilder ("High Rollin'"), whereas Mason's Lonnie surely has no interest in or awareness of such music. The South is changing: it still retains a certain regional flavor, particularly in its social structure, but, as Mason shows in her repeated references to popular culture, the South's cultural distinctiveness is being erased in the growing homogenization of America. Mason's pop culture references to fast food get distorted in Jewison's film as well. Mason very deliberately places Emmett and his friends at the local McDonald's every day: they attempt to reach some better understanding of themselves—or at least try to maintain a bond between themselves—within the context of the world's most homogenizing business. In the film, Jewison makes a clumsy alteration when he places Emmett and his friends at the local diner, a far cry from McDonald's or some other national chain. Again, Jewison misses Mason's point that the stereotypical old-fashioned small-town diner simply does not exist anymore. Curiously, though, in product placements for Pizza Hut and Dairy Queen, Jewison not only shows their signs and marquees but also lingers on the Pizza Hut sign for an inordinately long time. Perhaps Jewison thought this would suggest the encroachment of homogenized food on small-town Kentucky. His substitution, however, distorts Mason's point and represents careless filmmaking.

Jewison misses again when he fails to set the larger context of the southern landscape. Although Jewison to some degree suggests Dwayne's tie to the South, and though he retains Pete's map-of-Kentucky tattoo, these are but brief gestures to one of Mason's major themes. He does attempt to juxtapose flashbacks to Dwayne's letters and diary with scenes of Sam in Cawood's Pond, to re-create on some level the parallels between Vietnam and the South. But with Sam's tie to the southern landscape and the country missing from the movie and with no real discussion of the importance of these key symbols, Jewison's film fails to communicate Mason's point. "The larger resonances," says Kauffman, "are lost" (30).

Situated against Jewison's skewed depiction of landscape and the locale are his stereotyped renditions of southerners and their culture. Although Mason shows her characters going to church, eating traditional foods, and being obsessed with antiques, she shows them doing these things against a changing material background. Consequently, Jewison's filmic references to the disapproving old southern women Sam and Dawn face when they buy a pregnancy test kit, the old men playing checkers when Sam is running, and the old veteran named Bobby Ray are gratuitous. In fact, Mason specifically states in her short story "Shiloh" that "New shopping centers and industrial parks have displaced the farmers who used to gather around the courthouse square on Saturday afternoons to play checkers and spit tobacco juice" (4). For a while, however, his references to traditional southern food, taken as they are from Mason's text, seem responsible and true to southern experience. In fact, he deftly pulls together references to traditional fare with an indication of Sam's distance from her roots. When she visits at Mamaw and Pap's, she starts eating before grace, the ultimate display of rudeness and irreverence in such a household. Here, Jewison's instinct is right on, indicating the contrast between the old and the new and the level of Sam's removal from the old southern culture and traditions. But though Mason's characters eat greens, fried chicken, and barbecue, food is not usually the sole thing on their minds. Jewison's ending, therefore, stretches the topic of food and other southern traditions to the point of caricature. Mason's novel ends with a moment of epiphany, with Sam looking on as Emmett cries when he sees one of his buddies' names on the Vietnam Memorial. But Jewison's film ends, remarkably, as Emmett, Sam, and Mamaw leave the memorial, with Emmett providing the final voice-over: "Y'all wanna get some barbecue?"

Also interesting in Jewison's depiction of southern culture is his addition of references to southern blacks. One could argue that he correctly offsets Mason's peculiarly narrow view of a Kentucky populated entirely by whites. Unfortunately, his gestures strike the viewer as mere tokenism. Sam's lover, Tom, operates an auto repair business in an old shack. In the scene where Tom shows Sam the VW he has for sale, a black man can be seen leaving the shack deep in the shot's background. Nothing is done with this visual reference again, and the viewer—if he or she even sees the man—is left to wonder whether he is an employee or a customer. Other token visual references to blacks include the sole black veteran at the dance and a Sunday morning run that takes Sam past a black church. Apparently, neither Spielberg nor Jewison could resist including black church scenes.

The most distressing of Jewison's stereotypes, however, is his depiction of Mamaw and Pap. Mason provides Sam with two contrasting sets of grandparents: Grandma and Granddad Smith, as up-to-date, middle-class, suburban southerners, represent the changing face of the South, while Mamaw and Pap Hughes function as reminders of the traditional and poor-white South. And more important, Sam enjoys a lively relationship with the Smiths and is most frequently aligned with the changing and modern South, while she has an almost nonexistent relationship with Mamaw and Pap. Hence, Mason establishes a story in which the main character not only comes to terms with the role of Vietnam in her life but also travels back in time to her cultural roots as she drives further into the country to visit her paternal grandparents. Jewison apparently does not recognize any of this complexity. Instead, he collapses the two sets of grandparents, particularly the grandmothers, into one, choosing the more primitive rather than the more typically modern. Jewison's casting of Peggy Rea as the grandmother makes this even more problematic. Rea is easily recognizable as the stock "hick" grandmother figure. She played Aunt Rose on *The Waltons,* replacing Olivia and Grandma as the show's matriarchs, and later played a similar role on *The Dukes of Hazzard.* Her jolly plumpness, lilting "white trash" accent, straw bonnets, and sleeveless blouses endear her to directors who wish to portray the enduring southern poor white mama. Jewison's Pap is no less a caricature. He is the stereotypical cornball farmer, complete with white hair and a white droopy mustache. Their truck is old, splattered with paint, and the vague sounds of chickens are heard whenever the truck is around. Add to that their son Dwayne's heavy accent as he narrates his letters and diary and his statements such as "I miss mama's fried chicken," and Jewison is following out of the persistent genre of hillbilly movies.[7] Mamaw and Pap may be a bit more capable than Ma and Pa Kettle, but there is no real suggestion that anyone would want to get to know them or spend time with them. More important, because Jewison conflates the two sets of grandparents, there is no sense that Sam is struggling to come to terms with her southern, particularly her rural, heritage. Though Mason's Sam has a very strained relationship with Mamaw, and though she identifies much more closely with her other, more modern grandmother, Jewison's Sam is much more at ease in this backwoods South.

If Jewison can blithely distort this key relationship, it should not be surprising that he also garbles Mason's work on gender roles. In the novel, for example, Mason creates the character of Sue Ann, who leaves her husband Jim to find a new life for herself in Lexington. Thus, Jim goes to the Vietnam Vets dance alone. In the movie, however, the explanation for Sue Ann's absence from the dance is profoundly different: her husband says she is staying home from the dance because she is on the "Jesus diet" ("You can't cheat on Jesus"). Clearly, an enormous gap exists between staying home because of a diet and leaving home to create a new life. In addition, the close relationship between Sam and Emmett, one of the most refreshing and liberating aspects of Mason's novel, becomes difficult to understand in the movie. Although Jewison retains Emmett's love of cooking and his insistence on wearing his skirt, he fails to capture the essence of Emmett as a new southern man. Where Mason's Emmett happily does "women's work," wears skirts around the house because they are more comfortable and allow him to challenge gendered prescriptions for dressing, and has a relaxed attitude toward traditional southern values (e.g., he sees nothing wrong with premarital sex), Jewison's Emmett shows little affection for Sam and spends most of the movie "bossing" her around.

In Country's most important character, Sam, does retain some of the characteristics Mason imbued her with. She longs to be more, to be free, to figure out her place in her society. Her longing for the car is as important in the movie as in the novel. And her relationship with Lonnie is not as important to her as Dawn's relationship is with Kenny. In fact, one of her key statements in the novel is used in the film as well: "Lonnie's not the main thing on my mind right now." Despite this, Jewison still misses part of Sam's essence. The movie, in short, does not stress the degree to which she wrestles with making choices about her role in southern society. We do not frequently see her trying to make peace between what she senses as her obligation to her family (Emmett) and her past (Mamaw and Pap) and her need to move ahead and "be more." In fact, her relationship with Emmett is so unpleasant in the movie that it is hard to understand why allegiance to him would be a factor in her decision at all. Jewison indicates the level of distortion of gender roles in his movie in the bedroom scene between Tom and Sam. Psychologically wounded by the war, Tom cannot make love to any woman, including Sam. Defeated by a problem he cannot overcome, Mason's Tom, eschewing prescriptions for masculine behavior, asks Sam to hold him. Jewison, however, reinforces gender roles by having Sam ask Tom to hold her.

Finally, Jewison garbles Mason's central point. The ending of Mason's novel shows that the characters have not yet fully worked out the issues they face: the novel ends with Emmett's tears as he views his friend's name on the memorial and with Sam having not yet articulated a decision about college. Jewison, however, wraps things up quite neatly: Emmett feels good enough at the end of the movie to suggest getting barbecue and Sam announces to her mother that she will move to Lexington. Though Mason's readers might anticipate both of these resolutions, Mason deliberately avoids including them in her novel. Her text remains focused on choice, on change, on the need for southerners to play an active role in determining their future course. Jewison's film, however, requires no such participation from the audience.

If the novel is about the changing South, the film is about America's need to come to terms with the Vietnam legacy. As in Spielberg's *The Color Purple,* Jewison's *In Country* creates yet another situation in which the South is erased so that mainstream audiences can find the story accessible. One must wonder about the consequences of this erasure when an actor such as Bruce Willis plays the lead. Jay Scott, for example, reports that "one preview screening failed 'to work' . . . because the young audience, ignorant of the subject, applauded the name Bruce Willis and then apparently kept waiting for him to go berserk, pull out an M-16, and waste half of Kentucky" (12). Such a film might have been a neat fusion of *Rambo* and *The Texas Chainsaw Massacre.* But just because Jewison spared us that travesty, we should not be lured into thinking that the *In Country* he did make is any less damaging. For in skirting the deeper issues Mason inscribed in her text and by replacing them with stereotypes and caricatures as placeholders for the real South, Jewison plays a role in perpetuating the image of the South as a backwoods and backwaters place any reasonable person would want to escape.

Jewison and Spielberg are not particularly interested, then, in situating Mason's and Walker's novels within their specific sociocultural contexts or in reading them according to the authors' agendas. To paraphrase Martin Nystrand, they bring little "knowledge of which differ-

ences count" (76) to their readings of the novels and little understanding
of the world "as it relates to the writers' purposes" (79). Rather, they
seek to impose a "schema" of universality on these texts, transforming them into harmless and palatable stories intended for middle-class
white America. In *The Color Purple,* Spielberg looks for a feel-good story
about the triumph of good over bad and finds it; Jewison approaches *In
Country* as a Vietnam story and discovers only that. What Spielberg and
Jewison have seen has clearly depended on how they looked.

Why did Spielberg and Jewison approach Walker and Mason with
such expectations? Why, indeed, do many contemporary readers join
them in this approach? Both Walker and Mason have been touted as
major writers, Walker often being cited as a leading black woman writer,
Mason as a prominent southern writer. Walker's southernness—and,
hence, her radical message about African Americans' relationship to
the South—is not noted by many critics and readers. Indeed, Walker
might be much less popular and more taboo if her truly subversive messages were noted; instead, the fairy-tale story Spielberg latched onto and
brought to millions of Americans renders her text powerless but also
accords her greater revenues.

Similarly, though Mason is often cited as one of today's leading southern writers, readers have not read the southern aspects of her work very
carefully. Rather, like Jewison, many readers have been all too willing to
engage only the surface level of her work. As her own metaphor suggests,
however, readers need to "squeeze one layer deeper" to discover all the
richness in her texts. Consequently, Mason's popularity with nonsoutherners (as evidenced by her frequent publication in *The New Yorker*) may
be the result of pervasive misreading. In other words, while northerners
tend not to like more obviously "southern" works—as a northerner will
sometimes put it, "I just can't read any more of that southern shit"[8]—the
surface of Bobbie Ann Mason's texts reinforces what they long to know:
that the South is becoming just like the rest of the nation and is full of
"white trash" who shop at K-Mart. Consequently, many readers think
they "get" Mason when in actuality they have only grasped her often
misleading surface. Again, one suspects that if readers worked harder to
"squeeze one layer deeper" they would find Mason a little more difficult

to swallow and would be forced to confront more complex issues about the South.

Walker's and Mason's "success" as southern women writers, then, can be attributed in part to a pervasive lack of reader comprehension. In filming misreadings of the novels, Spielberg and Jewison are only giving the country what it wants and, in essence, are filming readings of the novels not all that far from the skewed readings of many white northerners. Walker's argument about the relationship of African Americans to the South and Mason's examination of the still-vital relationship between southern identity and (cultural) geography are all but lost in their appropriation by white mainstream America.

As readers who fail to follow the interpretive maps at the centers of Walker's and Mason's novels, Spielberg and Jewison are unfortunately symptomatic of (northern) white male readers in general who misread southern women's texts. The tension between the cultural and social limits placed on women—particularly as artists, writers, and politicians—and between women's need to express themselves as they wish is highlighted in the gulf separating these novels and their film adaptations. If southern women are to have any hope of making their voices heard, they will need to control and own access to media that can provide a vehicle for their voices. Though a few independent filmmakers, such as *Daughters of the Dust* director Julie Dash, are achieving success with visual media, an increasing number of presses owned and/or operated by women and minorities are providing opportunities for southern women's texts to find an audience. Only when southern women writers have full access to publishing and to other media will they be able to counteract the totalizing discourse of reinforcers of dominant ideology like Spielberg and Jewison. Only then can southern women disrupt the master narratives that seek to define and control them and tell instead what Molly Hite calls "the other side of the story."

SIX

THE SOUTHERN WILD ZONE:
VOICES ON THE MARGINS

African women drew
threads through their teeth
and speech began.
A woman's mouth—
language and the loom.
Yet men say a black
woman has no right
to weave herself

a story . . .

I will not shut my mouth.

I file my teeth, sharpen
the points of my loom,
and recall
the origin of language.
    JEANNE LEBOW, "Needle Picture"

We are publishing the fiction, poetry and drama of writers who are working at
the cultural edge, whose writing tends to reshape the way we see the world.
    Catalog for Carolina Wren Press

*S*ince at least the Civil War, southern women have been writing texts
that foreground the sense of talk at the center of southern women's
lives. Mary Chesnut's personal account of life in the Confederate South
is filled with hundreds of pages of women's talk, gossip, and conversation, suggesting that to understand the true story of the Confederacy one
need only listen more attentively to women's voices. Kate Chopin's short
stories, particularly those in the *Bayou Folk* collection (1894), point to

storytelling as a key vehicle for building strong bonds between women, while the powerful and lively self-revelatory talk in Zora Neale Hurston's *Their Eyes Were Watching God* (1937) not only binds women together in deeper friendship but also leads them to greater self-understanding. Images of women talking intimately with each other—in gardens and yards, on the road and on trains, and especially in kitchens—are rife in works such as Elizabeth Madox Roberts's *The Time of Man* (1926), Carson McCullers's *The Member of the Wedding* (1946), Katherine Anne Porter's "Old Mortality" (1937), and Harriette Arnow's *The Dollmaker* (1954). And in novels like *Delta Wedding* (1946), *Losing Battles* (1970), and *The Optimist's Daughter* (1972), Eudora Welty weaves together fragments of stories, bits of conversation, and a general sense of joy and delight, suggesting the lively cacophony at the heart of southern women's talk. From Chesnut to Chopin, from Roberts to Welty, southern women writers weave a verbal quilt of women's talk.

The recent resurgence of southern women's fiction is predicated on the persistent belief that talk constitutes the most significant fact in southern women's experience. The large majority of southern women novelists continue and even expand the emphasis on talk and voice. Toni Cade Bambara's *The Salt Eaters* (1980); Rita Mae Brown's *Six of One* (1978); Dorothy Allison's *Bastard out of Carolina* (1992); Bobbie Ann Mason's *In Country* (1985), as well as her short stories; Alice Walker's *The Color Purple* (1982); Karen Osborne's *Patchwork* (1991); Shay Youngblood's *The Big Mama Stories* (1989); Jill McCorkle's *July 7th* (1984), *Tending to Virginia* (1987), and *Ferris Beach* (1990); Lee Smith's *Oral History* (1983), *Fair and Tender Ladies* (1988), and *The Devil's Dream* (1992); and even Gloria Naylor's southern-influenced *Mama Day* (1988) are just a few of the works that are simultaneously created out of and give life to southern women's voice. Not coincidentally, these works also belong to the current movement of narrative-based fiction, which stands in opposition to the dominant movement of postmodernism. These writers are neither conspicuously experimental in technique nor overtly political in subject matter; thus, they are perceived as being conservative and as removed from the center of contemporary fiction. Postmodernists, on the other hand, engage not only in formal experimentation but also often overtly interrogate basic cultural assumptions and seek to decenter and destabilize political, social, and linguistic authority.

But as Jay Clayton argues, the increasing move toward narrative in minority fiction—and, I would add, in southern women's fiction—is decidedly not a conservative move; instead, it is precisely a subversive move, perhaps even more radical in its intent and effect than the more overtly political fiction of recent postmodernism. Clayton pits traditional narrative and realistic fiction against self-reflexive, metafictional, experimental, postmodernist fiction. Because those who control the dominant discourse define what can be articulated and what constitutes serious literature, the work of white males—primarily postmodernism—is perceived as being at the center of current literary trends, and the work of women and minorities—largely realistic fiction that depends heavily on narrative—is deemed traditional, conservative, old-fashioned. Yet as Clayton points out, narrative is increasingly seen "by novelists today as an oppositional technique because of its association with unauthorized forms of knowledge" (378). And in fact, he goes so far as to claim, "The rich mixture of traditional narrative forms and contemporary political concerns found in minority writing represents the most important force transforming the North American novel of the eighties" (379). The resurgence of southern black and white women writers is playing a similar role in the revitalization of the American novel.

Increasing numbers of critics and writers are beginning, as Clayton points out, to recognize the dynamic power of narrative. Joanne S. Frye's 1986 study, *Living Stories, Telling Lives: Women and the Novel in Contemporary Experience,* foregrounds the particular importance of narrative in women's fiction: "[W]e use the process of creating narrative shape," says Frye, "to identify our place in the world" (19). In other words, we tell stories about our lives to make sense out of them, and because novels are an extension of oral narrative, we can use them to remake our lives (20–21). In its effectiveness as a tool for self-definition, narrative is subversive as it allows women to rewrite the terms of their existence and to seize interpretive and expressive control of their lives. Frye argues, "[A]s novelistic narrative is an agent of interpretation, it becomes as well a possible agent of *re*interpretation, not only giving form but also altering accepted forms" (21). As women give voice to their own narratives, they necessarily disrupt, revise, and replace the male-defined master narrative that seeks to control them.[1] In Molly Hite's words, such subversive narratives tell "the other side of the story."[2]

Women's knowledge, says Toni Morrison, is often "discredited," because "people say it is no more than what women say to each other" (qtd. in McKay 428). Perceived as senseless chitter-chatter by men, women's talk is seen as unimportant and irrelevant. This has presented a particular problem for southern women novelists who place women's talk at the center of their work. The pages and pages of family chatter in *Losing Battles* may frustrate the northern reader who wants Eudora Welty to get on with the story; the southern reader, however, knows that the chatter *is* the story. As countless family members put in their two-cents' worth, as threads of stories get picked up repeatedly by various speakers, and as other speakers make seemingly irrelevant comments, Welty depicts the family dynamics of the Renfro clan and constructs an alternative method of creating knowledge and consensus. Women's talk figures prominently in this, as in so many other southern women's novels. As women tell their stories to one another—whether in the one-on-one conversation between Janie and Pheoby or in the collective talk of McCorkle's Pearson family—they create their own perception of the world and weave alternative responses to dominant male discourse.

Southern women's narrative is subversive in that it seeks to disrupt the prevailing paradigm: it poses a challenge to the accepted story (the master narrative) and seeks to revise and replace that text with the alternative story the master discourse seeks to suppress. Many southern women's texts—black and white—implicitly tell the story of women on the margins of societal power and, consequently, on the fringes of dominant discourse. Increasingly a forum for southern women's discontent, southern women's fiction in its most recent phase suggests that these women are questioning the roles assigned to them and are actively redefining their position in the South. As more and more independent and small presses provide a forum for these disrupting and revisionary voices, they participate in the displacement and replacement of the master narratives that seek to control and obscure southern women's lives. Access to publishing and to wider audiences becomes a final element in giving textual life to southern women's voices.

Unfortunately (though not surprisingly), women—as well as people of color, both male and female—are profoundly underrepresented in both ownership and management of establishment presses. Most southern women—particularly southern women of color—find themselves locked out of the traditional mainstream press, that organ which plays a fundamental role in creating universal standards, both in terms of what can be legitimately articulated and in terms of how it can be articulated. Southern women, therefore, inhabit one of the wildest discourse zones in America. Elaine Showalter defines the "wild zone" as the "spatially, experientially, [and] metaphysically" wild "no-man's-land" of women's discourse ("Feminist Criticism" 262) and shows that, though men's and women's social and cultural experience and expression overlap to a great extent, two thin crescents on either side of this shared experience represent the gendered zones to which the "other" gender does not have access. If we overlay this diagram of gender difference with racial and regional difference as well, we can see that southern women's cultural expression at its deepest levels is relegated to a very thin but very wild zone, densely packed with difference.

On the one hand, then, we have the traditionally silenced voices in the wild zone—that range of women's expression which is unheard, unrealized, denied by those outside the zone—and on the other, we have the increasingly insistent voices in that zone, voices that will not be silenced, voices that demand to be heard. As women and minorities have asserted their right to expression, more and more independent and radical feminist presses have sprung into existence. As Showalter argues, the creation of radical feminist presses is tightly linked to the enaction and articulation of the wild zone ("Feminist Criticism" 263). Therefore, despite formidable obstacles, the last decade has seen a lively resurgence of southern fiction, particularly southern women's fiction, and this resurgence is tied to the corresponding rise of independent and small quality presses in the South.

Among such presses are the more commercial Peachtree (Atlanta),

Longstreet (Marietta, Georgia), and Algonquin Books (Chapel Hill), as well as the radically independent Naiad Press (Tallahassee), Banned Books (Austin), Carolina Wren Press (Carrboro, North Carolina), Crones' Own Press (Durham), and the now-defunct Daughters, Inc., which, though based outside the South, focused on texts by southern lesbians. These smaller publishers seem much more receptive to southern writers—some, such as Algonquin, take that as their primary goal—and tend to support their writers more than do mainstream publishers. In addition to book publishing, the South has also seen a resurgence of journals, bookstores, writers' conferences, and writers' organizations. Periodicals currently published in the South and fostering, at least in part, creative writing by southerners include *The American Voice* (Louisville), *Atalanta* (Atlanta), *Callaloo* (Baton Rouge), *IRIS: A Journal about Women* (Charlottesville), *Kalliope: A Journal of Women's Art* (Jacksonville), *Nkombo* (New Orleans), *Obsidian II* (Raleigh), *Southern Exposure* (Durham), and *Feminary: A Feminist Journal for the South* (Chapel Hill). These small journals and magazines often self-consciously promote southern women writers. Also fostering new southern fiction are the academic and scholarly journals such as *SAGE: A Scholarly Journal on Black Women* (Atlanta), *Sewanee Review* (Sewanee, Tennessee), *Phylon* (Atlanta), *Southern Review* (Baton Rouge), and *Virginia Quarterly* (Charlottesville), which publish creative writing, and *SIGNS* (Durham), *Southern Literary Journal* (Chapel Hill), *Southern Quarterly* (Hattiesburg, Mississippi), and *Mississippi Quarterly* (Starkville), which focus on scholarship and criticism. Rounding out the southern literary scene are bookstores, such as The Regulator in Durham, Oxford Books in Atlanta, and Square Books in Oxford, Mississippi; writers' conferences such as Womonwrites, a southeastern lesbian writers' conference held each June in rural Georgia; and writers' organizations, such as the North Carolina Writers' Network.

Among the smaller, independent presses,[3] feminist presses, especially lesbian presses, have played a key role in the southern literary scene of the last twenty years. Self-publishing feminist presses sprang up all over the United States in the 1970s as part of a general proliferation of small, independent presses. By creating spaces in which all women, regardless of their ethnicity, sexual orientation, class, or region, could express themselves, independent presses helped create a larger mainstream demand for works by women. In many ways, the success of feminist presses partially accounts for the success of major feminist writers, especially those of color, such as Toni Morrison and Alice Walker. Although feminist presses in general have contributed to the stimulation of women's writing, lesbian presses in particular have played a vital role in creating radical space for women's voices. Indeed, Mab Segrest says lesbian-feminists "realized that, to create our own networks to subvert patriarchal culture, we would have to seize some of the means of producing books," and she points specifically to the role of southerners in fostering this "network of feminist presses and journals" in the seventies (57). Daughters, Inc., was one of the earliest lesbian presses, and, though originally located in Vermont, then in New York, and finally in Texas, it was founded by and actively supported the work of southern women writers, including Bertha Harris, June Arnold, and, most significant, Rita Mae Brown. Their publication of Brown's *Rubyfruit Jungle* in 1973 was the first bestseller that a feminist press produced and, in fact, was eventually sold to a large paperback publisher. Though Daughters, Inc., lasted only eight years (from 1972 to 1980), it published many books by southern lesbians and set the tone for other independent southern presses, such as Naiad Press, Banned Books, and Carolina Wren Press, all of which emphasize the political nature of the books they publish.

If southern women writers in general have difficulty getting published and finding an audience, black southern women are in a particularly frustrating position. They inhabit a uniquely dangerous wild zone, a space and a difference that threatens the dominant hegemony. Factors affecting the paucity of published black southern women are myriad. They are not seen as marketable or profitable; they are not in positions of power in the publishing industry or in the larger literary world; if they do get published and even if they achieve "major" status, they may find themselves out of print (as in the case of midwesterner Toni Morrison in the early 1980s); and, perhaps most important, their ability to write at all may be hampered by their socioeconomic oppression. If a black woman does get her work published by the mainstream press, her work is usually not promoted with alacrity or understanding. As black women's works are rejected or mispromoted, "[t]he public . . . is allowed to think that black women are generally incapable of literary creation" (Stetson 89). Worse, black women may themselves internalize this message and wind up engaging in self-censorship. Forbidden by law in the past to read or write, they are now discouraged from believing that what they think, say, and write has worth in the larger society. "[I]t is not," argues Mae G. Henderson, "that black women . . . have had nothing to say, but rather that they have had no say" (24)—and this situation continues largely unabated in the contemporary South.

Independent presses correct this situation to some degree because they publish precisely those volumes mainstream publishers will not touch. Like feminist presses, black independent presses grew out of a growing awareness that the black community must have control over its own voice. Though they have struggled for the small successes they have achieved, the alternative presses have played a crucial role in fostering literature by writers of color: ". . . the most politically incisive and artistically innovative works by black women are usually published by small or alternative presses, and many black women who now experience a measure of general popularity had published two or three volumes privately before their works were accepted by publishers" (Stetson 89). Most important, as Toni Morrison points out, though some books by women of color "get through," these rare publications do not "reflect the numbers of quality writers out there." Independent black presses, Morrison asserts, increase "the chances of women-of-color writers getting published" (qtd. in Moran 38). Although many independent black presses across the country, such as Kitchen Table: Women of Color Press, publish or distribute the work of a few southern women of color, most do not focus on regional writing and instead often see themselves as a vehicle for writers of color throughout the United States.

Yet the record-setting migration of blacks back to the South (Bronstein A1) and an increasing realization that *southern* blacks have something unique to contribute to African-American literature have stimulated an ever livelier black southern artistic community. As blacks move back to the South, they may, as Walker suggests in *The Color Purple,* try to make peace with the region of oppression, to look for wholeness and new ways of articulating and understanding that wholeness. Blacks' increasing interest in the South may finally result in, as Toni Cade Bambara and Leah Wise predicted in 1975, "the new re-emergence . . . of the Southern Black School of Literature." Given the dramatic change in demographic patterns in the South, African Americans' increasing interest in coming to terms with the South, and the generally heightened attention to writers of color throughout the country, the next decade or two should see a sustained and lively resurgence of black writing in the South.

Two presses of particular importance in helping southern women writers—black and white—make their voices heard are Carolina Wren Press, an independent press based near Durham, and Algonquin Books, a small press located in Chapel Hill. Not coincidentally, both presses are situated in or near North Carolina's "Triangle," encompassing Durham, Chapel Hill, and Raleigh, the center of the resurgence in southern fiction. A nonprofit, tax-exempt small publishing house, Carolina Wren Press was founded in 1976 by Judy Hogan. It has a "strong interest in new women's writing," is a particularly "supportive press for black Southern writers" (Frank 95), and stands out in its fusion of community interest and support, on the one hand, and the artist's need for creative expression, on the other. In other words, it actively looks for ways to give expression to voices in the wild zone. Carolina Wren publishes a range of southern women writers as it seeks "to provide an alternative to the books mass-marketed by the commercial presses" (Catalog [7]), among them Gloree Rogers, Margaret Stephens, Judy Hogan, Rebecca Ranson, Randee Russell, Jaki Shelton-Green, and Linda Beatrice Brown. Also important is its anthology of current North Carolina fiction and poetry, entitled *A Living Culture in Durham* (ed. Hogan et al. 1987). The press's publication of Linda Beatrice Brown's *Rainbow Roun Mah Shoulder* (1984) stands as its greatest success (it was later picked up in paperback by Ballantine) and as a prime example of the power of the independent press in giving voice to southern black women writers.

Less political in nature, perhaps, but just as crucial to the vitality of serious fiction in the South, are the small quality presses that emphasize aesthetics over politics. The leader in this regard is Algonquin Books of Chapel Hill, founded by Louis D. Rubin, Jr., in 1983. A division of Workman Publishing in New York, Algonquin is not an independent press but is small and local enough to play a conscientious role in stimulating the southern literary scene. It publishes the work of southern writers such as Jill McCorkle, Dori Sanders, and Kaye Gibbons, as well as Clyde Edgerton, Larry Brown, Margaret Skinner, Kelly Cherry, Jaimy Gordon, Shelly Fraser Mickle, Sylvia Wilkinson, and an impressive collection of nonfiction scholarship in southern studies. It also publishes Shannon Ravenel's yearly anthology, *New Stories from the South: The Year's Best,* probably the single most important ongoing forum for contemporary southern writers. While not as overtly radical as some independent presses, Algonquin is political in the sense that it provides a vehicle for writers locked out of the northern establishment presses. Algonquin's publication of works by southern women writers like McCorkle, Sanders, and Gibbons gives tangible life to voices previously unheard and provides a culturally significant corrective to the myopic male vision of southern women.

Whether the new press in the South is political in its orientation (for example, Naiad Press, Banned Books, and Carolina Wren Press) or whether it seeks to stimulate a resurgence in high-quality southern fiction (Rubin's goal with Algonquin Books), the rise in the number of independent and small presses in the South is directly linked to the increasing number of southern women, black and white, who are currently writing fiction and giving voice to women's experience in the South. Voices in the wild zone—previously unrealized, unheard, and denied—are now given free and unfettered expression; the subversive message at the center of these works, that women's talk is of and in itself revolutionary and revisionary, finds tangible expression in the new southern press.

Linda Beatrice Brown's 1984 novel, *Rainbow Roun Mah Shoulder* (first published under her previous name, Linda Brown Bragg), focuses on a southern woman's gifts of prophecy and healing, on the connections between voice and empowerment, on the creation of alternative community. As such, it falls squarely within the twin African-American traditions of the evangelical woman preacher and the black woman writer. Brown's explicit use of the prophetic tradition and implicit use of the writer-as-prophet tradition allows us to read her novel as a rich allegory of the southern black woman writer's dangerous position both in the dominant culture and within her own community. As protagonist Rebecca Florice confronts and accepts her spiritual gifts, she moves from denying her powers, to reluctantly accepting them, and finally to passing them on to her spiritual granddaughter, Ronnie. This culminating act of engendering spiritual life in Ronnie is a permanent—if single—act of displacement. Well on the road to accepting and using her spiritual powers more actively, Ronnie stands as a direct and dynamic challenge to racist, classist, and sexist oppression in the South. By the end of the novel, Rebecca Florice has given spiritual birth to Ronnie, who will become a more assertive expression of her own voice; in this way, like many other protagonists from African-American women's novels, she moves from "voicelessness to voice, from silence to tongues" (Henderson 24).

Through accepting her spiritual gifts and, by symbolic extension, finding her voice, Rebecca Florice creates a revisioned alternative family of unrelated women. It is only when Rebecca Florice accepts and uses her gifts, only when she allows herself to express her vision in and of the wild zone, that she is able to discover the healing power of revisioned community, the nurturing strength of the matrix. Using her gifts of healing, Rebecca Florice creates an alternative family with Alice, Harriet, and Ronnie, uses her home to create a safe and nurturing space for troubled young women, and conducts herself outside her home as a strong, assertive woman. Thus she authorizes herself and those around her as self-defined, self-empowered women. As bell hooks might say, Rebecca Florice uses her position on the margins of social power and discourse as a "site of resistance, as location of radical openness and possibility" ("Politics" 22). Though voiceless in the dominant culture, she nevertheless finds expression in her own wild zone; though cut adrift from the larger black community and from her own blood family, she discovers and exercises spiritual strength through her alternative family, the weave of women who resist and challenge the southern patriarchy.

Rebecca Florice is not the first African-American woman to weave a tapestry from an increasingly empowered voice, from a mystical sense of alternative spirituality, and from a matrix of loving, supportive women. Though the tradition of black women's subversive and radical discourse finds its roots in the traditional African-American link between religion and rebellion, a particularly radical form of black preaching arose as black women began to assert their own authorization as preachers and evangelicals. In their autobiographies, nineteenth-century black women preachers Jarena Lee, Zilpha Elaw, Julia A. L. Foote, and Rebecca Cox Jackson made literal the connection between black women's preaching and black women's literary self-expression. Moreover, orators and political writers such as Sojourner Truth and Ida B. Wells (who often published her writing in church weeklies) continued to highlight the connections between prophecy, politics, and writing. As women with the gift of prophecy, Lee, Elaw, and Foote were expected to confine themselves to "exhorting," a position that would have relegated them to the lowest rung of the church hierarchy and required them to seek the male minister's permission before doing even that (Andrews, *Sisters* 14). But these women took seriously their calls to preach, and each deliberately and boldly flaunted church policy.

These women's own comments in their autobiographies suggest their profound awareness of their positions on the margins of dominant discourse. "[W]hy should it be thought impossible, heterodox, or improper," asks Jarena Lee, "for a woman to preach?" (36), and she later describes her thwarted desire to preach as "a fire shut up in my bones" (42). Similarly, Zilpha Elaw wonders, "[H]ow can I be a mouth for God!—a poor, coloured female" (89). Likewise, Rebecca Cox Jackson "found 'fellowship' (more accurately 'sistership') among other black women who organized 'praying bands' that met in small groups in each other's house to pray, discuss the scripture and sing, and sustain each other in the arduous task of following the 'true' voice within them" (Walker, "*Gifts of Power*" 76).

As these women became more confident in their preaching and increasingly bold in the range of congregations they would address (Elaw even went on a preaching journey to England), they "began to feel empowered, indeed authorized by God, to listen to and act upon their intuitions, their long-suppressed ambitions, their idealized self-images" (Andrews, *Sisters* 16). This growth toward "authentic, individually authorized selfhood" (16) evolved into a concern with textual authority: "[F]or the spiritual autobiographer," says William Andrews, "appropriating God's word to his or her individual purposes constituted an especially bold form of self-authorization" (1). Andrews, in fact, claims that Jarena Lee, Zilpha Elaw, and Julia Foote were the "foremothers of the black feminist literary tradition in the United States" (22). These women became spiritual and textual leaders, asserting their mystical visions as well as the primacy of their own discourse, speaking from an especially dangerous position within the wildest of zones.

Twentieth-century southern black women's fiction exhibits similar instances of black women longing for or seizing authority to speak. As I have noted throughout this study and as many other scholars have noted, Hurston's *Their Eyes Were Watching God* depicts Janie's self-authorizing narrative of the events in her life and her increasingly self-empowered response to them. But Janie's desire to seize linguistic authority does not spring up in isolation; rather, it stems from her grandmother's yearning to control the text of her own life. As Nanny tells Janie early in the novel, "Ah wanted to preach a great sermon about colored women sittin' on high, but they wasn't no pulpit for me" (15). Though Nanny in many other ways oppresses, even abuses, Janie, here she passes on a legacy of frustrated voicelessness to her granddaughter, telling her that she has "save[d] de text for you" (16). Nanny never gets the chance to preach her sermon, to gain her voice, but her granddaughter does seize linguistic authority and moves from "voicelessness to voice, from silence to tongues."

Hurston's literary granddaughter, Alice Walker, also foregrounds the issue of black women's voices, both those silenced (as in *The Color Purple*) and those that find a vehicle for expression. Perhaps there is no greater example of the latter than her second novel, *Meridian* (1976), which weaves together many stories of strong, resisting southern black women—among them the slave, Louvinie, who had her tongue cut out because she told her master's children such a chilling horror story that one of the children was literally scared to death. Louvinie knew that "[w]ithout one's tongue in one's mouth or in a special spot of one's choosing, the singer in one's soul [is] lost forever to grunt and snort through eternity like a pig" (44). Therefore, she chose to plant the tongue under a "scrawny" magnolia tree on the plantation and thus to make an active choice about the fate of her tongue—both literally and figuratively. Her "tongue" indeed spread her message of subversion decades after her death. "Other slaves," writes Walker, "believed it [the tree] possessed magic. They claimed the tree could talk, make music, was sacred to birds and possessed the power to obscure vision" (44). Most significant, "[o]nce in its branches, a hiding slave could not be seen" (44). The power of Louvinie's tongue and the Sojourner tree (as it was named) still resonated in the mid-twentieth century, as students at the college that was built on the site of the Saxon plantation continued to revere it. In this brief story of Louvinie and the Sojourner tree, Walker evokes the dangers and possibilities of black women's discourse.

Building on the traditions of the black female evangelists/autobiographers as well as on the fictional images of black women's voices on the margins, Linda Beatrice Brown's *Rainbow Roun Mah Shoulder* traces the connections between black women's spirituality and the bold claims of their writing, between women's unfettered expression and the creation of revisioned community. A woman of "tall spirit" (3) and "controlled raging" (2), "the real priest" according to her friend Father Theodore (5), Rebecca Florice is overwhelmed by the astonishing power and sheer enormity of her spiritual gifts of prophecy. Throughout the novel, Brown implies that "prophecy" can include both the gift of seeing the future (or seeing what to most people is invisible) and the gift of healing. In this regard, Rebecca Florice can be seen in the rich history of fictional women healers and prophets—Gloria Naylor's Mama Day, Toni Morrison's Baby Suggs, Julie Dash's Nana Peazant, Lee Smith's Granny Younger and Rhoda Hibbitts, Toni Cade Bambara's Minnie Ransom, and Kaye Gibbons's Charlie Kate. Though her gifted goddaughter Ronnie seems to have a much stronger gift for "seeing" (she can, for example, see that "Miss Florice carries the light . . . in a circle hangin' on her arm" [144]), it is the gift of healing that is more pronounced in Rebecca Florice. Her reluctant acceptance of this power prompts a string of occasional and secret healings, such as her first "patient," a man with syphilis who simply shows up at her door saying he sensed she had "the gift" (27), and later a boy who has been bitten by a snake (88–90). Significantly, Rebecca Florice first becomes aware of her abilities when "the words [are] given" to her: "Blessed with power. You. Blessed with power. Heal. Heal and love. You are blessed with power. . . . Rain on the vine. Spill the rain and be at peace. Rain on the vine. Who was to be for others a fountain, let the waters flow" (7–8).

Though she has been given a rich and powerful gift, its price is very high: the community suppresses, rejects, and fears the mysterious Rebecca Florice, and as a result she herself silences the gift. The gift creates an unbridgeable chasm between Rebecca Florice and her husband, Mac, who misunderstands, fears, and rejects her deep and wild spirituality. Similarly, the entire community distrusts her; she has to defend herself silently against those in her church who accuse her of playing with the Devil, has to hide her gifts in fear of being discovered and run out of town, and so finds herself always on the "outside of one thing or another" (33). Because of her powers, traditional marriage is denied to her; though she deeply loves Robert, a married minister, and though he loves her and encourages her gift, he is nevertheless terrified of surrendering completely to their love. The strangeness of her abilities engenders fear and distrust in the people around her; she becomes the archetypal witch whose capacity for power and healing relegates her to the fringes of her community, the margins of social power and discourse.

In reaction to this community oppression and, in fact, because of her own fear of her spiritual powers, Rebecca Florice hides and disguises her acts of healing and thus oppresses and silences herself. Much of the novel details her embattled relationship with her spirituality. Each time the gift makes itself known to her, she tries to push it away. As she prepares to leave New Orleans and move to a new life in North Carolina, for example, the gift manifests itself "against her will": "the sun beg[ins] to shine on the inside," and she responds by "rock[ing] in a rhythm of disbelief and overwhelming love for the fear [of the gift]" (7). Whether in the inner pain they engender, in the tension they cause between the prophet and her loved ones, or in the positioning of the prophet on the "outside" of community power and social discourse, spiritual gifts clearly come at a high price.

Not until Rebecca Florice can accept her spiritual gifts and express her wild vision of life from the margins of societal discourse, that is, not until she finds and uses her symbolic voice, can the true healing power of her gift be made known. While she never fully accepts the gift, she nevertheless does find ways to express it and to experience it throughout her life—particularly in her creation of an herb garden and in her construction of home as a site of resistance. When she moves from New Orleans to North Carolina, she brings her herbs with her, "intending to replant her herb garden wherever they ended up staying" (16). Rebecca Florice is said to be "uncommonly good with plants," and folks in her community notice that there is "something about her garden that [is] special" (17). Her "lush garden" is filled with all types of healing and soothing herbs: "fennel seed, thyme, allspice, basil, rosemary, mace, nutmeg, mint, parsley, and sweet false chamomile" (17). Wherever she lives, Rebecca Florice always plants her herb garden, using it to tend to those around her who are ailing: she "soothed the mind with presence of Spirit, and the body with innumerable cups of herbal tea. She provided a warm shoulder and a cool head. The herbs were now in the backyard of the rooming house and everyone who lived there felt welcomed by the sight of Miss Florice's herbal garden" (53). Rebecca Florice—"she of the mysterious lore and herbs that made others whole" (65)—tends her garden and tills her soil, finding a way to use her gift to heal and nurture others.

Although she spends many of her years living with family members or in temporary rooming houses, Rebecca Florice is finally "given" a house on the college campus where she cooks. She is asked to become a caretaker for the campus house and to use it as a place of refuge for troubled women students. In this capacity, the house becomes a radical extension of her herb garden and an even more important site for healing and wholeness, a place where Rebecca Florice can provide a "little mothering" (58) to young women. Her first such student is Harriet, who is young, pregnant, and scared. She stays with Rebecca Florice for two weeks, during which time Rebecca Florice nurtures her, listens to her, and counsels her. Here, as in other instances, not only is the "patient" healed and made whole, but the sense of women's community is also expanded and strengthened. Through this act of healing and nurturing, Harriet becomes a key person in Rebecca Florice's evolving circle of close women friends, and the result of this pregnancy is Ronnie, who becomes Rebecca Florice's spiritual granddaughter. Rebecca Florice's house thereby becomes an empowering "site of resistance," mirroring other southern women's homes—from Ellen Chesser's "snug dry room" to the Peazant family's natural sanctuary, from Edna Pontellier's "pigeon house" to Virginia's grandmother's house, where "the history and knowledge are solid." But it is here, in Rebecca Florice's house, that bell hooks's description of women's space becomes most evident: "[H]ouses belonged to women, were their special domain . . . , places where all that truly mattered in life took place—the warmth and comfort of shelter, the feeding of our bodies, the nurturing of our souls" ("Homeplace" 41). Rebecca Florice's house is, in every sense, a site of resistance and empowerment, a place where "family" members are nurtured, fed, and comforted.

Through her creation of her herb garden and her construction of home as a site of resistance, Rebecca Florice finds ways of expressing her inner spirituality, of accepting the wildness of her life on the fringe. Only when she allows herself this access to the power of her gift, to the challenge of her voice, can community be revisioned. Finding it impossible to live in a traditional marriage, she remains single most of her life and expresses her love and maternal instincts through the creation of a symbolic kin network, much like the one Youngblood depicts in *The Big Mama Stories*. Her "family" consists of Alice, her best friend; of Harriet, the young female student she heals and befriends; and Ronnie, Harriet's daughter and Rebecca Florice's goddaughter and spiritual granddaughter. Other "sometime" members of the family include Peaches, a troubled woman who has been ostracized by the larger African-American community;

Maye, Alice's daughter, who is raped and psychologically destroyed by a white man; and a young foster child whom Rebecca Florice suspects is Alice's grandson. In her relationships with these women and children, Rebecca Florice tends to their physical and psychological needs, avenges wrongs against them as necessary (as when she severely attacks Maye's rapist in his sleep), and constructs a living circle of love, a matrix of female empowerment.

The revisionary dimension of this community is made especially clear during those moments when Rebecca Florice uses her domestic space, her voice, her gift to avenge and counter the brutal hurts against black women's bodies and souls. In this way, she actively rewrites community, dismantling patriarchal brutality and substituting the secret discourse of the matrix. Perhaps her most subversive use of her spiritual gifts comes in her relationship with Peaches, a woman whom the black community ostracizes and ridicules. Always one to look out for the underdog, Rebecca Florice reaches out to Peaches with the healing power of love and friendship. When Ronnie discovers the bones of a hand in Peaches's shed, and when Rebecca Florice recalls the unsolved murder of a white woman whose hand had been chopped off, she realizes that Peaches killed her employer in cold blood. Rather than turn her in, however, Rebecca Florice decides to find out if love and friendship have indeed healed Peaches's soul. She causes Peaches's dog to run off; though the dog is the only thing she can truly call her own, and though she grieves deeply, Peaches stops short of murdering Rebecca Florice in her anger and hurt. Rebecca Florice knows that if Peaches will not murder in this instance, she will never murder again. Convinced that Peaches has passed the test, Rebecca Florice disposes of the bones so that no one will ever know the truth. This scene parallels a similar scene in Gibbons's *A Cure for Dreams* and suggests that women on the margins—Rebecca Florice and Ronnie—can read the signs of other marginalized women in pain. It also shows Rebecca Florice's subversive use of her gifts, as she suppresses the facts of Peaches's transgression against the community. Rather than deferring authority to the police, she takes the matter into her own hands, leaving Peaches on the road to psychological recovery and, she presumes, the community in an unthreatened position. In this way, she literally redefines Peaches's position in the community and rewrites community on her own terms.

Rebecca Florice's final use of her spiritual gift to revision community is also its most permanent use: she passes it on to Ronnie, who as a member of a younger generation will be able to make bolder use of it. As she teaches Ronnie spiritual lessons, she passes onto her spiritual granddaughter not only her own gift but also, by symbolic extension, her voice as well. Now her gift has taken on a generative power, creating new spiritual life in Ronnie; in this way, her voice, like Elizabeth Madox Roberts's children, continues forever and ever. Significantly, during their final moments together, Rebecca Florice passes on her lessons to Ronnie through a song, underscoring the expressive dimensions of this gift:

> Evahwhuh I, whuh I look dis mawnin
> Looks lak rain, looks lak rain.
> I gotta rainbow, tied all roun mah shoulder
> Ain gonna rain, ain gonna rain.
> I'm gonna break right, break right pas dat shooter
> I'm goin home, Lawd, I'm goin home.
> I gotta rainbow, tied all roun mah shoulder
> Ain gonna rain, ain gonna rain.
>
> (159)

In this final lesson, Rebecca Florice initiates Ronnie into the weave of women, telling her, "[Y]ou're almost sixteen now, almost a woman" (159), paralleling the moment of womanly initiation the narrator of *The Big Mama Stories* experiences. As she welcomes Ronnie into the nurturing matrix of female empowerment, Rebecca Florice also gives Ronnie advice about her spiritual gift. She tells her that she will have to "hear" the gift through her "inside" ear (136), echoing Alice Walker's description of Rebecca Cox Jackson and other "sisters of the spirit" who "sustain[ed] each other in the arduous task of following the 'true' voice within them" ("*Gifts of Power*" 76). And in urging Ronnie to accept and use her gift, Rebecca Florice implicitly encourages her, like Jarena Lee, to release the "fire in her bones" (Lee 42). While Jarena Lee, Rebecca

Florice, and countless others like them had their voices silenced and had
to ask why it should "be thought impossible, heterodox, or improper
for a woman to preach" (Lee 36), Ronnie and southern black women
of her generation may find more opportunities for "preaching," writing,
and releasing the fire inside them.

Rebecca Florice teaches Ronnie that, because the world—and the
South—is changing, Ronnie may be better able to accept her gift and to
let it flourish in a revisioned spiritual garden. Tellingly, Rebecca Florice
concludes by saying, "You know, Ronnie, God gave me a great opportunity to serve, but I don't think I ever saw it all the way through. . . .
I guess I did the best I could; it was never easy for me, but maybe it'll
be easier for you. It's a different world now. Things are changin' fast"
(158). Here, Rebecca Florice positions herself with previous generations
of black women prophets and poets silenced both by society and by
themselves; at the same time, this southern "grandmother" recognizes
Ronnie as an exemplum of the younger generation who will make itself
heard. The younger generation—successors to a long tradition of attempts at disruption and revision—makes that revision permanent, as
it displaces the prior story of cultural hegemony, making room for the
stories, voices, and spiritual and political visions of those in the wildest
zone of gender, racial, and regional difference.

Rebecca Florice has seen the possibilities for claiming one's spiritual gifts, for sounding one's voice, for revisioning community, and for
making that revision permanent and ongoing. Despite these lessons and
despite the loving alternative family she has created for herself, on some
level Rebecca Florice remains the solitary, isolated witch-prophetess, the
wild seer on the margins, the lone individual crying in the wilderness.
This is made clear in the two most important moments in her own personal encounter with the spiritual gift of prophecy and healing. Early
in the novel, when she realizes that she will finally have to confront her
gift, she goes with her husband to Bear Island in North Carolina. As
she makes the decision to choose the gift over her husband, she thinks
to herself, "[H]ere I stand in the wilderness" (11). When her husband
abandons her and she is stranded on the island for the night, she wraps
herself up and sleeps out in the open.

Years later, aware that she is dying, Rebecca Florice returns to Bear Island to relinquish her spirit to God. She has taken care of her earthly business: she has taught Ronnie her final lesson, made sure that Ronnie will inherit a house of her own in the North, and visited Robert and made her peace with him. Now she is ready to tend to her spiritual business. As she prepares for the ending of her life, she thinks back through her mother, reaching back to the initial womb of life: "She thought of her mother for the first time in a long time. Her mother. New Orleans. Darkness" (160–61). Longing to become one with the womb again, to merge with the rich fecund darkness, with the nurturing power of her mother, she travels back to the exact spot on Bear Island where she had accepted her spiritual gifts so many years before, where she had rejected worldly concerns and opened herself to the cosmic and mystical dimensions of life:

> The great water was a composition of softness. Gray, white, ivory, tan, a bell sound of silver outlined the waves, and they spoke of a gentle and grand music underlaid by the mother heart which never rests. . . .
>
> The wind had become quite cold. There was a small sheltered cove not far ahead. Just before the steel-colored clouds disappeared into blackness, Rebecca Florice settled into a slight depression in the sand. The Light around her shoulders rose to a crystalline incandescence, faded gently, and went out. (168)

Having returned to the natural landscape, Rebecca Florice, much like Edna Pontellier, achieves one final merge with Mother Earth and travels back into her own wild feminine essence. Having healed others— through her herb garden, her house, her weave of women, her sharing of the gift, and the bold expression of her symbolic voice—Rebecca Florice now settles into her own empowering, if final, moment of life, settles into and returns to the cosmic womb.

Although Algonquin Books has been one of the strongest catalysts in the second Southern Renaissance, perhaps no Algonquin writer articulates and enacts the subversive southern woman's voice better than Kaye Gibbons. Gibbons is an exceptionally prolific young writer, having published four successful novels: *Ellen Foster* (1987), *A Virtuous Woman* (1989), *A Cure for Dreams* (1991), and *Charms for the Easy Life* (1993), the first three published by Algonquin, the latest by Putnam, signalling her acceptance by the mainstream publishing establishment. Where McCorkle's *Tending to Virginia* (1987) foregrounded the ways in which women form empowering networks through talking to one another, Gibbons's *A Cure for Dreams* takes this idea one step further, showing the ways in which women not only create empowering networks through talk but also use these networks and this talk to subvert the men who would control them and to define in radical measures the terms of their existence. *A Cure for Dreams* opens space not only for women's voice but also for the alternative structures of women's networks. At the same time, it juxtaposes male misreadings of women's subversive texts with women's perceptive readings of these same texts. Gibbons depicts a world in which men are at best irrelevant, at worst abusive—and centers her vision on the women in the family and in the community, looking to them for the primary text of southern life in the first half of the twentieth century.

Gibbons herself highlights her position as an Algonquin writer in her dedication (to Louis D. Rubin, Jr., the press's founder and one of the most significant presences in southern literary scholarship), in her personal life (naming her youngest daughter, Louise, after Rubin), and implicitly in her epigraph, which is taken from a comment by W. T. Couch, the regional director of the Federal Writers Project: "With all our talk of democracy it seems not inappropriate to let the people speak for themselves." These extratextual references alert the perceptive and knowledgeable reader not only to Gibbons's exceptional gratitude to Rubin—the first professor who exposed her to southern literature and the first and most important person to have encouraged her writing— but also to the fact that her text can be taken as a literal enactment of the power of Algonquin Books. Like the WPA documents—from which Gibbons draws heavily in *A Cure for Dreams* and especially in *Charms for the Easy Life*—Algonquin and its writers give voice to people whose stories have not been heard before, and, even more than the WPA, the press foregrounds women's voices and places them at the center of this new democratization of southern literature. Gibbons and, by extension, all of the other southern women writers published by Algonquin and other independent and small presses are not only speaking for themselves but are also giving voice to characters who have rarely been heard from before.[4]

A Cure for Dreams tells the story of four generations of women—Bridget O'Cadhain, Lottie O'Cadhain Davies, Betty Davies Randolph, and Marjorie Polly Randolph. The connection between all mothers and daughters in this novel is made clear from the outset, as Marjorie begins the novel with a nested family tree, similar in spirit to those provided by McCorkle and Youngblood as the dedications to their texts. The novel's structure also indicates the multigenerational matrix, the layers of women's experience. Marjorie provides a very brief preface, in which she introduces a kind of oral transcription of the stories told to her by her mother Betty, who has just died. The bulk of the novel is Betty's, as she tells her mother Lottie's story and as she frequently incorporates bits and pieces of Lottie's verbal (italicized) text. In reporting what Lottie told her, Betty also includes Bridget's history. The novel ends with the story of Marjorie's "wild" birth and with a brief concluding commentary from Marjorie.

In its weaving together of women's stories, *A Cure for Dreams* stands as a contemporary example of the connections between quilting and American women's fiction Elaine Showalter outlines in "Piecing and Writing." According to Showalter, "[T]he process of making a patchwork quilt involves three separate stages of artistic composition" (223): piecing, patchwork, and quilting. Gibbons uses these processes to create her own verbal quilt, piecing together narratives from Marjorie, Betty, and Lottie, patching together an episodic structure built on the rhythms of women's daily lives, and quilting all this into one figure that suggests the organic matrix of female empowerment. Showalter goes on in her essay to say that theories of a feminine aesthetic have used "the metaphor of piecing . . . as a model for the organization of language in the wild zone of the woman's text" (226), and she quotes Rachel Blau DuPlessis as describing "a pure women's writing" as one that would be "nonhierarchic . . . breaking hierarchical structures, making an even display of elements over the surface with no climactic place or moment, having the materials organized into many centers" (226–27). Such is the case with *A Cure for Dreams,* which rejects linear male narratives defined by the "external" world and which instead embraces a more circular, decentered, quiltlike narrative, which begins with a mother's death and ends with a daughter's birth.

The novel's structure, narrative technique, key scenes, and depiction of women's relationships with each other and with men create a text that challenges traditional male readings of southern women and suggests the web of female empowerment, the matrix that has the power to disrupt and to counter the southern patriarchy. In her fusion of the quilt and the matrix, storytelling and empowerment, Gibbons echoes the work of other contemporary artists, among them painter and fiber artist Faith Ringgold, whose story quilts fuse narrative, painting, and quilting to tell tales of resistance and empowerment;[5] poet Jeanne Lebow, whose 1991 volume *The Outlaw James Copeland and the Champion-Belted Empress* foregrounds the connections between speaking and weaving, between "language and the loom" ("Needle Picture" 3); Karen Osborne and Whitney Otto, whose novels, *Patchwork* (1991) and *How To Make an American Quilt* (1991), respectively, piece together stories of female family members; and Alice Walker, whose evocative and lyrical account of women's creativity, of quilts, stories, and gardens, stands as one of the seminal essays in the developing theory of female aesthetics. All of these artists—whether southern or nonsouthern, black or white—make clear the empowering dimension of the quilt, the story, and weaves of women, but the subversive element of quilting, of textual control and linguistic authority, of women's relationships with each other, are often only implied. In this light, the words of Radka Donnell-Vogt, a Bulgarian quilt maker, are instructive: "I saw quilts as the bliss and the threat of the womb made visible, spread out as a separate object shaped by the imaginative wealth of women's work and body experience" (qtd. in Showalter 226). Like Donnell-Vogt's quilts, *A Cure for Dreams* makes tangible both "the bliss and the threat of the womb," the empowerment the matrix affords women as well as the subversive challenge it represents to the patriarchy.

In highlighting the "bliss" of the matrix, Gibbons repeatedly calls attention to the centrality of women's voices in southern discourse. In talking to each other, these women weave a fabric of resistance and strength, a fabric that is consistently empowering. The opening and closing of the novel—the threads holding the verbal quilt together— highlight the central role of women's talk and alert the reader to the fact that the novel is an explicit articulation of the wild zone. Marjorie initiates the novel's narrative by foregrounding the essential connection between her mother, Betty, and talk:

> To tell the truth, she died in a chair talking, chattering like a string- pull doll. I had spent my life listening to her, sometimes all day, which often was my pleasure during snow and long rains. I would need only say to her, Tell me about your mother and you, and Ken- tucky and Virginia and the wild way I was born. Tell me about the years that made you.
>   Then she would talk. Talking was my mother's life. (1).

Betty is a vivid and empowered talker, who passes on to her daughter the gifts of textual control and linguistic authority she inherited from *her* mother Lottie. Likewise, the novel's ending foregrounds the multi- generational, matrix-defined, ongoing conversation between the women. On the last page of the novel, Marjorie recounts her first memory. Be- cause her father is serving in the Navy during World War II, her first two years are spent in the company of her mother, her grandmother, and their black housekeeper, Polly. "I wish I could say that my first memory is of my father coming through the door," reports Marjorie,

> but I can't. The first true memory is sound. All sorts of sounds above my cradle, maybe moving with shadows of hands and shoul- ders, maybe my mother's face shape. But certainly there were the sounds, faint and loud and then shrill. Then, Hush! She's sleeping. Let her sleep.
>   But I wasn't sleeping, not for the sounds of the women talk- ing. (171)

Here, as throughout the novel, women's identity is shaped by "the sounds of the women talking," and because the novel ends, the primacy of women's discourse is underscored once again. The lives of Marjorie, Betty, and Lottie are defined, shared, and expressed within the wild zone, the "no-man's-land" of women's discourse.

Women's talk, then, allows these women the "bliss" of defining themselves, but it is also able to express the "threat" of the matrix as they band together in resistance against the southern patriarchy. In a typical scene, Betty tells of her early memories of her father, of her embattled relationship with him, and of his attempts to tear the weave of women apart:

> I remember one afternoon sitting on a rug, drawing pictures out of a book and enjoying my mother chitter-chattering when he came in from work. When the door closed behind him, I thought, He's come home to ruin our day. I assumed this was his intention. This was my first original thought of my father. (15)

Like her own daughter who will be unable to remember her first meeting with her father (because it is not particularly significant to her) and who will instead define herself by her earliest memories of women's talk, so Betty delights in her mother's "chitter-chattering," while simultaneously rejecting her father because of his threat to "ruin" their world. But Lottie constructs her world so that Charles has little real power in it, and thus his attempts to "ruin" their world are unsuccessful. Here, the "threat" and the power of the matrix becomes clear, as Lottie and Betty defiantly create a separate if parallel life to the one Charles leads.

Lottie constantly schemes to get her own way, to maintain the upper (though unseen) hand in her household, and to assert her own vision of life. When the unemployed Charles begins to spend more time at home, he is incensed at the life he discovers Lottie and Betty leading. Betty recalls:

> He was frenzied by the sight of my mother and I waking up and taking out our rollers, dressing in something clean and pretty, though old, and heading out to take our constitutional. My mother used to scream and tell him we'd been going through the same motions since my hair was long enough to hold a curl, and he'd merely missed it.

. . . *[N]ow you're here to witness our daily habits, which are none*
of your business and cost you nothing. We'll not stay in the house all
day. You stay here! We're bored! And what's it costing you, anyway?
(69–70)

This passage not only speaks to Lottie's insistence on defining the terms
of her own existence ("our daily habits . . . are none of your business")
but also to Charles's lifelong inability to read the situation accurately
(Lottie and Betty have been doing this all along and "he'd merely missed
it"). Ultimately, Charles becomes so frustrated and disempowered that
he commits suicide, leaving them with no insurance money and no other
financial security. Yet Lottie and Betty rebound quite gracefully from
what could have been a cataclysmic event and instead relish even more
their self-definition. By the time Marjorie comes on the scene, Lottie,
Betty, and Polly have created a warm, loving, nurturing household defined totally by women. Moreover, Lottie extends the "bliss and threat of
the womb" outside her home to the larger community, where she forms
a weekly rummy club for women, providing a forum for women's talk,
the sharing of secrets, and defiance against the rules imposed upon them
at home.

If *A Cure for Dreams* is a verbal quilt, a womb of "bliss" and "threat,"
it is woven together from scraps of women's conversations, from the
matrix of relationships between women, from the multigenerational connections between Marjorie, Betty, and Lottie, from women's subversive
and radical expression within the wild zone, and from the men's inability to understand women's wild voices. And if one were to pinpoint
the center square of this quilt/novel, to locate the episode, the piece,
that most fully articulates all of these concerns, one might choose chapter 5, which tells the story of Sade, one of the women in the rummy
club. The very title of this chapter—"An account of things which heretofore were unsaid, or a lesson for the tardy"—foregrounds the secret
discourse embedded in the chapter and, if the chapter is taken as the
center square of the novel, might suggest that the entire novel is "an
account of things which heretofore were unsaid." In other words, this
chapter—in its themes, images, and title—reminds us that Gibbons and
her characters are speaking from the wild zone.

In this chapter, Sade's husband Roy has just been murdered, and Sade has asked John Carroll, part-time deputy sheriff, to bring Lottie along with him, presumably to comfort and take care of Sade. In a masterful reworking of Susan Glaspell's play *Trifles*,[6] Gibbons details Lottie's discovery of the fact that Sade herself has murdered her husband. Lottie's clues include Sade's dirty dinner plate, Roy's clean plate, the tiny sliver missing from Sade's fresh and "lavish" pie, the absence of briar picks from Sade's stockings (though she says she has been out walking), and Sade's wailing that Lottie can tell is not *"the cry of a woman startled by death or relieved that it has finally come"* (43). Most compelling is the clue that Sade's quilt provides. Just as Mrs. Hale and Mrs. Peters in *Trifles* read the wild stitching of Mrs. Wright's quilt, so too Lottie can see that *"[a] woman would have to be extremely disturbed to sew that raggedly, and she would have to be sheerly distracted out of her mind to leave this slipshod stitching in"* (42). And just like Mrs. Hale and Mrs. Peters in the Glaspell play, Lottie "pull[s] out the ugly stitches and fixe[s] them right, listening all the time to Sade wailing in the kitchen" (42–43).

While Lottie is "inside fixing Sade chamomile tea and getting ideas" (42), John Carroll is "outside looking for his clues" (41). Like the men in *Trifles,* John's position as a male severely limits his ability to read Sade's text. He concentrates on "searching for bullet casings and footprints and all the other kinds of things a man would naturally look for" (41–42), but he is unable to see, as Lottie does, "everything that had taken place" (43). Betty states:

> He didn't know to examine cotton stockings for briar picks, and he didn't know how to see and judge clean and dirty plates, slivers of cut pie, wild stitches, and wailing. This had more to do with the fact that he was full-time male than it did with the fact that he was merely part-time deputy and neither bright nor curious. Details escaped him. (46)

Like Charles, and like most men throughout the South (and beyond), John Carroll is unable to read women's texts. As Annette Kolodny notes, Glaspell's text shows us that man "is a *different kind* of reader and that, where women are concerned, he is often an inadequate reader" (57; her emphasis). Moreover, "lacking familiarity with the women's imaginative universe, that universe within which their acts are signs, the men [in Glaspell's text] can neither read nor comprehend the meanings of the women closest to them" (58). Clearly, Gibbons means to make a similar argument about men's failed readings of women's texts.

Kolodny goes one step further to link the men's failed readings of women's texts to the essential dilemma of women writers. If women and men share a common language, yet are unable to read each other's texts accurately, and if men control the means of linguistic production, women writers will continue—as they have for so long in the past—to be misread, demeaned, ignored, and rendered invisible by their male peers. The power of women's texts to assert an alternative to the dominant hegemony, however, is also suggested by this key scene in Gibbons's novel. Though the last few stitches of Sade's quilting are "very wild and uneven and [make] no sense at all" (42), they nevertheless do create a text and do inscribe the pain and wild despair that Sade felt. They articulate her experience, so precisely, in fact, that Lottie can reconstruct in her mind the events that led up to Roy's murder. And when Lottie pulls out the old stitching and repairs it, she seals the pact of women's discourse, while presenting a safer text for male consumption. Like Rebecca Florice in *Rainbow Roun Mah Shoulder,* Lottie covers up the murder because she knows that it is a single act of self-preservation in the face of abuse and brutality. Sade and Lottie never speak of "the fixed reckless stitching" (48), of Lottie's comprehension—and rewriting—of Sade's dangerous text. And significantly, for all her love of talk, Lottie does not reveal Sade's secret to anyone for years. Eventually, she tells Betty, but makes Betty "swear not to tell, which was like asking me to carry a bomb in my mouth" (41). After this, both Lottie and Betty keep the secret until after Sade's death, but now Betty "can be free to tell" Sade's story to her daughter, Marjorie (41).

Sade's creation of a dangerous text, Lottie's accurate reading of the text and her rewriting of it to conceal the true power that lies within it, and Sade's eventual decision to display the quilt proudly in the parlor she has made out of Roy's old room—all show the power of women's text and the centrality of southern women's discourse, particularly as a tool for understanding and communicating with one another. And, in her conscious recuperation of Glaspell's play, Gibbons signifies on this paradigmatic feminist text so that the scene between Lottie and Sade resonates across literary generations. Just as Marjorie and Betty think back through their biological mothers, so Gibbons thinks back through Glaspell, one of her literary mothers. As she quilts her own narrative, she weaves in this "scrap" from Glaspell, using it as the center square for her own quilt, the square that makes clear the pattern and intent of the whole quilt. In this way, she provides another dimension to the ongoing lineage of women telling stories to women, speaking to and for each other.

Gibbons's emphasis on quilts is crucial to understanding her novel, for, as numerous writers and critics have shown, quilts constitute a particularly powerful symbol of women's text—both literally as women's creation of textile and figuratively as women's articulation of alternative text. The anonymous 1845 essay by a factory girl, "The Patchwork Quilt," makes clear the secret discourse embedded in the text of a woman's quilt. "Annette" writes,

> [T]here is the PATCHWORK QUILT! looking to the uninterested observer like a miscellaneous collection of odd bits and ends of calico, but to me it is a precious reliquary of past treasures; a storehouse of valuables, almost destitute of intrinsic worth; a herbarium of withered flowers; a bound volume of hieroglyphics, each of which is a key to some painful or pleasant remembrance. (150)

An "uninterested observer" will be unable to read this text successfully and will instead perceive it as "a miscellaneous collection of odd bits and ends," much as the unsympathetic reader of southern women's novels will be frustrated by the rambling chitter-chatter at the center of these works. The careful reader of the quilt and of the southern woman's novel, however, will be able to discern the "treasures," the "valuables," the "painful or pleasant remembrance[s]" embedded in these women's texts. To the unsympathetic reader, the quilt/novel is "a bound volume of hieroglyphics"; to the careful reader, however, it is a revealing tapestry.[7]

A revealing tapestry, *A Cure for Dreams* becomes a paradigmatic text of the current generation of southern women novelists; it is a tangible realization of the wild zone—of women's subversive and radical expression within that zone and men's inability to read that wild expression accurately. Paradoxically, it is the southern woman's very position on the margins of dominant discourse that allows her to subvert that discourse. Relegated to the wildest zone of gender, regional, and sometimes racial difference, southern women writers inhabit the thinnest margin of dominant discourse—a position that often renders them unheard but that also has the potential to empower them in their resistance. Aligning herself with "a wild crowd of known and unknown folks" (19), bell hooks argues that many contemporary women writers and writers of color choose "counter-hegemonic marginal space" as the "site of resistance, as location of radical openness and possibility" ("Politics" 22)— and that this site of resistance is often the woman's home. The rejection of postmodernist metafiction and the simultaneous embrace of realistic narrative is not a rejection of experimentation and politicization per se but, rather, a rejection of the totalizing discourse that obscures and denies the real experiences of women. Choosing to write from a position of marginality and to foreground narrative and storytelling, southern women novelists provide radical, resistant vehicles for southern women's voices.

CONCLUSION
AND ACKNOWLEDGMENTS

These narratives seek to bring us back to our own lives, to our own
female families' experiences, through immersion within their communal
language, and their specifically feminine vision of creativity. . . . The
writers bring us as readers into an ongoing lineage of women. They
challenge us . . . to examine our own histories, to restore our collective
past as women, to rewrite cultural narratives of female victimization and
marginality. . . . At last, we find in these women writers the joining of
our own experience of our female families. We find that the weariness
and the frustrations of our mothers had meaning that joins their life to
ours, allowing us to salvage their wisdom and their creativity from
portrayals of victimization, to acknowledge and reclaim our own past as
their daughters.

HELEN LEVY, *Fiction of the Home Place*

. . . so many of the stories that I write, that we all write, are my mother's
stories. . . . [T]hrough years of listening to my mother's stories of her
life, I have absorbed not only the stories themselves, but something of
the urgency that involves the knowledge that her stories—like her life—
must be recorded.

ALICE WALKER, "In Search of Our Mothers' Gardens"

A woman writing, to paraphrase Virginia Woolf, thinks back
through her mothers. Such has been the case for me in writing this
book. Like many of the characters in the novels discussed here, I have
found my own voice by recuperating the voices of my female ancestors.
Their stories, triumphs, and disappointments prompted me to examine the legacy of southern womanhood they bequeathed to me and to
explore its impact on my life and my ability to write my own story. Behind every page of this book lie my struggles as a white woman of the
working-class border South to redefine the terms of my social, personal,

and political existence, to break into an academy that renders those from my background powerless and invisible, and to find the voice and the empowerment to undertake and to express this revision and disruption. More important, the voices and concerns of all my female ancestors and relatives—my mother, my sister, my aunt, my cousin, and especially my grandmothers—are palpably behind every page of this study. Like all women writers—literary and critical—I think back through my female family, and this book becomes my own quilt of personal, professional, and critical experience. This study was motivated by my desire to understand and was sustained by the weaves of women in my own life. In this sense, I share credit for this book with the blood-defined matrix of female empowerment constituted by Julia Burrows, Louise Overbey, Laura Schneider, Marie Landsbury, Fanny Tate, and my much beloved mother, Bonnie Burrows; at the same time, I acknowledge the womb of friends who nurtured the creative possibilities in me—Terri F. Reilly, Monica Bear, Lisa Dlutkowski, and Amy A. Young.

A woman writing also thinks back through her textual mothers, the feminist critic building on the foundation of feminist scholars and colleagues, male and female, who encourage, challenge, stimulate, prompt, and respond. In this light, I am deeply thankful for the pioneering work of Anne Goodwyn Jones and Louise Westling; the thought-provoking theories of bell hooks; the encouragement and mentoring of professors I have known at the University of Missouri–St. Louis and the University of Wisconsin–Madison—Sylvia Jenkins Cook, Annis Pratt, Craig Werner, Walter Rideout, Jay Clayton, and William L. Andrews; the nurturing of Nellie Y. McKay, who more than anyone taught me to believe in my own ideas; the thoughtful insights of my colleagues at Wisconsin, Nancy J. Peterson, Tom Curtis, Jim Gray, and Elisabeth Mermann, who read much of the study in an earlier form; the day-to-day support of my colleagues at Shepherd College in West Virginia; the enthusiastic and insightful responses of my students, especially Rachael Meads, Kathy J. Shambaugh, and my tireless research assistant, Terri L. Erwin; the efforts of Ron L. Jones, who made sure that I had institutional support in the form of a course reduction; the support of a summer research grant from the West Virginia Humanities Council; the expertise of Amy Williams and Laura Neal, Shepherd College librarians, and of Tina Gomoll, of A Room of One's Own feminist bookstore in Madison, Wisconsin; the collaborative encouragement of Joy Kurland, who helped me discover my own story; the faith and hard work of Karen Orchard, Madelaine Cooke, Kelly Caudle, and Eric Schramm at the University of Georgia Press, a press and a staff that prove my contention that the progressive southern press is providing a vehicle for women's voices to be heard; and, above all, the always supportive contributions of Will Brantley, a colleague with whom I share years of conversation about southern women, about our southern upbringings, about what we are doing and why, about finding ways to say what we have to say and what has to be said. In large part or small, each of these individuals sustained, encouraged, and supported me in finding my own critical voice, in providing another vehicle for the voices of southern women writers to be heard, and in finding a way for the stories of my grandmothers and millions of southern women like them to find a place in the academy. Needless to say, any shortcomings or lapses are my own.

In writing this book and in searching for my own voice and a space from which to make it heard, I think back through the women who have come before me. In coming back to my grandmothers, to the poor white and working classes to which they belonged, to the multiracial heritage they left to me, and to the Souths they had known, I went on a symbolic immersion quest, not unlike the immersion quests undertaken by African Americans as they return to the South, to the region of oppression. Having made the ascent to the academy and to the middle class, I found (and find) myself longing for family connection and looking for ways to re-create community and interconnectedness with friends in new places, weaving new matrices of personal and professional empowerment. Like the characters in contemporary southern women's novels, and like many of their creators, I seek to reconnect, to make whole, to constitute new webs of empowerment, and to nurture the old. The trick, as for Virginia, is to be like my grandmothers while simultaneously becoming more than them, to perpetuate their feistiness while exercising greater personal, social, and political power.

To highlight empowering weaves of women, to value the vitality of women's voice, and to focus on the dynamics of women's space is not a retreat from political involvement, nor a conservative, nostalgic, essentialist step back to an era when southern women, black and white, were devalued, made powerless, and rendered invisible. Rather, my immersion in these concerns, my link back to the "ongoing lineage of women" (Levy 230), my own "ritualized journey into a symbolic South" (Stepto 167), affords me the opportunity to redefine southern women's lives, to make silenced voices heard, and to create my own site of critical resistance. Talking a new talk, I simultaneously speak and validate the old. Many voices are mingled in my mouth: those of southern women writers and of their characters; those of my mother and grandmothers; and, finally, my own. The matrix and the voice, the womb and the loom, become one, and in weaving the tales of many southern women, I come to know and to say my own.

NOTES

INTRODUCTION

1. I discuss the concept of the "southern lady" more fully in chapter 2. It is interesting to note here, however, that most upper-middle-class southern women themselves—in the nineteenth *and* twentieth centuries—rarely fit the stereotype of the chaste, unblemished, self-sacrificing "lady" on a pedestal that W. J. Cash argued inspired the white southern male practice of "gyneolatry" (89). Instead, as Anne Firor Scott shows in her landmark study, *The Southern Lady: From Pedestal to Politics, 1830–1930* (1970), southern women in the nineteenth century were leading "more varied and more demanding [lives] than the fantasies of southern men would suggest" (44). Moreover, as the South moved into the twentieth century, many southern white women began to realize that the image of the "southern lady" did not accurately describe their lives. White southern women had played important roles in the Civil War, whether as nurses or as de facto managers of plantations and farms. After the war, they were reluctant to give up their newfound independence and responded by striking out into the work force (primarily, like my Grandma Landsbury, as schoolteachers), working for the vote, and organizing themselves politically. Scott's pioneering work and subsequent work by Anne Goodwyn Jones in *Tomorrow Is Another Day: The Woman Writer in the South, 1859–1936* (1981) and by Louise Westling in *Sacred Groves and Ravaged Gardens: The Fiction of Eudora Welty, Carson McCullers, and Flannery O'Connor* (1985) suggest that the critical and scholarly framework of the upper-middle-class woman as "southern lady" is much too narrow and obscures an accurate view of white southern women's lives in both the nineteenth and twentieth centuries. For an excellent discussion of the "southern lady," see Jones (3–50); for an equally superb understanding of southern women's accomplishments both during and after the Civil War, see Scott (80–231).

2. The term "South" as a geographical category has long been a subject of dispute, with some scholars restricting its use to the eleven Confederate states (although Texas and Florida have been considered problematic) and others

opening it up to include culturally related border states. My definition includes the eleven Confederate states—Virginia, North Carolina, South Carolina, Georgia, Alabama, Tennessee, Louisiana, Arkansas, Mississippi, (north) Florida, and (east) Texas. In addition, "my" South includes West Virginia and Kentucky when this seems appropriate (in the case, for example, of Bobbie Ann Mason).

3. If white women were kept on their pedestals against their will, southern black women were forced to serve as the outlet for the white southern male's sexual frustration, creating a peculiarly tense relationship between black and white southern women, a relationship that is the subject of chapter 2. Relegated simultaneously to the positions of concubine and of "mule," southern black women have been virtually invisible in studies of southern history, culture, and literature.

4. Perhaps most illustrative of this exclusionary trend is *The History of Southern Literature* (Rubin and Simpson et al.), which claims to account for "the principal developments in the history of Southern literature" and to look at "the writings of those authors who have played significant parts in creating it" (1). The lens through which this literature is seen is quite narrow: the five senior editors are all male, four of them white. While the introduction makes gestures to a "racially integrated history," it says nothing about a gendered balance. The collection falls short of perfection on both counts. Looking just at the last section, "The Recent South, 1951–1982," for example, four of the twenty-three essays (not including the introductory essay) focus on white women writers, three of whom (Welty, McCullers, and O'Connor) might be more properly considered part of an earlier generation; two on individual black writers (Ellison and Gaines); one on black writers in general; and none on black women writers. Of the four "general" essays in the section, each takes only cursory notice of work by women and blacks. In fact, this notice is so bold in its perfunctoriness that Berry Morgan, a white woman, is listed as a black woman who has "produced some impressive writing" (585).

5. See William L. Andrews ("Mark Twain" 1–2) for a good discussion of the ways traditional southern literary criticism has excluded black writers and the ways African-American literary criticism has begun to correct that vision. For examples of critics who have begun to examine African-American contributions to southern literature, see Minrose Gwin's *Black and White Women of the Old South* (1985), Ladell Payne's *Black Novelists and the Southern Literary Tradition* (1981), Fred Hobson's *The Southern Writer in the Postmodern World* (1991),

and Will Brantley's *Feminine Sense in Southern Memoir: Smith, Glasgow, Welty, Hellman, Porter, Hurston* (1993).

6. For a discussion of the need to examine the role of class in southern literature, see Fred Hobson, *The Southern Writer in the Postmodern World* (1991, 20–23).

ONE. "ALL THE WOMEN": FAMILY, HOME, AND
HEALING IN THE CHANGING SOUTH

1. I refer here not to the oppressive southern male pastoral as described by Louise Westling in *Sacred Groves and Ravaged Gardens* (9–12) and by Elizabeth Jane Harrison in *Female Pastoral: Women Writers Re-Visioning the American South* (1–8) but to the ways in which southern women rewrite this mythology so that women's tie to the land is seen as empowering and liberating. For thoughts on this phenomenon, see Westling's discussion of Eudora Welty's *Delta Wedding* (65–93), which she refers to as "a pastoral hymn of fertility" (65), and Harrison's consideration of Ellen Glasgow, Margaret Mitchell, Willa Cather, Harriette Arnow, Alice Walker, and Sherley Anne Williams, all of whom participate in "creating an alternative female pastoral tradition" (9), revision the landscape as "an enabling force for the woman protagonist" (11), and depict woman's relationship with the land not as one of "passive association" but as one of "active cultivation or identification" (11). Importantly, Harrison notes that "female friendships and cooperative communities become an important part of the new southern garden for these women authors" (15).

2. The perception of family and home as constricting, rather than empowering, has been perpetuated by scholars and critics who have too often focused on the limiting aspects of family. For example, much of the Welty criticism in the past has focused on the suffocating aspects of family life in her work; Robert Penn Warren, in his 1944 essay "The Love and Separateness of Miss Welty," argued that isolation "provides the basic situation of [her] fiction" (250), and John Edward Hardy noted that the characters in *Delta Wedding* respond more to things than they do people (401), thus increasing what he sees as their already-existing isolation from each other. Likewise, critics too often ignore fictional depictions of women who find deep satisfaction through their homes. In this regard, the history of Roberts criticism is instructive. Virtually no critic to date has provided a sustained discussion of Roberts's woman-centered vision, and femi-

nist critics in particular seem singularly unable to acknowledge her revisionary approach to southern women's existence. My intent here is not to single out particular critics for blame or to call special attention to Welty or Roberts. Instead, my aim is to suggest in but the briefest of ways the pervasive tendency to see only the negative aspects of women's lives as depicted in southern women's fiction—or worse, to ignore those aspects altogether. Nor do I wish to suggest that all southern women writers depict home and family as empowering and liberating. Numerous southern women writers themselves have, of course, written novels treating home as a place of suffocation (see, for example, Ellen Glasgow's *The Sheltered Life* [1932], Edith Summers Kelley's *Weeds* [1923], Evelyn Scott's *The Narrow House* [1921], Shirley Ann Grau's *The Keepers of the House* [1964], Doris Betts's *Heading West* [1981], Anne Tyler's *Dinner at the Homesick Restaurant* [1982], and Gail Godwin's *A Southern Family* [1987]). Rather, my paramount goal here is to suggest that a number of key southern women writers have challenged the traditional perception that home and family must by necessity be demeaning and oppressive to women—and that southern and feminist scholars must begin to read and reread these texts in the light of this revisionary emphasis.

3. See Alice Walker, "In Search of Our Mothers' Gardens."

4. Note Roberts's insistence that "Life is from within" (quoted by Warren xxiii) and her emphasis on women's identification with the deeply internal:

> There is so much more to a woman than there is to a man. More complication. A woman is more closely identified with the earth, more real because deeper gifted with pain, danger, and a briefer life. More intense, richer in memory and feeling.
>
> A man's machinery is all outside himself. A woman's deeply and dangerously inside. Amen. (qtd. in Slavick xvi)

5. Although some critics and sometimes McCorkle herself refer to this character as "Ginny Sue," "Virginia" is clearer and less cumbersome. This difficulty faces not only critics. Indeed, part of the tension in this novel derives from Virginia's own ambivalence about which name to use. Thus, in one of the title's several meanings, she is "tending to Virginia," that is, tending toward using the more formal name.

Also note that I use "Virginia" to refer to the protagonist, the younger Virginia (Virginia Suzanne Turner Ballard), and "Virginia Suzanne" to refer to her dead great-grandmother (Virginia Suzanne White Pearson).

6. Several stories from the collection were also adapted for the stage in the

play *Shakin' the Mess Outta Misery.* It was first produced by the Horizon Theatre Company in Atlanta (1988).

TWO. RACE AND REGION: BLACK AND WHITE SISTERS OF THE NOW SOUTH

1. For example, Sarah and Angelina Grimké argued, "They [the female slaves] are our countrywomen—*they are our sisters.* . . . Women ought to feel a peculiar sympathy in the colored man's wrong, for like him, she has been accused of mental inferiority, and denied the privileges of a liberal education" (qtd. in Evans 26).

2. See, for example, Fox-Genovese, who writes, "Sharing the domination of white men—of the master—did slave and slaveholding women share bonds? participate in a sisterhood? The simple and inescapable answer is no" (34–35).

3. For an excellent fictional account of the relationships between white and black women in the antebellum South, see Sherley Anne Williams's *Dessa Rose* (1986).

4. Evans also acknowledges the role of northern women involved in the New Left movements against racism, poverty, and the Vietnam War.

5. This paper is the one in response to which Stokely Carmichael made the infamous statement, "The only position for women in SNCC is prone" (qtd. in Evans 87).

THREE. REVISIONING THE BACKWARD GLANCE: NEW VIEWS OF SOUTHERN HISTORY

1. Tate used this famous phrase in his essay "The New Provincialism" to describe what he called "the peculiar historical consciousness of the Southern writer" (546).

2. It is not surprising to note that Woodward, in editing the most acclaimed edition of Chesnut's work to date, exhibits his bias as a male historian. Woodward's guiding principle in editing the diary was not to respect Chesnut's intentions as a writer but, rather, to manipulate the text as it best serves the purposes of a historian interested in what Chesnut had to say about "public and external forces." As Chesnut worked on the more artful rendering of her diary in the 1880s, she deleted a number of passages written in the 1860s and added new passages as well. Woodward reinserted many of the passages Chesnut herself

had cut while deleting many of the passages written in the 1880s, often because he felt they were "cryptic," "unrelated," "obscure," or "unintelligible"—criteria not clearly defined in his introduction. Indeed, Woodward's defense of these editorial decisions underscores his bias as a historian and his lack of respect for Chesnut as an artist. He states: "I think she [Chesnut] never completed anything, and I think that exonerates me from this charge of infidelity to the author's intent. She didn't know what she intended" (Meriwether 280). For a more thorough discussion of problems with the Woodward edition, see Hayhoe.

3. For a good discussion of the WPA interviews, see Rawick's introduction to volume 1 of *The American Slave: A Composite Autobiography* (xiii–xxi). This volume also reprints (167–78) the front matter of the WPA's *Slave Narratives: A Folk History of Slavery in the United States from Interviews with Former Slaves* (Washington, 1941).

4. Gwin notes that there are more than six thousand written and orally transmitted slave narratives by blacks. Though "fewer than thirty women's slave narratives . . . were published as books during the authors' or subjects' lifetimes," there apparently would still be a substantial number of accounts with which Brown might have worked (53).

5. These brief quotations, and the ideas that follow, were taken from a variety of useful background sources on Appalachia, including Campbell, McNeil, Frost, Fox, Semple, Shapiro, Kephart, S. W. Jones, and Daniel.

6. Cunningham's remarks come from a paper he presented at the March 1990 meeting of the Appalachian Studies Conference, "She Do the Police in Different Voices: Alterity, Polyphony, and Presence by Erasure in Lee Smith's *Oral History*."

7. For thoughts on the Renaissance, see Baber and Sullivan.

8. Smith's emphasis on the family links her to McCorkle's and Youngblood's concern with family. The Cantrell family is a hybrid of the traditional southern extended family, as in McCorkle, and of the alternative family, or symbolic kin network, as in Youngblood.

9. For an excellent history of the development of country music and its debt to mountain music, see Malone.

FOUR. NO PLACE LIKE HOME: LEARNING TO READ
TWO WRITERS' MAPS

1. See, for example, Mars-Jones, Ross, Sadoff, Towers, and Weisenburger.

2. See, for example, Hite, Lupton, and Walsh. Walker's use of folk or fairy tale conventions extends back to *Meridian,* as Nadel argues.

3. From "Zora Neale Hurston: A Cautionary Tale and a Partisan View": "I have a photograph of her in pants, boots, and broadbrim. . . . She has her foot up on the running board of a car—presumably hers, and bright red—and looks racy" (88).

4. See, for example, Gilman, Hobson, L. White, Stewart, Kinney, and Brinkmeyer ("Finding One's History").

5. Robert H. Brinkmeyer's comments on this subject are typical of the standard approach: "Her focus is less on the Southern experience than on the American, and so for her a Southerner's quest for self-definition means coming to terms with America and not the South, except as an expression of the national experience. This focus leads her back to the era of the Vietnam War, a period that tested the American way of life from within and without. . . . [S]he, like many other contemporary Southern writers, is moving away from seeing the South as a region distinctively set apart from the rest of the nation" ("Finding One's History" 32).

6. See, for example, Molarsky and L. White.

7. For an excellent discussion of the ways in which Mason links Vietnam and the South, see Owen W. Gilman, Jr.'s discussion of the novel in *Vietnam and the Southern Imagination* (45–59).

FIVE. ERASING THE SOUTH:
THE CREATION OF "UNIVERSAL" FILMS

Epigraph quoted in Turner, "Spielberg," 60.

1. For an excellent overview of depictions of the South in film, see *Southern Quarterly*'s special issue on "The South and Film" (19.3–4, Spring-Summer 1988). French's introductory article is especially helpful for gaining an understanding of the "Southern." See also Kirby.

2. See, for example, Julie Dash's *Daughters of the Dust* (1991), as well as John McElwee's documentary *Sherman's March* (1987), which provides an intriguing look at new images of southern womanhood from a southern man's perspective. For an excellent discussion of the obstacles facing independent filmmakers (par-

ticularly women filmmakers or filmmakers of color), see Dash's essay, "Making *Daughters of the Dust*" (1–26) and her "Dialogue" about the film with bell hooks (27–67), both included in *Daughters of the Dust: The Making of an African American Woman's Film*.

3. I am adapting Kauffman's definition of Hollywood as referring to "white-[and nonsouthern-]controlled films made anywhere in America" ("Sign" 24).

4. Walker coined the term "womanist" to designate a more flexible and assertive alternative to feminism. Widely in use by a number of American women, the term is defined in the epigraph to Walker's *In Search of Our Mothers' Gardens: Womanist Prose*.

5. Spielberg states, "I didn't allow any of my own inadequacies as a male, Jewish director from Hollywood to interfere with what I thought was a story that I could tell quite subjectively and yet at the same time be objective in my overview of what was happening" (qtd. in Turner, "Spielberg" 59).

6. For an excellent discussion of Spielberg's problematic depiction of Mr. _____, see bell hooks's "Representations: Feminism and Black Masculinity" (69–71).

7. See Austin and French for descriptions of this genre.

8. Quoted by Beverly Lowry in Wilson (85).

SIX. THE SOUTHERN WILD ZONE: VOICES ON THE MARGINS

Epigraph is from "Needle Picture," part of a long-poem series entitled *The Outlaw James Copeland and the Champion-Belted Empress* (1991).

1. I take the model of disruption, revision, and replacement from Mae G. Henderson, "Speaking in Tongues: Dialogics, Dialectics, and the Black Woman Writer's Literary Tradition" (1989).

2. Hite's work in her 1989 study, *The Other Side of the Story: Structures and Strategies of Contemporary Feminist Narratives,* is helpful in showing how women read and write "otherwise" and in calling attention to the often unnoticed subversive qualities of contemporary women's fiction. Hite rejects the either/or positioning that labels contemporary experimental (male) fiction as postmodernist and nonexperimental (female) fiction as unworthy of consideration. Yet like many critics she turns her attention not to women's novels that employ "traditional" realism but to those that, while appearing to be realistic, are actually experimental in style and structure. While I applaud Hite's decision to read "otherwise" so that women's formal experimentation can be noted and appreciated, I question her perpetuation of the attitude that women novelists

who *choose* more traditional aesthetics (i.e., narrative) are not subversive or political. See 1–15.

3. I define an independent press as one that (1) fosters primarily nonmainstream writing, (2) maintains no connection with a major commercial press, and (3) is primarily nonprofit in orientation.

4. Shelnutt provides an opposing, but less convincing, view. She argues that the press only publishes fiction that "validates [Rubin's] codification of southern writing" (52).

5. For an example of her work, see Ringgold's children's book, *Tar Beach* (1991), an expansion of a story quilt from her "Woman on a Bridge" series, which she completed in 1988 and which is now housed in New York's Guggenheim Museum.

6. *Trifles* was first performed by the Provincetown Players in Provincetown, Massachusetts, on August 8, 1916. A year later, it was rewritten and published as a short story, "A Jury of Her Peers."

7. The anonymous passage about the patchwork quilt was cited in Elaine Showalter's 1986 essay, "Piecing and Writing," whose thoughts on the connections between quilts and women's narratives helped to sharpen my own.

WORKS CONSULTED

Algonquin Books. Fall catalog. Chapel Hill, N.C.: 1990.

Allison, Dorothy. *Bastard out of Carolina.* New York: Dutton, 1992.

Andrews, William L. "Mark Twain, William Wells Brown, and the Problem of Authority in New South Writing." *Southern Literature and Literary Theory.* Ed. Jefferson Humphries. Athens: U of Georgia P, 1990. 1–21.

———, ed. *Sisters of the Spirit: Three Black Women's Autobiographies of the Nineteenth Century.* Bloomington: Indiana UP, 1986.

Anello, Ray, and Pamela Abramson. "Characters in Search of a Book." *Newsweek* 21 June 1982: 67.

"Annette." [Harriet Farley or Rebecca C. Thompson]. "The Patchwork Quilt." *The Lowell Offering.* Ed. Benita Eisler. New York: Harper, 1977. 150–54.

Arnold, Edwin T. "An Interview with Lee Smith." *Appalachian Journal* 11 (1984): 240–54.

Arnow, Pat. "Lee Smith: An Interview." *Now and Then* 6 (Summer 1989): 24–27.

Austin, Wade. "The Real Beverly Hillbillies." *Southern Quarterly* 19 (Spring-Summer 1981): 83–94.

Awkward, Michael. *Inspiriting Influences: Tradition, Revision, and Afro-American Women's Novels.* New York: Columbia UP, 1989.

Baber, Bob Henry. "True Grit: Conversations on the Appalachian Literary Renascence." *Appalachian Journal* 14 (1987): 250–61.

Baker, Houston A., Jr. *The Journey Back: Issues in Black Literature and Criticism.* Chicago: U of Chicago P, 1980.

Bakerman, Jane. "The Seams Can't Show: An Interview with Toni Morrison." *Black American Literature Forum* 12 (Summer 1978): 55–60.

Bambara, Toni Cade. *The Salt Eaters.* New York: Random, 1980.

Bambara, Toni Cade, and Leah Wise. Introduction. *Southern Black Utterances Today.* Special issue of *Southern Exposure* 3 (Spring/Summer 1975): [i].

Bammer, Angelika. "Feminist Texts and the Nonestablishment Press." *Women in Print II: Opportunities for Women's Studies Publication in Language and Litera-*

ture. Ed. Joan E. Hartman and Ellen Messer-Davidow. New York: MLA, 1982.
117–37.

Berlant, Lauren. "Race, Gender, and Nation in *The Color Purple*." *Critical Inquiry*
14 (Summer 1988): 831–59.

Betts, Doris. *Heading West*. New York: Knopf, 1981.

Boorman, John, dir. *Deliverance*. Warner Brothers, 1972.

Bourne, Daniel. "*Artful Dodge* Interviews Lee Smith." *Artful Dodge* 16/17 (Fall
1989): 38–52.

Brantley, Will. *Feminine Sense in Southern Memoir: Smith, Glasgow, Welty, Hellman, Porter, Hurston*. Jackson: UP of Mississippi, 1993.

Brinkmeyer, Robert H., Jr. "Finding One's History: Bobbie Ann Mason and Contemporary Southern Literature." *Southern Literary Journal* 19 (Spring 1987):
22–33.

———. "In Print, Out of Print: Book Publishing in the '80s." *Southern Exposure*
9 (Summer 1981): 86–87.

Bronstein, Scott. "More Blacks Choosing Life in the South." *Atlanta Constitution*
10 Jan. 1990: A1, A8.

Brown, Linda Beatrice. *Rainbow Roun Mah Shoulder*. Chapel Hill, N.C.: Carolina
Wren P, 1984. New York: Random/Ballantine, 1989.

Brown, Rita Mae. *Bingo*. New York: Bantam, 1988.

———. *High Hearts*. New York: Bantam, 1986.

———. *In Her Day*. Plainfield, Vt.: Daughters, Inc., 1976.

———. *Rubyfruit Jungle*. Plainfield, Vt.: Daughters, Inc., 1973.

———. *Six of One*. New York: Harper, 1978.

———. *Southern Discomfort*. New York: Harper, 1982.

———. *Sudden Death*. New York: Bantam, 1983.

Bush, Trudy Bloser. "Transforming Vision: Alice Walker and Zora Neale Hurston."
Christian Century 16 Nov. 1988: 1035–39.

Butler, Robert James. "Making a Way out of No Way: The Open Journey in Alice
Walker's *The Third Life of Grange Copeland*." *Black American Literature Forum*
22 (Spring 1988): 65–79.

Campbell, John C. *The Southern Highlander and His Homeland*. New York: Russell
Sage Foundation, 1921.

Carolina Wren Press. Fall catalog. Carrboro, N.C.: 1990.

Cash, W. J. *The Mind of the South*. New York: Knopf, 1941.

Chesnut, Mary Boykin. *Mary Chesnut's Civil War*. Ed. C. Vann Woodward. New
Haven: Yale UP, 1981.

Cheung, King-Kok. "'Don't Tell': Imposed Silences in *The Color Purple* and *The Woman Warrior.*" *PMLA* 103 (Mar. 1988): 162–74.

Chew, Martha. "Rita Mae Brown: Feminist Theorist and Southern Novelist." *Southern Quarterly* 22 (1983): 61–80.

Chopin, Kate. *The Awakening.* 1899. New York: Avon, 1972.

———. *Bayou Folk.* Boston: Houghton Mifflin, 1894.

Clausen, Jan. "The Politics of Publishing and the Lesbian Community." *Sinister Wisdom* 1 (Fall 1976): 94–115.

Clayton, Jay. "The Narrative Turn in Recent Minority Fiction." *American Literary History* 2 (Fall 1990): 375–93.

Clinton, Catherine. *The Plantation Mistress: Woman's World in the Old South.* New York: Pantheon, 1982.

Collins, Patricia Hill. *Black Feminist Thought: Knowledge, Consciousness, and the Politics of Empowerment.* New York: Unwin Hyman, 1990.

Cunningham, Rodger. "She Do the Police in Different Voices: Alterity, Polyphony, and Presence by Erasure in Lee Smith's *Oral History.*" Appalachian Studies Conference, March 1990.

Daniel, Pete. *Standing at the Crossroads: Southern Life in the Twentieth Century.* New York: Farrar–Hill and Wang, 1986.

Daniels, Gabrielle. "Tell It Like It Is: Fighting Self-Censorship." West 153–59.

Dash, Julie, dir. *Daughters of the Dust.* American Playhouse, 1991.

———. *Daughters of the Dust: The Making of an African American Woman's Film.* New York: The New Press, 1992.

Davis, Thadious M. "Alice Walker's Celebration of Self in Southern Generations." *Southern Quarterly* 21 (Summer 1983): 39–53. Rpt. in Prenshaw 39–53.

———. "Southern Writers: Notes toward a Definition of Terms." *Southern Quarterly* 19 (Winter 1981): 10–16.

De Lauretis, Teresa. *Technologies of Gender: Essays on Theory, Film, and Fiction.* Bloomington: Indiana UP, 1987.

Denby, David. "Endless War." Rev. of *In Country,* dir. by Norman Jewison. *New York* 25 Sept. 1989: 129–30.

DePietro, Thomas. "In Quest of the Bloody Truth." Rev. of *In Country,* by Bobbie Ann Mason. *Commonweal* 1 Nov. 1985: 620–22.

"Dialogue on Film: Steven Spielberg." *American Film* June 1988: 12–16.

Dillman, Caroline Matheny. "Southern Women: In Continuity or Change?" Mathews 8–17.

Dixon, Melvin. *Ride Out the Wilderness: Geography and Identity in Afro-American Literature*. Urbana: U of Illinois P, 1987.

Dixon, Barbara. "Family Celebration: Portrayals of the Family in Fiction Published in the 1980s by Southern Women." *Southern Quarterly* 26 (Spring 1988): 5–14.

Douglas, Ellen. *Apostles of Light*. Boston: Houghton Mifflin, 1973.

——— . *Black Cloud, White Cloud*. Boston: Houghton Mifflin, 1963.

——— . *Can't Quit You, Baby*. New York: Atheneum, 1988. New York: Penguin, 1989.

——— . *A Family's Affairs*. Boston: Houghton Mifflin, 1962.

——— . "Faulkner in Time." *A Cosmos of My Own: Faulkner and Yoknapatawpha 1980*. Ed. Doreen Fowler and Ann J. Abadie. Jackson: UP of Mississippi, 1981. 284–301.

——— . *A Lifetime Burning*. New York: Random House, 1982.

——— . *The Magic Carpet and Other Tales*. Jackson: UP of Mississippi, 1987.

——— . *The Rock Cried Out*. New York: Harcourt, 1979.

——— . *Where the Dreams Cross*. Boston: Houghton Mifflin, 1968.

Douglass, Frederick. *My Bondage and My Freedom*. 1855. Ed. William L. Andrews. Urbana: U of Illinois P, 1987.

——— . *The Narrative of the Life of Frederick Douglass*. 1845. New York: New American Library, 1968.

Dubler, Linda. "Southern Exposure." *American Film* Apr. 1986: 39–44.

Elaw, Zilpha. *Memoirs of the Life, Religious Experience, Ministerial Travels and Labors of Mrs. Zilpha Elaw*. 1846. Andrews, *Sisters* 49–160.

Ellison, Ralph. *Invisible Man*. New York: Random, 1952.

Erdrich, Louise. *Tracks*. New York: Holt, 1988.

Evans, Sara. *Personal Politics: The Roots of Women's Liberation in the Civil Rights Movement and the New Left*. New York: Knopf, 1979.

Faulkner, William. *Absalom, Absalom!* New York: Random, 1936.

Fish, Stanley. *Is There a Text in This Class? The Authority of Interpretive Communities*. Cambridge: Harvard UP, 1980.

Foote, Julia A. J. *A Brand Plucked from the Fire: An Autobiographical Sketch by Mrs. Julia A. F. Foote*. 1879. Andrews, *Sisters* 161–234.

Fox, John, Jr. "The Southern Mountaineer." *Scribner's Magazine* Apr.–May 1901: 387–99, 556–70. Rpt. in McNeil 121–44.

Fox-Genovese, Elizabeth. *Within the Plantation Household: Black and White Women of the Old South*. Chapel Hill: U of North Carolina P, 1988.

Fraiman, Susan. "An Interview with Deborah E. McDowell." *Critical Texts* 6 (1990): 13–29.

Frank, Shirley. "Feminist Presses." *Women in Print II: Opportunities for Women's Studies Publication in Language and Literature*. Ed. Joan E. Hartman and Ellen Messer-Davidow. New York: MLA, 1982. 89–116.

Fraser, Walter J., Jr., R. Frank Saunders, Jr., and Jon L. Wakelyn, eds. *The Web of Southern Social Relations: Women, Family, and Education*. Athens: U of Georgia P, 1985.

French, Warren. "'The Southern': Another Lost Cause?" *Southern Quarterly* 19 (Spring-Summer 1981): 3–13.

Friedman, Jean E. *The Enclosed Garden: Women and Community in the Evangelical South, 1830–1900*. Chapel Hill: U of North Carolina P, 1985.

———. "Women's History and the Revision of Southern History." *Sex, Race, and the Role of Women in the South*. Eds. Joanne V. Hawks and Sheila L. Skemps. Jackson: UP of Mississippi, 1983. 3–12.

Frost, William Goodell. "Our Contemporary Ancestors in the Southern Mountains." *Atlantic Monthly* Mar. 1899: 311+. Rpt. in McNeil 91–106.

Frye, Joanne S. *Living Stories, Telling Lives: Women and the Novel in Contemporary Experience*. Ann Arbor: U of Michigan P, 1986.

Gaines, Ernest. *The Autobiography of Miss Jane Pittman*. New York: Dial, 1971.

Ganim, Carole. "Herself: Woman and Place in Appalachian Literature." *Appalachian Journal* 13 (1986): 258–74.

Gates, Henry Louis, Jr., ed. "The Black Person in Art: How Should S/he Be Portrayed? (Part II)." *Black American Literature Forum* 21 (Fall 1987): 317–32.

Gibbons, Kaye. *Charms for the Easy Life*. New York: Putnam, 1993.

———. *A Cure for Dreams*. Chapel Hill, N.C.: Algonquin, 1991.

———. *Ellen Foster*. Chapel Hill, N.C.: Algonquin, 1987.

———. *A Virtuous Woman*. Chapel Hill, N.C.: Algonquin, 1989.

Gilman, Owen W., Jr. *Vietnam and the Southern Imagination*. Jackson: UP of Mississippi, 1992.

Glasgow, Ellen. *The Sheltered Life*. 1932. New York: Harvest-HBJ, 1985.

Glaspell, Susan. *Trifles*. *The Heath Anthology of American Literature*. Ed. Paul Lauter. Vol. 2. Lexington, Mass.: Heath, 1990. 1078–87.

Godwin, Gail. *A Southern Family*. New York: William Morrow, 1987.

Grau, Shirley Ann. *The Keepers of the House*. New York: Knopf, 1964.

Gray, Richard. *The Literature of Memory: Modern Writers of the American South*. Baltimore: Johns Hopkins UP, 1977.

———. *Writing the South: Ideas of an American Region.* Cambridge: Cambridge UP, 1986.

Greenberg, J. Rev. of *The Color Purple,* dir. by Steven Spielberg. *Variety* 18 Dec. 1985: 16.

Gutman, Herbert G. *The Black Family in Slavery and Freedom, 1750–1925.* New York: Vintage-Random, 1976.

Gwin, Minrose C. *Black and White Women of the Old South: The Peculiar Sisterhood in American Literature.* Knoxville: U of Tennessee P, 1985.

Halprin, S. "'The Color Purple': Community of Women." *JumpCut* Mar. 1986: 1+.

Harrell, A. "The Look of 'The Color Purple.'" *American Cinematographer* Feb. 1986: 50–56.

Harris, Trudier. "From Victimization to Free Enterprise: Alice Walker's *The Color Purple.*" *Studies in American Fiction* 14 (Spring 1986): 1–17.

———. "On *The Color Purple,* Stereotypes, and Silence." *Black American Literature Forum* 18 (Winter 1987): 155–61.

Harrison, Elizabeth Jane. *Female Pastoral: Women Writers Re-Visioning the American South.* Knoxville: U of Tennessee P, 1991.

Harwell, Richard B., ed. *Kate: The Journal of a Confederate Nurse.* Baton Rouge: Louisiana State UP, 1959.

Havens, Lila. "Residents and Transients: An Interview with Bobbie Ann Mason." *Crazyhorse* 29 (1985): 87–104.

Hayhoe, George F. "Mary Boykin Chesnut: The Making of a Reputation." *Mississippi Quarterly* 35 (1982): 60–72.

Henderson, Mae G. "Speaking in Tongues: Dialogics, Dialectics, and the Black Woman Writer's Literary Tradition." *Changing Our Own Words: Essays on Criticism, Theory, and Writing by Black Women.* Ed. Cheryl Wall. New Brunswick, N.J.: Rutgers UP, 1989. 16–37.

Henning, Barbara. "Minimalism and the American Dream: 'Shiloh' by Bobbie Ann Mason and 'Preservation' by Raymond Carver." *Modern Fiction Studies* 35 (Winter 1989): 689–98.

Hite, Molly. *The Other Side of the Story: Structures and Strategies of Contemporary Feminist Narratives.* Ithaca: Cornell UP, 1989.

Hoberman, J. "Film: Color Me Purple." Rev. of *The Color Purple,* dir. by Steven Spielberg. *Village Voice* 24 Dec. 1985: 76.

Hobson, Fred. *The Southern Writer in the Postmodern World.* Mercer University Lamar Memorial Lectures 33. Athens: U of Georgia P, 1991.

Hogan, Judy, with Mary Ellen Priestley and Margaret Stephens, eds. *A Living Culture in Durham: A Collection of Writings by Durham Area Writers*. Durham, N.C.: Carolina Wren, 1987.

hooks, bell. "Homeplace: A Site of Resistance." *Yearning* 41–49.

———. "The Politics of Radical Black Subjectivity." *Yearning* 15–22.

———. "Representations: Feminism and Black Masculinity." *Yearning* 65–77.

———. *Yearning: Race, Gender, and Cultural Politics*. Boston: South End P, 1990.

Hurston, Zora Neale. *Their Eyes Were Watching God*. 1937. New York: Perennial-Harper, 1990.

Inge, Tonette Bond. *Southern Women Writers: The New Generation*. Tuscaloosa: U of Alabama P, 1990.

Jacobs, Harriet. *Incidents in the Life of a Slave Girl*. Ed. Lydia Maria Child. 1861. Ed. Jean Fagan Yellin. Cambridge: Harvard UP, 1987.

Jameson, Fredric. *The Political Unconscious: Narrative as Socially Symbolic Act*. Ithaca: Cornell UP, 1981.

Jewison, Norman, dir. *In Country*. Warner Brothers, 1989.

Jones, Anne Goodwyn. *Tomorrow Is Another Day: The Woman Writer in the South, 1859–1936*. Baton Rouge: Louisiana State UP, 1981.

Jones, Suzanne W. "City Folks in Hoot Owl Holler: Narrative Strategy in Lee Smith's *Oral History*." *Southern Literary Journal* 20 (1987): 101–12.

Kastor, Elizabeth. "Southern Seeds of a First Novel." *Washington Post* 6 May 1990: F1, F9.

Kauffman, Stanley. "In Several Countries." Rev. of *In Country*, dir. by Norman Jewison. *New Republic* 16 Oct. 1989: 30–31.

Kearney, Jill. "Whoopi Goldberg: Color Her Anything." *American Film* Dec. 1985: 25–27.

Kelley, Edith Summers. *Weeds*. New York: Harcourt, 1923.

Kephart, Horace. *Our Southern Highlanders*. New York: Macmillan, 1922.

King, Grace. *Monsieur Motte*. New York: Armstrong, 1888.

King, James R. "African Survivals in the Black American Family: Key Factors in Stability." *Journal of Afro-American Issues* 4 (1985): 153–67.

King, Richard H. *A Southern Renaissance: The Cultural Awakening of the American South, 1930–1955*. Oxford: Oxford UP, 1980.

Kingston, Maxine Hong. *Woman Warrior: Memoirs of a Girlhood among Ghosts*. New York: Knopf-Random, 1976.

Kinney, Katherine. "'Humping the Boonies': Sex, Combat, and the Female in

Bobbie Ann Mason's *In Country.*" *Fourteen Landing Zones.* Ed. Philip K. Jason. Iowa City: U of Iowa P, 1991. 38–48.

Kirby, Jack Temple. *Media-made Dixie: The South in the American Imagination.* Baton Rouge: Louisiana State UP, 1978.

Kolodny, Annette. "A Map for Rereading: Gender and the Interpretation of Literary Texts." Showalter, *New Feminist Criticism* 46–62.

Kopkind, Andrew. Rev. of *The Color Purple,* dir. by Steven Spielberg. *The Nation* 1 Feb. 1986: 124–25.

Lebow, Jeanne. *The Outlaw James Copeland and the Champion-Belted Empress.* Athens: U of Georgia P, 1991.

Lee, Jarena. *The Life and Religious Experience of Jarena Lee.* 1836. Andrews, *Sisters* 25–48.

Lesser, Ellen. "Voices with Stories to Tell: A Conversation with Jill McCorkle." *Southern Review* 26 (1990): 53–64.

Levy, Helen. *Fiction of the Home Place: Jewett, Cather, Glasgow, Porter, Welty, and Naylor.* Jackson: UP of Mississippi, 1992.

Lupton, Mary Jane. "Clothes and Closure in Three Novels by Black Women." *Black American Literature Forum* 20 (Winter 1986): 409–21.

McCorkle, Jill. *The Cheerleader.* Chapel Hill, N.C.: Algonquin, 1984.

———. *Crash Diet: Stories.* Chapel Hill, N.C.: Algonquin, 1992.

———. *Ferris Beach.* Chapel Hill, N.C.: Algonquin, 1990.

———. *July 7th.* Chapel Hill, N.C.: Algonquin, 1984.

———. *Tending to Virginia.* Chapel Hill, N.C.: Algonquin, 1987.

McElwee, John, dir. *Sherman's March.* 1987.

McKay, Nellie. "An Interview with Toni Morrison." *Contemporary Literature* 24 (Winter 1983): 413–29.

McNeil, W. K., ed. *Appalachian Images in Folk and Popular Culture.* Ann Arbor: UMI, 1989.

Malone, Bill C. *Country Music U.S.A.* Rev. ed. Austin: U of Texas P, 1985.

Manning, Carol S., ed. *The Female Tradition in Southern Literature.* Urbana: U of Illinois P, 1993.

Marshall, Paule. *Brown Girl, Brownstones.* 1959. Old Westbury, N.Y.: Feminist, 1981.

———. "The Making of a Writer: From the Poets in the Kitchen." *New York Times Book Review* 9 Jan. 1983. Rpt. in *Reena and Other Stories.* Paule Marshall. Old Westbury, N.Y.: Feminist, 1983. 3–12.

Mars-Jones, Adam. Rev. of *The Color Purple,* dir. by Steven Spielberg. *New Statesman* 11 July 1986: 27.

Martin, Elmer P., and Joanne Mitchell Martin. *The Black Extended Family.* Chicago: U of Chicago P, 1978.

Maslin, Janet. "Rural Wonderland." Rev. of *The Color Purple,* dir. by Steven Spielberg. *New York Times* 18 Dec. 1985: C18.

Mason, Bobbie Ann. *Feather Crowns.* New York: HarperCollins, 1993.

——. *In Country.* New York: Harper, 1985. New York: Perennial, 1989.

——. *Love Life.* New York: Harper, 1989.

——. *Shiloh and Other Stories.* New York: Harper, 1982.

——. *Spence + Lila* New York: Harper, 1988.

Mathews, Holly F. "Introduction: What Does It Mean to Be a Woman in the South Today?" Mathews 1–7.

——, ed. *Women in the South: An Anthropological Perspective.* Athens: U of Georgia P, 1989.

Meriwether, James B., ed. *South Carolina Women Writers.* Proc. of the Reynolds Conference. University of South Carolina. Oct. 24–25, 1975. Spartanburg, 1979.

Mitchell, Margaret. *Gone with the Wind.* New York: Macmillan, 1936.

Molarsky, Mona. "Back in the World." Rev. of *In Country,* by Bobbie Ann Mason. *The Nation* 18 Jan. 1986: 57–58.

Momaday, N. Scott. *The Way to Rainy Mountain.* Albuquerque: U of New Mexico P, 1969.

Moran, John. "Standing the Heat." *CAPITAL Region* [Albany, N.Y.] June 1987: 37–38.

Morrison, Toni. *Song of Solomon.* New York: Knopf, 1977.

Nadel, Alan. "Reading the Body: Alice Walker's *Meridian* and the Archaeology of Self." *Modern Fiction Studies* 34 (Spring 1988): 55–68.

Naylor, Gloria. *Mama Day.* New York: Ticknor & Fields–Houghton Mifflin, 1988.

Nobles, Wade. "Africanity: Its Role in Black Families." *Black Scholar* 15 (1974): 10–17.

Nystrand, Martin. "The Structure of Textual Space." *What Writers Know: The Language, Process, and Structure of Written Discourse.* Ed. Nystrand. New York: Academic Press–Harcourt, 1982. 75–86.

Osborne, Karen. *Patchwork.* New York: Harcourt, 1991.

Otto, Whitney. *How to Make an American Quilt.* New York: Random, 1991.

Payne, Ladell. *Black Novelists and the Southern Literary Tradition.* Athens: U of Georgia P, 1981.

Pearce, Richard, dir. *The Long Walk Home.* Miramax, 1990.

Porter, Katherine Anne. *The Collected Stories of Katherine Anne Porter.* New York: Harcourt, 1965.

Prenshaw, Peggy, ed. *Women Writers of the Contemporary South.* Jackson: UP of Mississippi, 1984.

Raboteau, Albert J. *Slave Religion: The "Invisible Institution" in the Antebellum South.* New York: Oxford UP, 1978.

Rawick, George P. *From Sundown to Sunup: The Making of the Black Community.* Westport, Conn.: Greenwood, 1972. Vol. 1 of *The American Slave: A Composite Autobiography.* 19 vols. 1972.

Ringgold, Faith. *Tar Beach.* New York: Crown, 1991.

Roberts, Elizabeth Madox. *The Great Meadow.* New York: Viking, 1930.

———. *The Time of Man.* New York: Viking, 1926.

Ross, Daniel W. "Celie in the Looking Glass: The Desire for Selfhood in *The Color Purple.*" *Modern Fiction Studies* 34 (Spring 1988): 69–84.

Rubin, Louis D., Jr., Lewis P. Simpson et al. *The History of Southern Literature.* Baton Rouge: Louisiana State UP, 1985.

Sadoff, Dianne F. "Black Matrilineage: The Case of Alice Walker and Zora Neale Hurston." *Signs* 11 (Autumn 1985): 4–26.

Sanders, Dori. *Clover.* Chapel Hill, N.C.: Algonquin, 1990.

———. *Her Own Place.* Chapel Hill, N.C.: Algonquin, 1993.

———. *Ideal Land for Farming.* Chapel Hill, N.C.: Algonquin, 1990.

Sayers, Valerie. *Due East.* Garden City, N.Y.: Doubleday, 1987.

Scott, Anne Firor. *The Southern Lady: From Pedestal to Politics, 1830–1930.* Chicago: U of Chicago P, 1970.

Scott, Evelyn. *The Narrow House.* New York: Boni and Liveright, 1921.

Scott, Jay. "Mirror, Mirror. . . ." Rev. of *In Country,* dir. by Norman Jewison. *Film Comment* Sept.–Oct. 1989: 11–14.

Segrest, M[ab]. "'Lines I Dare to Write': Lesbian Writing in the South." *Southern Exposure* 9 (1981): 53–62.

Semple, Ellen Churchill. "The Anglo-Saxons of the Kentucky Mountains: A Study in Anthropogeography." *Geographical Journal* 17 (June 1901): 588–623. Rpt. in McNeil 145–74.

Shapiro, Henry D. *Appalachia on Our Minds: The Southern Mountain and Moun-*

taineers in the American Consciousness, 1870–1920.* Chapel Hill: U of North Carolina P, 1978.

Shelnutt, Eve. "A Contemporary Southern Writer's Predicament: Removing the Rose-Colored Glasses." *Southern Quarterly* 30 (Fall 1991): 52–57.

Shelton, Frank W. "Alienation and Integration in Alice Walker's *The Color Purple.*" *CLA Journal* 28 (June 1985): 382–92.

Shomer, Enid. "An Interview with Bobbie Ann Mason." *The Black Warrior Review* 12 (1986): 87–102.

Showalter, Elaine. "Feminist Criticism in the Wilderness." Showalter, *New Feminist Criticism* 243–70.

———. "Piecing and Writing." *The Poetics of Gender.* Ed. Nancy K. Miller. New York: Columbia UP, 1986. 222–47.

———, ed. *The New Feminist Criticism: Essays on Women, Literature, and Theory.* New York: Pantheon, 1985.

Sigal, C. "The Color of Candy Floss." Rev. of *The Color Purple,* dir. by Steven Spielberg. *Listener* 17 July 1986: 34.

Silko, Leslie Marmon. *Ceremony.* New York: Viking, 1977. New York: Penguin, 1986.

Simon, John. "Black and White on Purple." *National Review* 4 Feb. 1986: 56.

Slavick, William H. "Ellen Chesser: A Journey of the Mind." Introduction. *The Time of Man.* By Elizabeth Madox Roberts. Lexington: UP of Kentucky, 1982. vii–xx.

Smith, Lee. *Black Mountain Breakdown.* New York: Putnam, 1980.

———. *Cakewalk.* New York: Putnam, 1981.

———. *The Devil's Dream.* New York: Putnam, 1992.

———. *Fair and Tender Ladies.* New York: Putnam, 1988.

———. *Family Linen.* New York: Putnam, 1985.

———. *Fancy Strut.* New York: Harper, 1975.

———. *The Last Day the Dogbushes Bloomed.* New York: Harper, 1968.

———. *Me and My Baby View the Eclipse.* New York: Putnam, 1990.

———. *Oral History.* New York: Putnam, 1983.

———. *Something in the Wind.* New York: Harper, 1971.

Smith, Lillian. *Killers of the Dream.* 1949. Rev. ed. 1961. New York: Norton, 1978.

Smith, Virginia A. "On Regionalism, Women's Writing, and Writing as a Woman: A Conversation with Lee Smith." *Southern Review* 26 (1990): 784–95.

Speir, Jerry. "Of Novels and the Novelist: An Interview with Ellen Douglas." *University of Mississippi Studies in English* 5 (1984–87): 231–48.

Spielberg, Steven, dir. *The Color Purple*. Warner Brothers, 1985.

Stack, Carol B. *All Our Kin: Strategies for Survival in a Black Community*. New York: Harper, 1974.

Stepto, Robert B. *From behind the Veil: A Study of Afro-American Narrative*. Urbana: U of Illinois P, 1979.

Stetson, Erlene. "Black Women in and out of Print." *Women in Print I: Opportunities for Women's Studies Research in Language and Literature*. Ed. Joan E. Hartman and Ellen Messer-Davidow. New York: MLA, 1982. 82–108.

Stewart, Matthew. "Realism, Verisimilitude, and the Depiction of Vietnam Veterans in *In Country*." *Fourteen Landing Zones*. Ed. Philip K. Jason. Iowa City: U of Iowa P, 1991. 166–79.

Sudarkasa, Niara. "Interpreting the African Heritage in Afro-American Family Organization." *Black Families*. Ed. Harriette Pipes McAdoo. Beverly Hills, Calif.: Sage Publications, 1981. 37–53.

Sullivan, Ken. "Gradual Changes: Meredith Sue Willis and the New Appalachian Fiction." *Appalachian Journal* 13 (1986): 38–45.

Tate, Allen. "The New Provincialism." *Essays of Four Decades*. Chicago: Swallow Press, 1968. 535–46.

Thigpen, Corbett H., and Hervey M. Cleckley. *The Three Faces of Eve*. New York: McGraw-Hill, 1957.

Toomer, Jean. *Cane*. New York: Boni and Liveright, 1923.

Towers, Robert. Rev. of *The Color Purple*, by Alice Walker. *New York Review of Books* 12 Aug. 1982: 36.

Tucker, Lindsey. "Alice Walker's *The Color Purple*: Emergent Woman, Emergent Text." *Black American Literature Forum* 22 (Spring 1988): 81–95.

Turner, G. "'The Color Purple': Allen Daviau, ASC." *American Cinematographer* Apr. 1986: 80–82.

———. "Spielberg Makes 'All Too Human' Story." *American Cinematographer* Feb. 1986: 58–64.

Tyler, Anne. *Dinner at the Homesick Restaurant*. New York: Knopf, 1982.

Wagner-Martin, Linda. "'Just the Doing of It': Southern Women Writers and the Idea of Community." *Southern Literary Journal* 22 (1990): 19–32.

Walker, Alice. "Beyond the Peacock: The Reconstruction of Flannery O'Connor." *In Search* 42–59.

———. *The Color Purple*. New York: Harcourt, 1982. New York: Washington Square Press, 1983.

————. "Everyday Use." *In Love and Trouble: Stories of Black Women.* New York: Harcourt, 1973.

————. *"Gifts of Power: The Writings of Rebecca Jackson."* In *Search* 71–82.

————. "In Search of Our Mothers' Gardens." *In Search* 231–43.

————. *In Search of Our Mothers' Gardens: Womanist Prose.* New York: Harcourt, 1983.

————. *Meridian.* New York: Harcourt, 1976.

————. *Once.* New York: Harcourt, 1968.

————. *Possessing the Secret of Joy.* New York: Harcourt, 1992.

————. *Revolutionary Petunias and Other Poems.* New York: Harcourt, 1973.

————. *The Temple of My Familiar.* San Diego: Harcourt, 1989.

————. *The Third Life of Grange Copeland.* New York: Harcourt-Harvest/HBJ, 1970.

————. "Writing *The Color Purple.*" *In Search* 355–60.

————. "Zora Neale Hurston: A Cautionary Tale and a Partisan View." *In Search* 83–92.

Walker, Margaret. *Jubilee.* Boston: Houghton Mifflin, 1966.

Wall, Wendy. "Lettered Bodies and Corporeal Texts in *The Color Purple.*" *Studies in American Fiction* 16 (Spring 1988): 83–97.

Walsh, Margaret. "The Enchanted World of *The Color Purple.*" *Southern Quarterly* 25 (Winter 1987): 89–101.

Warren, Robert Penn. "Elizabeth Madox Roberts: Life Is from Within." Introduction. *The Time of Man.* By Elizabeth Madox Roberts. Lexington: UP of Kentucky, 1982. xxi–xxxiii.

Weisenburger, Steven C. "Errant Narrative and *The Color Purple.*" *The Journal of Narrative Technique* 19 (Fall 1989): 257–75.

Welty, Eudora. *The Collected Stories of Eudora Welty.* New York: Harcourt, 1980.

————. *Delta Wedding.* New York: Harcourt, 1946.

————. *Losing Battles.* Greenwich, Conn.: Fawcett, 1970.

————. *The Optimist's Daughter.* New York: Random, 1972.

West, Celeste, ed. *Words in Our Pockets: The Feminist Writers Guild Handbook on How to Gain Power, Get Published and Get Paid.* Paradise, Calif.: Dustbooks, 1985.

Westling, Louise. *Sacred Groves and Ravaged Gardens: The Fiction of Eudora Welty, Carson McCullers, and Flannery O'Connor.* Athens: U of Georgia P, 1985.

White, Armond. "White on Black." *Film Comment* 20 (December 1984): 12.

White, Deborah Gray. *Ar'n't I a Woman? Female Slaves in the Plantation South.* New York: Norton, 1985.

White, Leslie. "The Function of Popular Culture in Bobbie Ann Mason's *Shiloh and Other Stories* and *In Country*." *Southern Quarterly* 26 (Summer 1988): 69–79.

Wilhelm, Albert E. "An Interview with Bobbie Ann Mason." *Southern Quarterly* 26 (Winter 1988): 27–38.

———. "Private Rituals: Coping with Change in the Fiction of Bobbie Ann Mason." *Midwest Quarterly* 28 (Winter 1987): 271–82.

Williams, Sherley Anne. *Dessa Rose.* New York: William Morrow, 1986.

Williamson, Joel. *The Crucible of Race: Black-White Relations in the American South since Emancipation.* New York: Oxford UP, 1984.

Willis, Susan B. *Specifying: Black Women Writing the American Experience.* Madison: U of Wisconsin P, 1987.

Wilson, Austin. "What It Means to Be a Southern Writer in the '80s: A Panel Discussion with Beverly Lowry, Reynolds Price, Elizabeth Spencer and James Whitehead." *Southern Quarterly* 26 (Summer 1988): 80–93.

Woodward, C. Vann. *The Burden of Southern History.* Baton Rouge: Louisiana State UP, 1960.

Woolf, Virginia. *A Room of One's Own.* 1929. New York: Harvest/HBJ–Harcourt Brace, 1989.

Wright, Richard. *Black Boy.* New York: Harper, 1945.

———. *Native Son.* New York: Harper, 1940.

Yates, Gayle Graham. *Mississippi Mind: A Personal Cultural History of an American State.* Knoxville: U of Tennessee P, 1990.

Youngblood, Shay. *The Big Mama Stories.* Ithaca, N.Y.: Firebrand Books, 1989.

Zollar, Ann Creighton. *A Member of the Family: Strategies for Black Family Community.* Chicago: Nelson-Hall, 1985.

INDEX

southerners in, 153–54; the South in, 153–54, 215 (n. 1.); role of Hollywood in, 154–55; the "hillbilly" movie as genre of, 169. *See also* Spielberg, Steven; Jewison, Norman

Fish, Stanley, 150

Foote, Julia A. L., 185–86

Fox-Genovese, Elizabeth, 213 (n. 2)

French, Warren, 153, 215 (n. 1)

Friedman, Jean E., 23–24, 26

Frye, Joanne S., 176–77

Gaines, Ernest, 117

Gardens, 175; as symbol of women's creativity, 14–15, 19–20; as works of art, 112; as vehicles for healing, 189–90, 194

Gibbons, Kaye, 25, 183; and Algonquin Books, 194–96. Works: *Charms for the Easy Life,* 187, 195; *Ellen Foster,* 195; *A Virtuous Woman,* 195. See also *Cure for Dreams, A*

Gilman, Charlotte Perkins, 21

Gilman, Owen W., Jr., 133, 136, 215 (n. 7)

Glasgow, Ellen, 48, 75

Glaspell, Susan, 201–3

Gone with the Wind (Mitchell), 74, 84, 85, 90

Gordon, Jaimy, 183

Great Meadow, The (Roberts), 74–75

Grimké, Sarah and Angelina, 49, 213 (n. 1)

Gutman, Herbert C., 34, 35

Gwin, Minrose, 44–46, 47, 51, 214 (n. 4)

Harris, Bertha, 180

Harrison, Elizabeth Jane, 211 (n. 1)

Haxton, Josephine. *See* Douglas, Ellen

Hayden, Casey, 49–50

Henderson, Mae G., 181, 184, 216 (n. 1)

Henning, Barbara, 114

High Hearts (Brown, R.), 7, 77–91; private vs. public domains of history, 79, 83, 87; women's contributions to Civil War in, 79–80, 81–88, 91; importance of understanding the past in, 79–82; author's motives for writing, 79–82, 88; as revisionary history, 79–91; women warriors in, 80, 83–88, 91; historical sources for, 80, 90–91; self-definition in, 81, 87; male misperceptions of women in, 83–88; myth of southern lady in, 84–85; relationships between black and white women in, 88–89; slaves' relationships with owners in, 88–89; problematic depictions of slaves in, 89–91; problems with historical sources in, 90–91

History: and women, 73–78, 79–80, 81–88, 91; as traditional, linear accounts, 74, 95, 96, 97–100, 101–2, 111; as public, external events, 74–75, 76, 77, 78, 79, 83, 87, 111; as private, individual events, 74–76, 77–78, 111; and orality, 75, 93, 94, 95, 96–98, 101–9, 110–11; as collective experience, 75–76, 77–78, 79, 83, 111; and African Americans, 79–80, 81, 82, 83, 88–91; revisionary, 79–91, 93–98, 101–11; as collaborative, dynamic, 93, 96–97, 105–11; and Appalachians, 93–111; southern concern with, 133

Hite, Molly, 161–62, 173, 176, 216 (n. 2)

Hobson, Fred, 134, 135, 211 (n. 6)

Hogan, Judy, 182

O'Connor, Flannery, 130
"Old Mortality" (Porter), 175
Optimist's Daughter, The (Welty), 175
Oral History (Smith, Lee), 7, 77–78,
    175, 187; orality and community
    survival in, 93, 97, 101–5, 109, 110–
    11; Appalachia as changing region in,
    93, 104–5, 109–10; sources for, 93–
    94; Appalachian culture in, 93–94,
    101–5, 110–11; revisionary history in,
    93–98, 101–9, 110–11; family tree in,
    94–95; structure of, 94–96; academic
    exploitation of Appalachia in, 95,
    96–101, 110; narrative strategies in,
    95–97, 105–9, 110–11; traditional
    linear history in, 95–101, 102; history
    as collaborative, dynamic process in,
    96–97, 105–9, 110–11; misreadings
    in, 96–101; destruction of Appalachia
    in, 98–99, 104–5, 109–10; mountain
    and country music in, 103–5; orality
    and healing in, 105–6, 108
Orality: and African Americans, 15, 38,
    39–42; and southern women, 15–16,
    20, 21, 22, 30–32, 38, 39–42, 174–
    75, 177, 183, 195, 196, 198–200, 203,
    204; and self-definition, 15–16, 91–
    92, 109; and healing, 30–32, 91–92,
    105–6, 108; and community survival,
    39–42, 91–92, 93, 97, 101–5, 109,
    110–11; and songs, 40, 92, 94, 101–2,
    103–5, 110; and history, 75–76, 93–
    98, 101–11; and contemporary ethnic
    writers, 91–92, 93, 111; and folktales,
    92–94, 101–3, 105, 110–11; and
    Appalachia, 93–98, 101–9, 110–11.
    See also Women's talk
Osborne, Karen, 175, 197
Othermothers, 33, 35, 36
Otto, Whitney, 197

*Outlaw James Copeland and the
    Champion-Belted Empress, The*
    (Lebow), 174, 197

Pancake, Breece D'J, 93
Patchwork (Osborne), 175, 197
"Patchwork Quilt, The"
    ("Annette"), 203
Phillips, Jayne Anne, 93
Porter, Katherine Anne, 175
Postmodernism, versus narrative-based
    fiction, 175–76, 204, 216–17 (n. 2)
Presses: mainstream, 4, 178, 180–81,
    202; small, independent, 173, 174,
    177–83, 194–96; feminist, 173, 178,
    179–80, 181; African-American, 173,
    181; lesbian, 179–80

Quilts: as symbol of women's creativity,
    18–19, 196–97, 203–4; as family
    history, 29; as works of art, 112; as
    feminine aesthetic, 196–97; as
    narrative structure, 196–98, 200,
    203; as symbol of women's text,
    201–4

Race relations, in the South, 43–51
Race-sex-sin spiral, 46–47, 50
Rainbow Roun Mah Shoulder (Brown,
    Linda Beatrice), 7, 31, 38, 182, 202;
    prophecy in, 183–85, 187–89, 192–
    94; healing in, 183–85, 187–92, 194;
    alternative spirituality in, 183–85,
    187–94; women on margins of
    dominant discourse in, 184, 185, 187–
    89, 193; and tradition of the black
    woman preacher, 184, 187, 192–93;
    self-silencing in, 184, 188–89;
    revisioned community in, 184–85,
    187, 189–94; voice and